The
CARIBBEAN:

BRITISH, DUTCH, FRENCH,
UNITED STATES

SERIES ONE   *VOLUME VIII*

A publication of the
SCHOOL OF INTER-AMERICAN STUDIES
*which contains the papers delivered at the eighth conference on the
Caribbean held at the University of Florida, December 5, 6, and 7, 1957.*

ISSUED WITH ASSISTANCE FROM
THE WALTER B. FRASER PUBLICATION FUND

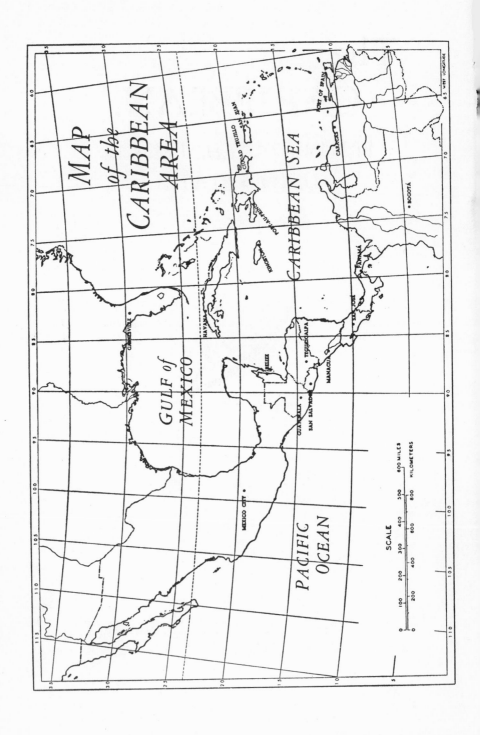

MAP of the CARIBBEAN AREA

The
CARIBBEAN:

BRITISH, DUTCH, FRENCH,
UNITED STATES

edited by A. Curtis Wilgus

1963

UNIVERSITY OF FLORIDA PRESS
Gainesville

A University of Florida Press Book

COPYRIGHT, 1958, BY THE
UNIVERSITY OF FLORIDA
ALL RIGHTS RESERVED

LIBRARY OF CONGRESS
CATALOGUE CARD NUMBER: 51-12532

FIRST EDITION, 1958
LITHOPRINTED EDITION, 1963

LITHOPRINTED BY DOUGLAS PRINTING COMPANY, INC.
JACKSONVILLE, FLORIDA

Contributors

PETROAMÉRICA PAGÁN DE COLÓN, Director, Bureau of Employment Security, Department of Labor, Commonwealth of Puerto Rico

FREDERIC W. GANZERT, Former Director, Bermuda Division, American International College

CORNELIUS J. GRIFFIN, Member of the Board of Directors, Esso Standard Oil, S. A., Havana

G. V. HELWIG, Specialist Teacher, Central Technical School, Toronto

HANS G. HERMANS, Head, Netherlands Information Bureau, Curaçao, N. W. I.

SIDNEY W. HOCKEY, Director, Eastern Caribbean Regional Library, Port-of-Spain, Trinidad

ROLAND DENNIS HUSSEY, Department of History, University of California, Los Angeles

MELVIN H. JACKSON, Department of History, University of Miami

CARL L. LOKKE, Archivist in Charge, Foreign Affairs Branch, The National Archives, Washington, D. C.

ARTURO MORALES CARRIÓN, Under Secretary of State, Department of State, Commonwealth of Puerto Rico

CÁNDIDO OLIVERAS, Chairman, Puerto Rico Planning Board, Commonwealth of Puerto Rico

J. J. OCHSE, Consulting Engineer, Tropical and Subtropical Agriculture, University of Miami

v

FRANKLIN D. PARKER, Department of History and Political Science, Woman's College of the University of North Carolina, Greensboro

BERNARD L. POOLE, Department of History, Erskine College, Due West, South Carolina

LOWELL J. RAGATZ, Department of History, Ohio State University, Columbus

J. WAYNE REITZ, President, University of Florida

W. ADOLPHE ROBERTS, Author and President, The Jamaica Historical Society, Kingston

FRANCES McREYNOLDS SMITH, Foreign Affairs Officer, Office of Dependent Area Affairs, Department of State, Washington, D. C.

PETER M. STERN, Assistant Research Director, The Conservation Foundation, New York

REXFORD G. TUGWELL, Professor Emeritus of Political Science, University of Chicago

ANDRÉ L. VAN ASSENDERP, Department of Political Science, Florida State University, Tallahassee

A. CURTIS WILGUS, Director, School of Inter-American Studies, University of Florida

DOUGLAS WILLIAMS, Colonial Attaché, British Embassy, Washington, D. C.

Foreword

THE EIGHTH ANNUAL Caribbean Conference, held at the University of Florida December 5, 6, and 7, 1957, considered the Caribbean area by political and geographical components. These proceedings of the conference will contribute to a broader understanding of the nature of contemporary government, economy, society, and culture within the political entities treated by participants in the conference. Here is considered, as a family of political groups within the Caribbean area, these aspects of life in the British, Dutch, French, and United States areas.

As in previous proceedings of the Caribbean Conference Series, which began in 1950, no single subject or area is considered exhaustively, but the general overview presented so ably by so many participants will, we believe, enable the reader to acquire an understanding of the peoples of these areas, of their potential, and of their increasing international significance.

The School of Inter-American Studies of the University of Florida enjoyed the cooperation of Esso Standard Oil, S.A., in the presentation and organization of this conference, and we are grateful for its collaboration. In the publication of these proceedings we have had, as in previous years, the generous assistance of Mr. Walter B. Fraser of St. Augustine, who has an abiding interest in inter-American cultural activities. The University of Florida Press has set a high standard in designing the format and in publishing this series. We hope that you will find these proceedings as valuable and useful as previous ones which have been so widely and well received by readers at home and abroad.

J. WAYNE REITZ, *President*
University of Florida

The Caribbean Conference Series

Contents

Introduction

THE UNIVERSITY COLLEGE
OF THE WEST INDIES

ANY STUDY OF the British, Dutch, French, and United States areas of the Caribbean during the past decade or more must of necessity take into consideration the growth of schools and of educational interest in all of the island and mainland dependencies. Nowhere in the Caribbean, outside of Puerto Rico, has there occurred such a rapid educational growth as in the British areas now bound together in the West Indies Federation. The phenomenal development of the University College of the West Indies at Mona near Kingston, Jamaica, presents a picture of intellectual cooperation found in very few places on the face of the earth. In a symposium such as this volume presents, the story of the rise of the University College of the West Indies may be traced as one phase of the growing political and intellectual spirit of the British Caribbean. In the immediate future, certainly, the University College of the West Indies is destined by its very nature to play an increasingly important role in this newest of British commonwealths.

I

The relative poverty of the British Caribbean colonies through the centuries and the lack of British cultural interests in the area combined to retard the development of education in these

British overseas dependencies. Although these colonies were bound together by the common language of English, the French and Spanish languages were spoken also. Natives of the British islands with personal ambition and the necessary funds early developed the tradition of acquiring their advanced education in British universities or even in some continental universities, as well as in schools of higher learning in the United States.

The first so-called college of the British West Indies was Codrington College, founded in the year 1710 in Barbados. However, this was little more than a grammar school until it was reorganized by Bishop Coleridge in 1834. Its first buildings date from 1716, and by their architecture they established an academic flavor. In 1875 the school became affiliated with the University of Durham, and since that time its curriculum has emphasized theology and the classics. Many clergymen, schoolmasters, and lawyers in the late nineteenth century owed their education to this school. With modest ambitions and inadequate endowment, the school has never attempted to provide the needs of the British Caribbean area for higher education. However, this college has been called the "first academic institution in the area."

In 1870, when the capital of the island of Jamaica was moved to Kingston, the governor proposed to convert the square in the old capital city (called Old Spanish Town) into a college quadrangle, using the Georgian-type buildings around the square for university instruction. Thus Queen's College was founded in 1876. The new school, however, was short-lived. The first principal, an Oxford man, died of yellow fever, and the college succumbed a little over a year after its founding.

In 1890 an attempt was made to establish near Kingston a University College in connection with the already existing Jamaica College, a secondary school for boys. Students were to be trained in this school to take the external degrees of the University of London. But financial and other problems necessitated the abandonment of a separate University College, and in 1902 it was incorporated with Jamaica College. This combination has produced an excellent boys' school that remains on this site to the present time.

For a time it seemed most important to devote energies and finances in the British Caribbean to developing good secondary schools from which graduates could go to higher education in England and other countries. However, the topic of creating a new university was not dropped, and a number of groups in the colonies and in the mother country organized committees to keep alive interest in a school of higher learning in the area. One important such committee was finally created in 1926 for the colonies, and in 1938 in Jamaica a similar committee was created.

At long last, in 1943 in Britain the Asquith Commission was appointed to inquire into higher education in the West Indian colonies, as well as in the colonies in Africa and Malay. After examining the Caribbean problem, the commission appointed a special West Indies Committee, often referred to as the Irvine Committee since its chairman was Sir James Irvine, Vice Chancellor of St. Andrews University. The other members of this most important committee were Sir Raymond Priestley, Vice Chancellor of Birmingham University, Miss Margery Perham of Oxford University, and two men whose destinies have been very closely connected with the present University College of the West Indies: Mr. Philip M. Sherlock of Jamaica and Mr. H. W. Springer of Barbados. Although this committee was appointed in January, 1944, during World War II, it began to work immediately. The British members arrived in Trinidad by mid-February, and during the next three months the whole committee visited several Caribbean colonies where in many instances they invited local leaders to give advice and suggestions. By the end of August, 1944, they had finished their examination of the problem. The committee's report, generally called the Irvine Report, was presented to Parliament in June, 1945, and was circulated throughout the British West Indian colonies, where it was enthusiatically received.

In substance this report recommended that a University Col-

lege be established in Jamaica to provide teaching and research
in the faculties of arts, natural science, and medicine, and that
it should resemble in its constitutional structure the universities
of Great Britain. The committee recommended that the University College should be governed by a council which would include representatives of all the governments concerned, as well
as of its own academic staff. All academic questions and problems should be under the control and supervision of a senate
composed of representatives of the academic staff. The college
should have residential halls in which students would reside
throughout their academic year. The committee recommended
that a financial grant should be made from the Colonial Development and Welfare Funds in order to get the project under
way, but it was agreed that in the future current expenses
would have to be borne by the colonies connected with the
project.

It was generally agreed that all the British Caribbean would
benefit from the establishment of this new institution. In this
geographical area were included Barbados, British Guiana,
British Honduras, Jamaica, the Leeward Islands, Trinidad and
Tobago, and the Windward Islands. The immensity of this
group was appreciated by the committee, and distances proved
an important handicap for many students, as later appeared.
An appreciation of the extent of this large area in comparison
with Europe can be made as follows: If British Honduras is
placed over London on the map, then Jamaica is roughly in
the vicinity of Danzig in the Baltic, Trinidad is at Odessa on the
Black Sea, while the Windward and Leeward Islands would
stretch far to the east of Moscow, with British Guiana in Asia
Minor. Yet in this vast area there are only about three million
people, of which Jamaica has about half. Partly for this reason
and also for others, Jamaica was chosen to be the site of the new
University College.

The Asquith Commission, viewing the problem of education
in all of the British colonies, recommended that all university
institutions which might be developed in colonial territories

should have as a "foster mother" the University of London. It was also decided that before each university reached full university status and awarded its own degrees, the students were to work for the University of London degrees. Thus the new University College was to be in a special relationship with the University of London, but having the initiative of proposing the syllabus of each examination. The examination boards were to include members of the University College staff as well as examiners appointed by the University of London. In this way, it was believed, the staffs would acquire important experience and the proper sense of responsibility in order to help them make the transition to a full university as soon as possible. In October, 1948, the University of London set up special arrangements to accomplish these objectives.

II

In October, 1946, a principal was appointed for the new institution, reaching Jamaica in November. In January, 1947, the Provisional Council decided to implement the Irvine Report and to get the university opened. Consequently, representatives of seven of the colonial areas met with Sir James Irvine and Sir Raymond Priestley in Jamaica. Since the university had no constitution, one of the first problems considered was how the University College might become a corporation in the legal sense, empowered to acquire and own property and to enter into various contracts. It was finally decided to ask for a grant of a Royal Charter. In January, 1949, a charter similar to those granted other British universities was passed under the Great Seal, after having been submitted to the Privy Council and approved. Unfortunately this document was lost when an aeroplane in which it was carried disappeared without a trace between Bermuda and the Bahamas in January, 1949. Since it was illegal to issue a new Charter, the Privy Council agreed to issue Letters Patent recording the existence of the lost charter. The British King consented to become the Visitor of the University College and to nominate the chancellor.

A further step in organizing the University College was the creation of a coat of arms, which was granted by the College of Heralds in 1949. The university motto was eventually selected: *Oriens ex occidente lux*. Another early problem was the question of academic dress. Because black academic costumes absorb a great deal of heat in the tropics and were in too great contrast with bright tropical colors, it was decided to copy the academic regalia used in St. Andrews University which provided a handsome scarlet undergraduate gown.

One of the most important questions that had to be settled immediately was the problem of a site for the university. Because the University College was to have a hospital, it was agreed that it must be near a population center, and the city of Kingston or its vicinity was decided upon. The question of beauty of environment was also carefully considered. Finally at Mona, about seven miles from the center of Kingston in a valley with the foothills of the Blue Mountains rising to the north and east, a little over a square mile of ground was selected which was turned over by the government of Jamaica to the University on a lease of 999 years at a peppercorn rent. The site has proved to be a most beautiful and functional one, and the campus area will enable the university to expand almost indefinitely for at least a hundred years. Since the island is subject to numerous earthquakes, it was decided that all buildings should be low and long with ample space between them and with some buildings connected by covered walkways. An area of about eighty acres was set aside for athletic purposes, thus providing for one of the most beautiful cricket grounds anywhere in the world. A firm of London architects was employed to design buildings and their campus location. There were to be resident halls for men and for women undergraduates, lecture rooms, laboratories, a library, and other necessary buildings, including, in a beautiful section of the campus, houses for the academic staff. In the early months a number of temporary wooden buildings, used during the war to house refugees from Gibraltar and Malta, were set aside for offices and other purposes. By October, 1950, the first undergraduate residence hall, to house 162 students and some bachelor members of the staff, was opened. In the next two years a handsome functional library was erected, and the hospital and medical school buildings were constructed.

III

In February, 1950, the first chancellor of the University College of the West Indies was installed amidst inspiring and brilliant ceremonies. The school, however, had been functioning since October, 1948, largely with a staff which had been obtained wherever possible. At first it had been hoped to employ on the staff a number of West Indian natives, but the war and other world problems caused the appointment of staff members from as far apart as New Zealand and Great Britain, with some few from Canada.

The financial problems of the University have always been important. It had originally been agreed between the British government and the governments of the colonies that capital needed for buildings and equipment should be provided from the higher education allocation of the Colonial Development and Welfare Funds, while the capital needed for current expenditures (salaries, wages, departmental grants, and other running expenses) should be contributed from the revenues of the individual colonies. In 1947 at Montego Bay representatives of the British West Indian colonies had agreed upon a ratio of providing funds for the years 1947–53, according to their populations. Thus, Jamaica agreed to bear 45.4 per cent of the cost of the University, Trinidad 17.9 per cent, British Guiana 12.9 per cent, the Windward Islands 10.3 per cent, Barbados 7.4 per cent, Leeward Islands 3.9 per cent, and British Honduras 2.2 per cent.

From the very beginning it was decided that the University College of the West Indies should have as one of its primary functions research in the social sciences, the natural sciences, the humanities, and in medicine. One of the most important early divisions of the University was an Institute of Social and Economic Research established through financial support from the Colonial Social Science Research Council. In 1948 the first director was appointed. He is Dr. H. D. Huggins, born in the Island of Nevis and educated at Cornell and Harvard in the United States. At present there are on the campus three faculties: of arts, of natural sciences, and of medicine. Wide course offerings are available in all of these faculties.

A most important division of the University College is the Department of Extra Mural Studies which was originally and still is under the direction of Mr. Philip M. Sherlock, one of the members of the Irvine Committee. This department, somewhat like the extension division in American universities, carries the influence and the facilities of the University College of the West Indies into the remote areas of the British Caribbean. In each of the Caribbean British colonies is a resident tutor whose function is to organize the extension work. The resident tutor's duties include that of a public relations officer, a registrar, and a general fount of knowledge for all types of questions pertaining to the University College. Through this officer many excellent students of six races and from an area of 2,000,000 square miles are recruited for the University College. Students from the remote areas of the British Caribbean are provided with one round-trip passage between their home and University College. The newly arrived student finds many conditions and habits new to him. He lives on the campus with other students, he associates with them in the classroom and in campus activities, his health is carefully guarded, he is subject to a general university disciplinary control, and he must meet certain standards of qualifications and attainment or leave the university. No one under the age of seventeen can be admitted as a student. In order to maintain certain standards all students must be qualified to matriculate in the University of London and to follow the appropriately prescribed courses. In some professional and technical studies the students actually make equipment for classrooms and laboratories. All students are required to take

well coordinated courses which provide them with the degrees
they desire. These include, besides the bachelor's degrees, the
M.Sc., the M.A., and the Ph.D. In all advanced degrees also
the students must be able to meet the standards maintained by
the University of London.

IV

After only a decade it is much too soon to attempt to measure
the influence which the University College of the West Indies
has had upon the cultural and intellectual life of the Caribbean
area. Suffice it to say that the founding of the University College
was a milestone on the intellectual highway which leads the
educated youth out of his small Caribbean world into a world
of greater opportunities and wider geographical extent. The
University College of the West Indies already has many alumni
and friends throughout the world who are spreading good will
and friendship for this great and growing institution. The further development of the University College of the West Indies
will be watched with interest during the coming years.

A. CURTIS WILGUS, *Director*
School of Inter-American Studies

Note: I am indebted to many sources of information for this discussion
of the University College of the West Indies, but particularly to a most
helpful pamphlet entitled *The University College of the West Indies* by
T. W. J. Taylor (later Sir Thomas Taylor), reprinted from the *Universities
Review* (1950). The "Pamphlet of Information," October, 1957, a catalog
of the University College of the West Indies, was also of value. Conversations in the summer of 1956 with University College Registrar H. W.
Springer, Dr. H. D. Huggins, and other faculty members in Mona not only
provided me with valuable information but with several delightful hours of
beneficial and pleasant friendships. I especially wish to thank Mr. Springer
for invaluable suggestions which he made after reading this paper.

Part I

THE BRITISH AREAS

Douglas Williams: CONSTITUTIONAL DEVELOPMENTS IN THE BRITISH WEST INDIES

IN 1958 A NEW POLITICAL ENTITY will appear upon the Caribbean scene. A federation of ten island governments, to be known (after much debate) as The West Indies, will come formally into existence in January and will hold its first elections in March. In April its first legislative assembly will meet in Trinidad which (again after much debate and some hard feelings) has been chosen as the site of the federal capital.

This long-heralded development has already received some publicity in the American press. It was the subject of a typically frank and illuminating lecture by Mr. Albert Gomes, then Minister of Labor in Trinidad, to the sixth conference on the Caribbean held in Gainesville in 1955. It will doubtless receive still more publicity during 1958, partly because Princess Margaret is due to attend the inaugural ceremonies and partly because the West Indies have claimed the present United States naval base at Chaguaramas in Trinidad as the place for their federal capital.

The pomp and circumstance of inaugural ceremonies and the debate and argument about the capital site are comparatively ephemeral things which we can well leave the journalists to take care of. What is about to happen in the British Caribbean has many points of much more permanent significance, and it is on one of these—the constitutional aspect—that I wish to make a few observations in this paper.

I

This Federation of the West Indies will, broadly speaking, follow the Australian rather than the Canadian pattern. That is to say, a few specific subjects will be reserved exclusively for the Federal Government to deal with; there will be an important number of concurrent subjects with which both the federal and the individual territorial governments can deal, federal law prevailing in case of any discrepancy; while residual subjects will remain with the individual territories. The Federal Legislature will consist of a Senate and an elected House of Representatives. Executive power will be vested in a Governor-General, who in exercising it will be bound, except in a few limited instances, to accept the advice of the Council of State. This Council of State, which is in fact a cabinet following the usual British Parliamentary pattern, will be appointed on the advice of the Prime Minister, who will have been elected by the House of Representatives. The Council of State will therefore be dependent for its existence and for carrying through its policies upon the confidence of the Federal Legislature. In short, from the outset of its existence The West Indies will enjoy responsible self-government. It is the hope of all of us that in due course The West Indies will move on to full independence within the Commonwealth; and the West Indian leaders themselves have every confidence that they will attain this goal within five or ten years.

II

These facts are already well known. What is not so well known is that this development has set off a whole chain of constitutional advances within the individual territories themselves, all designed to put greater power into the hands of the elected representatives of the people and to bring them nearer to the goal of complete responsible self-government. Some of these changes have been announced already. Some have only been foreshadowed.

In Jamaica, for example, it seems already to have been agreed in principle that the island shall have full internal self-government under a new constitution, though its final introduction will have to await the next general election since it would involve an increase in the size of the House of Representatives. As an interim measure, proposals have already been approved whereby the Executive Council will become a Council of Ministers, presided over by the Chief Minister instead of the Governor and consisting exclusively of ministers with no official members. The Colonial Secretary and the Financial Secretary will cease to be members of the Legislative Council and will be replaced by elected ministers, leaving the Attorney General as the only official member of that body. Under this system the Governor appointed by Her Majesty the Queen will continue to be responsible only for defense, external affairs, and certain matters relating to the public service. Dampier in his *New Voyage round the World,* published in 1697, tells us that the Moskito Indians "take the Governour of Jamaica to be one of the greatest Princes in the World." Like other "great Princes," he is rapidly being reduced to the status of a constitutional monarch.

Similar changes have already been announced for Barbados and may shortly be announced for Trinidad. In Barbados the principal instrument of government policy is known as the Executive Committee. Prior to 1946 under the old constitution of Barbados, the Executive Committee was appointed by the Governor and was responsible only to him. It thus reproduced the fatal flaw of the "old representative system" of colonial government—the system operating in the American Colonies before 1776—whereby "an irremovable executive confronted an irresponsible legislature." In 1946, however, following an election on a new and wider franchise which brought the Barbados Labor party to power, the Governor invited the majority leader in the House of Assembly to submit names for appointment to the Executive Committee. In that moment Barbados was firmly placed upon the road to responsible self-government—the system wherein a ministerial executive depends for its existence upon the support of an elected legislature. The Executive Committee accepted collective responsibility then to the House of Assembly. In 1954 those members of the Executive Committee who were also members of the House of Assembly became full-time ministers. As a result of the further changes just announced, the full direction and control of government in all internal matters will pass to the Premier and his ministers meeting as a cabinet, with the officials (the Attorney General, the Financial Secretary, and the Chief Secretary) attending only on request.

It is not yet possible to give the full details of the similar changes which, as is now public knowledge, are being contemplated for Trinidad. It can be confidently predicted, however, that their general features are likely to be the same; that is to say, they will produce an executive exclusively chosen from, and responsible to, a popularly elected legislature.

As in the case of Barbados, it is internal political changes within Trinidad itself which even more than the stimulus of outside events such as the establishment of federation have produced this far-reaching result. It is the development of the party system and in particular the growth of one party to win the allegiance of a majority of the electorate and gain command of a majority of the seats in the legislature. In Barbados that party was Sir Grantly Adams' Labor party. In Trinidad it is Dr. Eric Williams' Peoples' National Movement. This is the essential prerequisite of the final step to responsible self-government on the British Parliamentary pattern—the growth of a party strong enough to rule, and of course the growth of other parties strong enough to provide an alternative to its rule.

III

What we are in fact witnessing in the British Caribbean is not simply the growth of systems of responsible self-government; it is also the demise of the Crown Colony system. The time is therefore perhaps ripe to consider the place of the Crown Colony system in the development of the West Indies and to write its obituary notice.

In the West Indies the Crown Colony system is only about 90 years old. Prior to the emancipation of the slaves in 1834, most of the British West Indian islands were governed under what was known as the "old representative system." This was the system common in all the settlements in America and the West, including the thirteen colonies which ultimately became the United States. It has in fact left a permanent mark on the Constitution of the United States to this day. The basic features of the system were the strict separation of the powers. The governor, appointed by the Crown, was in charge of the executive branch of government. He exercised his power with the advice—and sometimes the consent—of a council which he had himself appointed. Legislative authority was vested in an assembly, generally elected on a restricted franchise, but having in its hands the great power conferred by the exclusive right to initiate or amend money bills. Broadly speaking, therefore, the constitution of the West Indian islands in 1834 reproduced the constitution of England as it emerged from the "glorious revolution" of 1689.

The fatal flaws of the system always were that under it there was no link between the executive and the legislative parts of government, while the head of the local executive, the governor, also had to be the representative of an external power—namely the United Kingdom. The views of this external power by no means always coincided with those of the local groups who had control of the local legislatures. The emancipation of the slaves in 1834 brought all these difficulties to a head. It was carried through by the United Kingdom Government in the teeth of opposition from all those interests which held power in the West Indian legislatures. (One consequence of this was that Jamaica openly threatened to join the United States!) The freeing of the slaves created problems with which the old legislatures, partly because of their unrepresentative character in the new circumstances, were quite incapable of dealing. In the words of a Colonial Secretary's despatch of 1868, "the Population at large, consisting of uneducated Negroes, neither had nor could have any political powers; they were incapable of contributing to the formation of any intelligent public opinion; and the consequence was that the Assemblies performed their office of legislation under no real or effective responsibility."

For thirty years all attempts to deal with this situation failed. It needed a Negro revolt in Jamaica in 1865 and the panic which it caused to bring the system to an end. Everywhere, except in Barbados, Bermuda, and the Bahamas, the "old representative system" was then abolished and replaced by the Crown Colony system, with both executive and legislative councils almost wholly nominated by the governor.

Constitutionally this was an undoubted retrogression; but politically it was a case of *reculer pour mieux sauter*. As one writer has said, "Only with the establishment of Crown Colony government did the Negroes really begin to taste the proper fruits of emancipation." Sir Hilary Blood in a recent article has been even more forthright and draws from these events conclusions which have an application far outside the West Indies. He writes: "Now the Queen's Governors were in a position to see to it that the new freemen of the West Indies had equal treatment, fair shares in such social and political benefits as were available, and, as time went on and the basis of the Governors Councils could be widened, a voice in the government of their country. Here is a valuable lesson which the West Indies has to teach: namely that at a certain stage in the history of a mixed society it is necessary to limit the political rights of a more advanced section of the community until the less advanced section can catch up."

Thus the wheel is about to come full circle. It may soon be possible to say again as it was said in the early nineteenth century that "the smallest rock in the West Indies exhibits a sort of miniature of the British Constitution"; but it will be the British Constitution of the middle of the twentieth century and not that of 1689.

IV

So much for the past. What of the future? As everywhere, a good deal of the success or failure attending these political developments will depend on economic and social factors outside the scope of this paper—upon how well these new governments can exploit the natural resources of the islands, develop their communications, and cope with their growing populations. Politically, however, their success will, I think, be determined by the success or failure of the federal experiment itself, and I want now to hazard a few observations on this topic.

The problems facing any newly established federation are difficult and complex. There is above all the problem of establishing loyalty to itself without damaging the existing loyalties to its constituent parts. In the case of the West Indies there is a further problem in that the number of subjects exclusively reserved to the Federation are few. On the other hand, the number of subjects on the concurrent list over which the Federation can, if it so wills, assume control is wide and far-reaching. It can therefore draw strength to itself if it so wishes. Is that going to be the will of the leaders who will emerge to take charge of its destinies? A great deal will depend on whether the men of real political ability in the West Indies—who at their best can more than hold their own with any political leaders either within or without the Caribbean area—are going to choose to associate themselves with federal politics or remain in the service of their island governments. The answer to this question will not be known until the federal elections. A great deal may also depend on whether the Federal Government is of approximately the same political complexion as the island governments. The West Indies will not be able to afford feuds and friction over "states rights."

Many forces have worked against these islands coming together in the past. Some of them still continue to operate. It would be wrong to pretend that federation is coming about as a result of wide popular demand. Nevertheless, we believe there are a sufficient number of people in public life in the West

Indies with the vision and ability to make it work. We have every expectation that they will be successful, and it will be interesting to see in the years to come what effect this new nation, reared in the Anglo-Saxon political traditions, is going to have on the affairs of what has hitherto been—politically speaking—predominantly a Latin American zone. We must all hope that the Federation of the West Indies will grow and prosper and provide its own unique and colorful contribution to the life of the free world.

Bernard L. Poole: ECONOMIC TRENDS
IN THE BRITISH WEST INDIES

THE ECONOMIC PROBLEMS of the British areas in the Caribbean present few unique aspects. Indeed, they may be considered representative of the economic maladies which have afflicted the region as a whole for more years than we care to remember. The pattern of complex problems which British officials and local authorities alike have been attacking with increased vigor these last two decades is therefore a familiar one.

I

Early settlement of the Caribbean islands was effected chiefly for the purpose of providing sources of tropical products, notably sugar. Since the industry proved to be extremely profitable, large sugar estates were developed by British planters as the basis of great fortunes in the Caribbean area. By the eighteenth century the West Indies were ranked among the most flourishing segments of the British Empire.

A series of disastrous reverses in the nineteenth century, however, forced the industry into a period of decline from which it has never fully recovered. The abolition of slavery left the planters with an uncertain labor supply. Competition with foreign producers became more strenuous with the rise of costs

11

of production and the elimination of prohibitive duties on foreign sugar in the mother country. By the middle of the century the West Indies had lost the monopoly they had enjoyed in England, and they were forced to compete on equal terms with sugar produced by slave labor in Brazil and Cuba.

During the closing years of the nineteenth century the economy of the British Caribbean territories was further weakened by a serious epidemic of cane disease and the increased importation of beet sugar into the United Kingdom. At the end of the century the sugar industry, supplying four-fifths of the export trade of the Caribbean colonies, experienced the most serious crisis in its history. This was a period of widespread bankruptcy among the planters and a marked reduction in cultivation of sugar cane.

Early in the present century some improvement was achieved by the substitution of other tropical crops and sea-island cotton for sugar cane. This program was pursuant to recommendations of a Royal Commission in 1897, which also urged the replacement of large estates by small peasant holdings. The elimination of bounties on beet sugar after 1903 was another factor in improving, to some degree, the position of the West Indian planter in the world market. A measure of prosperity was thus restored with the transfer of considerable acreage to the cultivation of bananas, cocoa, coconuts, citrus fruits, and sea-island cotton. So significant was this trend that sugar cultivation was reduced to a secondary role in the economies of Jamaica, Trinidad, and a few of the smaller islands.

The sugar industry was artificially revived during the war period from 1914 to 1918 chiefly because the United Kingdom was cut off from its supply of beet sugar. However, high prices invited increased production in other areas and improved production techniques in the British territories. Hence, after the war sugar production began to exceed world demand.

Even though the British Government granted significant preference to sugar imported from the colonies, the position of the industry in the West Indies did not improve. In 1937 exports from the Caribbean and other sugar-producing areas were limited by a quota system established in an International Sugar Agreement. These restrictions led to increased unemployment which was not relieved until World War II established a world-wide demand for increased production.

In the meantime the tropical products which had been sub-stituted for cane at the close of the preceding century failed to provide more than a temporary halt of the economic decline. Indeed, the producers of cocoa, citrus fruits, limes, bananas, coffee, rice, and nutmeg suffered great loss from plant disease and hurricane damage, resulting in a return of considerable acreage to the cultivation of sugar.[1]

II

Just before World War II the West India Royal Commission, under the direction of Lord Moyne, carried out a searching in-vestigation of the declining economy of the Caribbean terri-tories. In its report, published in full in 1945, the Moyne Commission stressed a need for long-term remedies to attack the economic problems of the area at their sources. The Commis-sion proposed a number of measures directed toward broad social and economic reforms. Included in the proposals was an agricultural program based upon greater production of food-stuffs at home and a resulting reduction of dependence on im-ports from abroad. It was suggested that planning should include projects designed to distribute West Indian crops abroad in markets more stable than those associated with the sugar industry. The Commission further recommended fostering local industries to provide employment for a portion of the rapidly expanding laboring population.[2]

1. Bernard L. Poole, *The Caribbean Commission: Background of Co-operation in the West Indies* (Columbia, S. C., 1951), pp. 1–10.
2. West India Royal Commission, *Report Presented by the Secretary of State for the Colonies to Parliament by Command of His Majesty* (London, 1945), pp. 426–453.

The Commission's inquiries focused greater attention on an urgent need for development projects which the colonies were obviously unable to finance from their own resources. Indeed, a similar program, applied to the Empire as a whole, had been under consideration since 1929. For the Caribbean areas the Moyne Commission recommended the establishment of a welfare fund of £1,000,000 annually, to be financed from the British Exchequer for a period of twenty years. The British Government accepted the main recommendations of the Commission but provided the needed assistance from funds appropriated in the Colonial Development and Welfare Act of 1940. Under the direction of a newly appointed Comptroller and staff of advisors in various fields, a broad social and economic program was launched in the West Indies.

All planning for implementation of the new undertaking was done locally, and no attempt was made to decrease the privileges of the local governmental organizations, since the functions of the Comptroller were essentially advisory in nature. However, approval by the Secretary of State for the Colonies and concurrence of the United Kingdom Treasury were required for all Development and Welfare Funds projects. Thus, the major responsibility for formulating and executing social and economic development plans was transmitted to the colonial governments.[3]

Development and Welfare policies naturally aroused apprehension that assistance from Imperial funds would prejudice the chances of the colonies to become self-supporting and ultimately self-governing. It was obvious, of course, that permanent subsidies from the British Government would not foster conditions in which the Caribbean territories could become self-sustaining. The fact is that financial dependence is hardly compatible with political responsibility.

The principle that self-government to be meaningful must rest upon solid economic foundations was recognized by the British in planning the new approach. Subsidies made from

3. Sir John Macpherson, *Development and Welfare in the West Indies, 1945–1946* (London, 1947), pp. 1–2.

Imperial funds were intended only to supplement local efforts to produce more wealth and improve standards of living. Economic development was designed to produce sufficient wealth to provide a self-sustaining status, achieved by West Indians themselves as responsible members of the world community.[4]

Total grants of £7,500,000 were approved for various social and economic projects by the end of 1944.[5] While the Moyne Commission in 1945 recommended that the West Indian governments foster the expansion of industry, it expressed disapproval of any program of financing "speculative industrial enterprises." It observed that new industries could provide employment for a small portion of the population only, since any effective economic policy must be essentially an agricultural policy with the objective of expanding production of foodstuffs for home consumption rather than for export.

The Commission acknowledged that a program of eliminating dependence on imports, especially food, would require many years of work and planning. Meanwhile, measures should be undertaken to foster local industries which would not raise the costs of living. In short, the Commission viewed the problem of the West Indies as an agrarian one with industrial development to be a supplementary remedy to provide employment to a limited degree only.[6]

In general the Development and Welfare program followed this cautious industrial policy until it became apparent that an expansive welfare design cannot successfully be based on an entirely agrarian economy. It is impossible to escape the conclusion that such an approach will, of necessity, result in what Professor Thomas S. Simey has termed "planning for poverty." While it is true that the Caribbean areas have been exploited

4. Thomas Spensley Simey, *Welfare and Planning in the West Indies* (Oxford, 1946), pp. 122–125.

5. Sir Frank Stockdale, *Development and Welfare in the West Indies, 1943–1944* (London, 1945).

6. Royal Commission Report, 1945, pp. 443–444.

in the past by the so-called "vested interests," history has shown
that the total resources are poor and that the standard of living
cannot be materially improved by a mere redistribution of
existing wealth.[7]

Consequently, in 1945 a new Colonial Development and
Welfare Act was approved by Parliament to increase the scope
of the new program with greater emphasis on industrial development. The West Indies were allotted £15,500,000 for a
ten-year period, but the colonial governments were urged to
use local funds in financing development projects to the fullest
extent consistent with their resources.[8]

Planning for expansion of economic activities, however, revealed that more capital than had been provided to date would
be required. Hence, in 1948 Parliament created the Colonial
Development Corporation with a capital of £110,000,000 financed partly from the British Exchequer and partly from other
sources. The primary function of this organization was to
finance projects designed to stimulate colonial industrial and
trade development and expand the production of foodstuffs.
The Corporation was authorized to undertake such ventures on
its own initiative or in association with local governments.

Although the activities of the Colonial Development Corporation mainly concerned agricultural development, they included
a number of projects intended to expand industry and trade.
By the end of 1950 approved capital investments in 4 Caribbean
territories totaled £4,287,000, distributed among 10 enterprises.
These undertakings provided employment for 2,200 people in
the areas concerned. It was not expected that the operations
of the Corporation would result in large profits, but provisions
were made to reinvest any surplus in other colonial developments
or in offsetting losses incurred in other ventures.[9]

Scarce factors of industrialization in the Caribbean areas

7. Simey, pp. 124–127.
8. Macpherson, pp. 3–6.
9. Caribbean Commission, *The Promotion of Industrial Development in
the Caribbean* (Port-of-Spain, 1952), pp. 26–27, 69.

are capital and entrepreneurship. Large savings find their way into traditional fields of speculation in real estate and trade rather than into industry. Because of the lack of stock exchanges small savings are virtually excluded from investment in industrial enterprises. In addition serious difficulties are involved in the problem of attracting investment from abroad. International investment levels in general have declined because of unsettled economic and political conditions in various parts of the world. Further, the Caribbean area faces serious competition from a number of other undeveloped regions. In the United States domestic investment generally is relatively more attractive to large investors.

Government financial assistance will fill part of the void in the field of capital investments. The development of entrepreneurship, however, will depend on a number of factors which cannot be reduced to a simple formula. Certainly the emergence of initiative and enterprise should accompany the acquisition of technical skills and experience resulting from the promotional impetus and encouragement provided by the colonial governments.[10]

III

After the inauguration of the Development and Welfare program, the colonial governments devoted increasing attention to promotion of secondary industries through "pioneer industry" legislation and tax concessions. Local interest in industrialization grew, and numerous applications for pioneer status were made in Jamaica and Trinidad, while various ventures in processing agricultural products were undertaken in the smaller islands.[11]

Among new industries which have been inaugurated in Jamaica are those engaged in the production of cement, building

10. *Ibid.,* pp. 4–5.
11. Colonial Office, *Development and Welfare in the West Indies, 1951* (London, 1952), pp. 22–23.

board, cotton and knitted goods, clothing, shoes, and luggage. The most important achievement was the establishment of a bauxite industry in the island in 1952. In Trinidad 57 pioneer enterprises have been started, including the manufacturing of beer, cement, typewriters, cardboard, textiles, paints, lingerie, and bathing suits. Examples of progress in other areas are a modern arrowroot factory in St. Vincent, an aluminum plant in British Honduras, a tantalite mine in British Guiana, a canning factory in British Honduras, a ceramics factory in Antigua, and brick, fish-canning, and biscuit factories in Barbados.[12]

The industrial developments of the last decade, especially in Jamaica and Trinidad, have been encouraging. In Jamaica the local government has expanded incentive legislation offering income tax and customs duty concessions to stimulate investments and industrial output which have been increased to a significant extent. In 1955, for example, 881 more workers were added to the total employed in registered factories, which also increased in number from 722 to 732. During the same year capital investment in Trinidad increased by more than 5 per cent. Large manufacturing concerns increased from 230 to 250, and the total number of workers employed in these firms rose by 12 per cent. As in Jamaica, Trinidad's incentive legislation stimulated new enterprises, including the manufacture of tin-plate containers, gin, bathing suits, yeast, and nails. In British Guiana 54 companies with total capital of $15,700,000 were incorporated in a period of less than 2 years.

The two most important heavy industries in the area are oil in Trinidad and bauxite in Jamaica and British Guiana. Income tax and royalties from oil produce about one-third of all government revenues in Trinidad, and exports of petroleum and asphalt reach a total of approximately $128,000,000 annually. The growth of the bauxite industry in Jamaica has been spectacular. In 1955 Alumina Jamaica, Limited, embarked upon an

12. J. E. Heesterman, "Industry," *The Caribbean*, X, 4 (November, 1956), 112.

expansion program to be completed in 1958 which is estimated to involve costs of £12,000,000. Financing of this project will raise the company's capital investment in Jamaica to £34,000,000. Kaiser Bauxite Company and Reynolds Jamaica Mines also engaged in expansion projects increasing capital investments. In British Guiana a new plant for the processing of undried bauxite into alumina is being constructed at a cost of some $60,000,000. This new industry is expected to provide employment for 700 people.[13]

Many of the industries which have been established in the last decade have had no direct association with the agricultural products grown in the West Indies. While such enterprises can be introduced, as in other regions of the world, with generally beneficial results, the most promising basis for existing and potential industrial expansion lies in the processing of raw materials provided by domestic agriculture, livestock, and forestry. Caribbean agricultural products fall into three broad categories: those raised primarily for export, such as sugar cane, cocoa, coffee, tobacco, and spices; those produced mostly for home consumption, including rice, corn, vegetables, and root crops; and fruit crops cultivated both for export and domestic consumption.[14]

As early as 1764 an attempt was made to relate scientific methods to agriculture when the Botanical Gardens were established in St. Vincent. This was followed by similar ventures in Jamaica and Trinidad. In the nineteenth century progressive planters formed agricultural societies to distribute information concerning the most recently developed agricultural methods. Government did not assume a significant role in these early activities until the 1880's when government botanists were appointed and an official Botanic Research Station was established in Barbados where eventually sugar cane was successfully

13. Sir Stephen Luke, *Development and Welfare in the West Indies, 1955–1956* (London, 1957), pp. 29–31.

14. Caribbean Commission, *Caribbean Economic Review*, V, 1, 2 (December, 1953), 20–21.

grown from seed for the first time. In time Barbadian seedlings replaced the less hardy strain which previously had been cultivated in the West Indies for a century.

The chief link between government and the application of scientific knowledge to local agricultural endeavor was the Imperial Department of Agriculture, founded by Joseph Chamberlain as Secretary of State for the Colonies. From the work of this organization the Imperial College of Tropical Agriculture emerged. Established in Trinidad in 1921 and financed jointly by the British and local governments, this institution conducts research and advisory projects, trains agricultural officers for the whole empire, and provides technical assistants for West Indian estates.[15]

IV

In his report for 1951 the Comptroller of Development and Welfare suggested a re-examination of agricultural policies in the light of experience derived from the preceding ten years of planning. The needs most emphasized were for large production of export crops, increase in the local production of foodstuffs, more efficient use of the land, and improvement of peasant farming methods. In planning for increased production the small landholder will be the key figure. It is on the peasant farms that the most significant progress in agriculture must begin if a stable, self-sustaining economy is to be established for the area as a whole.

During the first decade of its operation, the Development and Welfare program emphasized the work of equipping and preparing departments of agriculture for productive action, and little was done relative to expanding actual food production on a large scale. In effect the early phase of financing agricultural development was a preliminary period during which the territories were equipped to attack the most basic problems.

15. Agnes M. Whitson and Lucy F. Horsfall, *Britain and the West Indies* (London, 1948), pp. 50–51.

In this respect activities of the first decade were of great value, but it cannot be said that agricultural production increased to an appreciable degree.[16]

In recent years two of the most urgent problems attacked by the Development and Welfare organization have been those associated with increasing local food production and improving marketing facilities. A primary objective has been to reduce imports from abroad of those commodities which can be produced within the area. This objective requires the production of specialized crops in the various regions most suited for their cultivation and the distribution of production in a manner designed to eliminate periods of surpluses and shortages which now regularly occur. Problems of marketing have been the special province of a marketing organizer, who assumed duty late in 1955. Among his recent proposals to improve facilities and techniques are provision of adequate domestic marketing facilities, formation of food-crop producer associations, maximum use of government marketing departments, and expansion of central grading and packing facilities. These recommendations have been endorsed by both the Regional Economic Committee and the Advisory Council on Agriculture.[17]

Sugar remains the outstanding agricultural enterprise in the British Caribbean, roughly equaling, with its by-products, the total cash value of all other crops. The Commonwealth Sugar Agreement, effective to the end of 1964, has provided a measure of stability for the industry. Under this arrangement exports from Commonwealth producers are restricted to 2,375,000 tons, with the quota of the Caribbean areas at 670,000 tons for which a remunerative price is guaranteed by the British Government.[18]

The sugar industry has the distinction of being the most technically progressive agricultural enterprise in the area. While

16. *Development and Welfare . . . , 1951,* pp. 28–31.
17. Luke Report, 1955–1956, pp. 35, 41–42.
18. *Ibid.,* p. 21.

sugar producers are constantly increasing efficiency of production, progress in other agricultural industries is lagging. By contrast with industrial countries, Caribbean agriculture is obviously inefficient. Seasonal employment is the rule, and the average return per worker is no more than $500 annually. Production per acre is much lower than the domestic crops permit. The inefficiencies associated with non-sugar agriculture reflect general lack of skilled management due rather to an inadequate number of managers than to deficiencies of intelligence and initiative.

This condition continues to exist in spite of large expenditures to expand and diversify agriculture. Agricultural services and research have been increased in all the territories. But only a very small portion of Development and Welfare funds has been spent on the sugar industry, which finances its own research. In other agricultural activities the progress which has occurred has not been due to natural evolution. What has been accomplished has been achieved by the promotional impetus and encouragement provided by government agencies. Most of the money spent to date has been devoted to education and research. But it cannot fairly be stated that these fundamental methods of encouraging expanding production have achieved significant results. There are no signs of an agricultural revolution similar to that which is taking place in industrial development of the area.[19]

V

Except in Barbados, there were few organized fishing activities in the British Caribbean as late as 1945. The industry was carried on mainly by individual fishermen, mostly on a part-time basis. Methods were inefficient, and working conditions offered little to attract competent young men seeking steady employment. Since the beginning of Development and Welfare operations,

19. A. L. Jolly, "Agriculture," *The Caribbean,* X, 4 (November, 1956), 80–81.

however, much attention has been devoted to promoting the fishing industry as a means of increasing local food production. In most of the territories definite progress has been made, although the tendency to avoid the industry as a source of employment has not been entirely eliminated.

Since 1946 the local governments have enacted legislation to stimulate and organize fishing activities. Exemptions from customs duties or rebates on fishing gear, marine engines, and fuel have been provided in Barbados, British Guiana, Jamaica, and Trinidad. Price controls on fish have been removed in British Honduras and Trinidad. Fisheries officers have been working successfully to arouse public consciousness to the importance of fish as a valuable natural resource. In Jamaica a Fish Farming Experimental Station is carrying on important research in the field. Marketing and storage of fish have been improved with the establishment of modern sanitary fish centers in many of the territories. One of the outstanding developments in the fishing industry has been the formation of cooperatives as the foundation of group action to provide facilities beyond the resources of individuals. Loans on reasonable terms are now made available through committees of the cooperatives. The major technical improvement in recent years has been the introduction of engines, purchased in many instances with government loans.[20]

VI

Forestry has always been an important economic factor in British Guiana and British Honduras. In the other Caribbean territories the forests serve primarily to supply local needs for lumber, to hold water supplies, and to prevent erosion of the soil. Within the last decade, however, Trinidad has implemented with considerable success a program of controlled regeneration and development of its teak and mora forests. How-

20. "Fisheries," *The Caribbean*, X, 4 (November, 1956), 91–94.

ever, the most important progress achieved in forestry development has been the adoption of long-term policies designed to
preserve and improve the production potential of the area's
forest resources. The regeneration scheme adopted in 1948
in British Honduras is indicative of the prevalent philosophy
that foresight and planning are the first requisites for preservation of the wealth of the forests.[21]

VII

The natural beauty and mild climate of the Caribbean area
have formed the foundations of an expanding tourist industry
during the last decade. Jamaica's Tourist Board, publicly financed, has general jurisdiction over this phase of the island's
economy. In 1956 more than 160,000 tourists spent £7,000,000
in the territory. In Trinidad, where a Tourist Board also is
in operation, visitors spent $9,500,000 in 1955, and most of the
other islands experienced an upswing in the tourist traffic. All
areas have benefited from the abolition in 1956 of the United
States tax on travel to the Caribbean. Most of the territories
are members of the Caribbean Tourist Association, an international organization originally established under the sponsorship
of the Caribbean Commission. The objective of the Association
is to stimulate development of tourism in the Caribbean by closer
cooperation of the nations concerned with territorial responsibilities in the area.[22]

VIII

Revenues of the local governments have soared in the period
since 1939. There is no commonly accepted method, however,

21. Colonial Office, *Report on British Honduras for the Year 1954* (London, 1956), pp. 55–59; "Forestry," *The Caribbean*, X, 4 (November,
1956), 95–97.
22. Luke Report, 1955–56, p. 32; *The Caribbean*, IX, 9 (April, 1956),
193.

of measuring degrees of inflation which have occurred in different areas. Indeed, local authorities, in spite of augmented income, have been hard pressed to meet serious problems arising from high living costs, high prices of consumer goods, and financial demands imposed by increased government activity in development projects. In these circumstances all colonial governments have experienced considerable financial strain.[23]

While increased revenues have permitted local governments to expand economic activities to a remarkable extent, colonial authorities still face problems of varying degrees of complexity. Rising costs of labor and materials have projected government expenditures to new high levels. Another complication has been the rapid expansion of the population, which increased by some 500,000 from 1948 to 1955 to reach a total of more than 3,500,000. These basic statistics graphically emphasize the serious nature of the difficulties involved in expanding public services to keep pace with constantly increasing numbers to be served.

Nevertheless, the local governments are addressing themselves with increasing vigor to the task of expanding agricultural and industrial production. To this end they are striving to create a favorable climate for capital investment from sources at home and abroad. At the same time they are broadening the scope of basic government services necessary for intensive economic development. Special attention is accorded to farmers, both large- and small-scale, through provision of research and training facilities, extension of capital and credit, improvement of market facilities, and by every means to increase the farmer's efficiency and to promote the best use of the land. Agricultural planning is directed toward the ultimate objective of diversifying production with proper regard to market prospects for new crops.

Grants and loans provided for Colonial Development and Welfare schemes during the sixteen years to March 31, 1956,

23. Sir Stephen Luke, *Development and Welfare in the West Indies, 1954* (London, 1955), p. 21.

reached a total of slightly less than £36,000,000. The existence
of the Development and Welfare organization will be terminated
early in 1958 when most of its functions will be taken over by
the new British Caribbean federation. The West Indian economy remains vulnerable because, while it has become diversified
to some degree, it is still a specialized one depending on future
prospects in overseas markets for a limited range of tropical
products. Nevertheless, the Comptroller of Development and
Welfare in his latest report makes special note of the existing
atmosphere of activity and confidence. New hands are seizing
responsibility, and aroused interest in the problems of social
and economic betterment prevails everywhere. In little more
than a single decade intensive planning for comprehensive
economic development has become a characteristic feature of
government policies in the British Caribbean areas.[24]

24. Luke Report, 1955-1956, pp. 5–6, 18–19.

G. V. Helwig: SOCIETY IN THE
BRITISH WEST INDIES

THIS PAPER IS BASED on intimate first-hand knowledge
of one territory over a long period of years and on information
of the other territories gained at second hand. Society in
Jamaica, the territory I know best, will be treated the most fully,
and the pattern of society in Jamaica will be used as a convenient
standard for comparison. Jamaica has the largest population,
over 1,600,000, which is about half the population of all the
territories. It is the largest island territory, though it is a great
deal smaller in area than either of the mainland territories of
British Guiana and British Honduras. Nonetheless, other islands
and territories have in their societies special features not found
in Jamaica.

I

Society in Jamaica comprises peoples of different races:
Europeans, Negroes, Indians, Chinese, Jews, and Syrians, with
the inevitable blending of the races. The outstanding features
of society are the variety of types and the overwhelming predominance of peoples of mainly African origin or type—folk
who are usually described locally as "colored," the term
"Negro" or "Negroid" being less acceptable to them and often
regarded as derogatory. The predominance of African types

27

exists throughout the territories except in Trinidad and British Guiana, where these types are equalled or exceeded by people of East Indian race. Another exception is the Cayman Islands, with people of predominantly European race.

Traces of the aboriginal inhabitants, Arawaks and Caribs, are rare and have to be sought for. These island Amerindians were almost completely wiped out by the Spaniards within a short period after their discovery of the New World. There are few, if any, Caribs of pure race in Dominica, in Grenada, and in St. Vincent. The Arawaks, a less hardy and warlike race, continue to exist only on the mainland in British Guiana and in the blood of some of the descendants of escaped slaves, the Maroons, in Jamaica.

One can hardly escape a feeling of regret at the passing away of the Arawaks, who were peaceful and hospitable. Their first contacts with Columbus and his men are described from original sources in Samuel Eliot Morison's book about Columbus.[1] In his letter to his sovereigns Columbus laid stress on the gentleness and generosity of the natives. The Spaniards are usually charged with their destruction, and it is only fair to them to recall the persistent efforts of one of their priests, Las Casas, the Apostle of the Indians, to save them.

The racial pattern in the majority of the island territories is similar to that of Jamaica: a small minority of white people, chiefly of United Kingdom stock, with an overwhelming majority of black and colored people. The territories which do not conform to this pattern are Trinidad, British Guiana, and the Cayman Islands, as noted above.

In British Guiana the East Indians are in the majority, and there is a large community of people of Portuguese descent. In Jamaica the Chinese minority is comparable in numbers with the whites. There East Indians are more numerous but less influential than whites or Chinese. There also are to be found Jews, whose ancestors found refuge in Jamaica a long time ago

1. *Admiral of the Open Sea: a Life of Christopher Columbus* (Boston: Little, Brown & Co., 1941).

when they fled from persecution in Spain and Portugal. The
economy of Jamaica has been enriched by industries brought
there by Cubans of Spanish descent and by the wealth brought
in by refugee French families from Haiti, whose descendants are
now indistinguishable from other white or colored Jamaicans
except by their French names.

In Trinidad and in St. Lucia there are people with French
blood whose native speech is French or a dialect derived from
the French language. In Barbados, the island among the first
settled by the British (in 1625) and the only one which has
always remained in British hands since its settlement, there is a
greater proportion of whites in the population than in any other
territory. The population is composed of whites, blacks, and
colored almost exclusively. It is a small island, more fully
developed economically than any other, carrying the densest
population per square mile to be found in the territories, perhaps
the densest in any agricultural country in the world (over 1340
people per square mile in 1953). It is greatly to the credit of
Barbados that it has reached the furthest of any territory in providing universal education for its citizens. A high standard of
education is provided especially in the secondary schools.
Colored and white Barbadians are to be found settled throughout all the British Caribbean territories. Emigration is stimulated
by pressure of population. Moreover, Barbadians are well suited
by education and native energy to be successful settlers.

II

If one of the basic features of the society is variety in racial
type, with African predominating, or African and Asiatic (Indian) sharing the predominance, the other paramount feature
is the social ferment due to political advance, to recent and
rapid changes from government by a colonial power (Great
Britain) to or towards representative and responsible government. These changes have been aided and encouraged by the
mother country, and have gone furthest in Jamaica, in Barbados,

and in Trinidad. All three islands now have legislatures elected by universal adult suffrage and have forms of cabinet government with the administration in the hands of a chief minister and ministers appointed from the elected members of the legislature.

At the turn of the century these islands were administered by the British Colonial Office with the aid of a legislature elected on a limited franchise which had more or less circumscribed powers. In effect government was mainly by Colonial Office officials from the mother country and planters descended from English settlers. This form of government continued until about twelve years ago when World War II ended, except that in the course of years the racial composition of the legislatures had changed to include more and more colored representatives of the people. In the most advanced territories politically, the racial composition of the legislatures now conforms closely to the racial type of the majority of the electors, and the racial composition in the government services is changing rapidly to conform in the same way. The Colonial Office officials appointed by the mother country used to occupy the senior posts in the service. Now as these posts become vacant, they are filled as a general rule by locally born officials.

There has never in my lifetime been in Jamaica any discrimination against colored people founded on law, nor any avenues in the professions, in commerce, or in industry, which were not open to colored and white. I have always from childhood known, or known of, colored persons and some of pure, or almost pure, African race who were respected ornaments in the various professions, in the government service, and in trade and commerce. It was once true that a greater share of the wealth of the country lay in the hands of the whites and with it the economic power and influence derived from their wealth and that the white inhabitants had an advantage because of their race. Any advantage based on race or on the historical ascendancy of the whites has lessened and is lessening, and with it is passing the exclusiveness, the tendency for isolation of a ruling minority from the majority, as more and more men and women of color swell the ranks of the professions and gain wealth and power in trade and industry. With these political and economic changes there has developed a greater sense of solidarity and friendship between people of different races, derived from schooling at the same secondary school, from friendly competition in games at school and in clubs, from contacts in the practise of the professions or in commerce and industry.

It is easy for an observer to sense in the young people a strong feeling of emergent nationalism, a sense of excitement even, in the taking over of the government and the management of public affairs by the elected representatives of the people, and to recognize in these young people a sense of purpose, of determination to build soundly and well for their advancement, so that they may be citizens of a nation of which they may be proud. This sense is particularly evident among young graduates from universities and in students at the University College of the West Indies in Jamaica, at universities in the United Kingdom, in Canada, in the United States. Wherever there are groups of West Indian students, there are likely to be associations of these students. Anyone who is privileged to meet one of these groups is likely to be very favorably impressed by the politically conscious young men and women in the group. They have a strong belief in the future of their countries and an eagerness to play their part in the progress and advancement of the territories. A few perhaps have thoughts of political careers. The majority envisage for themselves careers in the professions and in the government services. They feel that they are wanted and valued, that they will have ample opportunities to render service and to earn due rewards and recognition.

III

Society is essentially conservative, tenacious of longstanding customs and habits, slow to change and adopt new ways. The pattern and shape of any society are based on its origins and

past history. In the West Indies, though the European now
forms a small part of the community, he has been on the scene
the longest, has had the greatest influence in government, in
education and religion, in industry, and has shaped society to
follow the pattern of Western democracy as practised in the
United Kingdom. The peoples brought from Africa as slaves
had little opportunity to preserve their social organization and
their customs. Such preservation was obstructed by planters
because any association of slaves was likely to help them to
organize and to rebel against their owners. The outcome in
Jamaica is a social organization almost entirely derived from
Britain, the mother country, with vestigial survivals of African
customs. This does not hold good in the same way in Trinidad
and British Guiana. There the pattern is predominantly that
of western European democracy, but the religious beliefs and
practices and the social customs of the East Indians are largely
derived from India, though many Indians are converts to
Christianity.

Society in the West Indies is still a stratified society with
merging upper and middle classes, with the laboring classes,
skilled labor in particular, aspiring to the middle classes. The
large majority of the people are poor agricultural workers and
peasant farmers, manual and unskilled laborers, domestic servants, and the unemployed.

The middle classes and those aspiring to middle-class status
conform closely in beliefs, ideals, standards of behavior, customs, and habits to those of the middle classes in the United
Kingdom. Though greatly outnumbered now by laboring
classes (unskilled low-wage earners and unemployed), the middle classes set the standards to which the lower classes aspire,
and as economic development proceeds and standards of living
improve, the middle-class ranks are being swelled more and more
from the laboring classes and their standards adopted ever
more widely.

In the book *Family and Society in Jamaica*[2] there is a study

2. F. M. Henriques (London: Eyre and Spottiswoode, 1953).

mainly of middle-class society. In it are described features different from English middle-class society, such as the tendency of economically successful Jamaicans to marry women fairer than themselves and the social and economic advantages of those with fairer complexions. Counterbalancing the undoubted tendency of ambitious Jamaicans to marry up the color scale, there is the growth of a real sense of pride among the blacks in their own race, which growth was fostered in the United States and in Jamaica, for the first time, by Marcus Garvey.[3] He was born in Jamaica and had a notable career in the United States, though it ended with his expulsion and his return to Jamaica. Lloyd Braithwaite's study[4] on social stratification in Trinidad shows that brown- and fair-skinned persons have economic and social advantages in Trinidad as in Jamaica. The same is no doubt true throughout the West Indies.

IV

Most of the studies made of society in the West Indies are made of the laboring classes. At one extreme there are the unemployed or under-employed groups. In the cities to which these unemployed tend to gravitate from the rural areas, they provide recruits at the lowest extreme for criminal groups, slum dwellers, and practitioners and followers of the occult arts, witch-craft, and obeah derived from African witch-doctor lore. These unemployed or under-employed groups find avenues for self-expression and means of preserving their self-respect in Poco-mania and revival cults, such as those described by George Eaton Simpson,[5] which practise possession by spirits and trances. Members of the groups who become more successful economically tend to join recognized Christian churches.

3. Edmund David Cronon, *Black Moses: the Story of Marcus Garvey and the Universal Negro Improvement Association* (Madison: University of Wisconsin Press, 1955).

4. "Social Stratification in Trinidad," *Social and Economic Studies,* University College of the West Indies, II, 2, 3 (1953).

5. "Jamaican Revivalist Cults," *ibid.,* V, 4 (1956).

The standard of living of these lower classes is too low for them to aspire to stable family life, and the percentage of illegitimate births is very high. Men and women joined in "common-law unions" usually find the cost of getting married prohibitive, for couples are expected to conform to the established practice of expensive weddings. Moreover, a wife expects more from a husband than from a common-law partner, and a husband who is a low-wage earner may find himself unable to support his wife in the way she expects to live. Thus a marriage can disrupt what has been a stable common-law union.

In these classes there is then by established custom freedom in sexual behavior and irresponsible paternity, and the burden of rearing the offspring is very often left to the mother, who may in turn pass it on to her own mother or aunt. There is an established matriachal family pattern, with the fathers making little or no contribution to the rearing and training of their children.

Edith Clarke[6] and Madeline Kerr[7] have studied and reported on typical lower-class groups in Jamaica. The free sexual habits of the males and the matriachal family groups spring from the disruption of the families under slavery—from the encouragement of promiscuous breeding to keep up the supply of slaves, from the discouragement or prevention of the teaching of religion to the slaves, and from the practice of white overseers and owners of estates in cohabiting with selected female slaves. It was only later when the period of emancipation was approaching that ministers of religion were able to begin their missionary work among slaves. The teaching of the Christian religion, though largely accepted by the people emerging from slavery, has not been effective in establishing the practice of Christian marriage and stable family life for the masses, though it is accepted as an ideal to be achieved if possible.

6. "Land Tenure and the Family in Four Communities in Jamaica," *ibid.*, I, 4 (1953).

7. *Personality and Conflict in Jamaica* (Liverpool: University of Liverpool Press, 1952).

For the future the prospects seem to be that as the economic development of the territories advances, as universal education becomes available to help raise productivity and income, there will be fewer illegitimate births, fewer children without the care and affection of both their parents, and perhaps a more stable population in numbers, even though a recent study shows that more children (in proportion) are born of married than of unmarried parents, and the children born in wedlock have better prospects of growing to maturity.[8]

V

The peoples in the British Caribbean territories are on the threshold of further political advance, and the next step in their advance will be the federation of those of the territories which have agreed to unite. These territories and peoples are becoming better known to the peoples of the mainland countries of America because of their political advance, because of the strategic positions they occupy in relation to the United States and to Central and South America, because of their trade, and perhaps especially because there are more and more people from the United States and the United Kingdom who are finding the territories beautiful, healthy, and attractive places to visit for holidays and to live in. A well-known governor of Jamaica in the early years of this century wrote a book about the island. The title of his book *Jamaica, the Blessed Island*[9] is equally applicable to almost any of the British island territories. The islands are blessed in many ways, but not in economic resources; and the inhabitants still have many problems to solve before they will have a satisfactory standard of living for all. The inhabitants are fully aware of the difficulty of the tasks ahead, of the need for all the help they can get in technical aid, guidance, and capital investments from abroad. But there is already a sense

8. D. Ibberson, "Illegitimacy and the Birth Rate," *Social and Economic Studies*, University College of the West Indies, V, 1 (1956).

9. Baron Sydney Haldane Olivier (London: Faber & Faber, Ltd., 1936).

of initial achievements of which the inhabitants may well be proud. Not the least of the achievements are the cooperation and unity of peoples of diverse races and origins in the early stages of their progress to the full stature of nationhood.

POPULATION AND RACIAL DISTRIBUTION IN
BRITISH CARIBBEAN TERRITORIES

FROM CENSUS REPORTS AND ANNUAL GOVERNMENT REPORTS

Barbados	1946 Census
European	m. 4,301
	f. 5,538
African	m. 67,334
	f. 81,589
Asiatic	m. 78
	f. 58
Mixed	m. 13,980
	f. 19,848
Total	192,726
1953 Estimate	222,942

British Guiana	1946 Census
Amerindian	4.4%
Portuguese	2.3
Other European	.7
African	38.2
East Indian	43.5
Chinese	1.0
Other Asiatic	.1
Mixed	10.0
Total	369,400
1953 Amerindian	18,136
Others	447,280
Total	465,416

British Honduras	1946 Census
Amerindian	10,030
White	2,329
Black	22,693
East Indian	1,366
Syrian	128
Chinese	50
Carib	4,112
Mixed	18,360
Not stated	152
Total	59,220
1953 Estimate	75,780

Cayman Islands	1943 Census
Black	1,051
Coloured	3,518
White	2,050
Total	6,619

Jamaica	1943 Census
Black	78.1%
Coloured	17.5
White	.4
Chinese	.6
Chinese coloured	.4
East Indian	1.7
East Indian coloured	.4
Syrian	.1
Other races	.8
Total	1,237,000
1956 Total	1,600,000

Trinidad and Tobago	
1954 Census total	697,550
East Indian	36

Turks and Caicos Islands	1943 Census
African	4,081
Mixed	1,935
European	122
Total	6,138
1952 Estimate	6,500

RACIAL DISTRIBUTION *(Continued)*

Leeward Islands	1946 Census			Total 108,840
	White	Black	Asiatic	Mixed
Antigua	1.7%	86.0%	.2%	12.1%
Barbuda	.1	52.9	—	47.0
Montserrat	.5	92.9	.1	6.4
St. Kitts	2.6	85.9	.3	11.0
Nevis	.6	90.7	.7	8.0
Anguilla	1.8	79.9	.1	18.0
Tortola	.5	87.0	—	12.4
Other Virgin Islands	.6	87.9	—	11.5

Windward Islands	1946 Census			Total 251,770
	Windward Islands	Dominica	Grenada	St. Lucia	St. Vincent
Carib	.16%	.08%	.16%	.02%	.39%
White	1.2	.3	.9	.5	3.1
Black	60.0	24.9	73.7	58.1	73.1
Asiatic	3.2	.1	4.9	3.8	3.0
Mixed	35.5	74.6	20.4	37.6	20.5

Note: I am indebted to Dr. H. D. Huggins, Director of the Institute of Social and Economic Research, for access to the Library of the Institute, and for opportunities to consult with workers at the Institute. The latest population figures given here were culled from publications in the Library of the Institute.

Sidney W. Hockey: AN EMERGING CULTURE
IN THE BRITISH WEST INDIES

AN ATTEMPT TO SURVEY the cultural pattern of the British West Indies by a professional librarian whose nine years in the area have been fully occupied with the policy and practice of establishing public library service may appear a presumption. But since library service aims at bridging the gap between the reading and life of the community by the provision of books and reading material to every man, woman, and child who can use them, it may be conceded that such service is the keystone upon which the development of the culture of the community rests, and that the quality and nature of library work, which is related to the expressed needs of library users, will be a fair indication of the cultural life of the community. The question of a "West Indian" culture can arouse controversy as passionate as that engendered by a political campaign, and I hope that I may steer a middle course between the scholarly and sociological study which I am not competent to undertake and the nebulous and often pretentious writing to which this subject so easily lends itself.

I

The area with which we are concerned consists of the islands of Trinidad and Tobago, Barbados, the Windwards and Leewards, and Jamaica, which are scattered in a great arc of some

39

2,000 miles between British Guiana and British Honduras, the two colonies on the American mainland. British Guiana, Jamaica, and Trinidad account for 2,500,000 of the total population of some 3,000,000. This small population group is fragmented into smaller groups which owing to distance and bad communications have had little contact with one another, and the present cultural pattern reflects the history of these islands since they were fought over by the great powers in the period of colonial expansion, with the resulting importation of Africans as slaves and later East Indians as indentured labor. While the large and powerful East Indian group has preserved its traditional way of life and religious observances, the Africans, their tribal life shattered by their original uprooting and their subsequent dispersal in the sugar plantations, have absorbed the culture of the governing metropolitan powers, modified though it may be by vestigial tribal customs and practices, the social and economic background, and a tropical climate. The Spanish and French influences of the early days of colonization still remain in varying degrees, both in the speech and folklore of many of the country districts and in the rather self-conscious cultivation of both these cultures by a number of the creole groups.

The island of Trinidad which contains every element of the multi-racial society in these islands may be described as the melting pot where all these components meet and where, considering their diversity, they coexist in reasonable amity. The smaller islands, with an average population of 70,000, form more homogeneous and often startlingly different groups, each one self-contained and until recently knowing and caring little about its neighbors. The short flight from Barbados to St. Lucia, for example, will plunge the traveler into an exuberant patois-speaking French and Roman Catholic background, just as he has accustomed himself to the stratified social atmosphere of "Little England" where, most suitably, the buses plying to the suburbs bear the names of some of the more respectable English watering places.

In spite of a considerable improvement in standards of living during recent years, the general background of this predominately rural society is one of poverty and a low standard of life. The social and economic background of the area has been dealt with more fully in another session of this conference, and this brief summary is intended only to place in perspective the following discussions on the cultural activities of its people and also to make the point that the society, the economy, and the culture are closely interrelated, a fact which is not always accepted by those whose thinking is colored, understandably, by the long and often bitter struggle, first for freedom, and latterly for self-government, and the consequent urge to cast off colonial domination. The culture of a nation is the expression of its way of life, and its evolution is shaped by every aspect of the development of the nation; it cannot be drafted like a constitution or superimposed by a set of statutes. Moreover it cannot exist in a vacuum, and it is subject to the law of demand and response.

II

It is inevitable, therefore, that the indigenous culture of these islands is mainly to be found in the music and dance of the people, these reflecting the hard and often primitive lives of many of the inhabitants of the remoter country districts and the different backgrounds of the various islands. Poverty, lack of educational facilities and social services, coupled with a plantation economy, have resulted in a lack of traditional craftsmanship, good husbandry, and the usual expressions of rural life in stabilized village communities. The result is a continual drift to the urban areas of the larger islands, particularly from the eastern Caribbean to Trinidad, and it is here that all the various influences meet and make themselves seen and heard. Again the main original contribution in music and speech comes from the class usually described as "the common people," in the extraordinary development of the steel band and the salty wit of the Calypso which, incidentally, suffers a sad sea change on its way to the United States. These spring from the annual celebration of carnival and find their true place during the two days in the year when Trinidad abandons itself to dance and song, and its people express their innate appreciation of color, rhythm, and the sheer enjoyment of life.

It is therefore not surprising that many West Indians have become international figures in the world of entertainment and sport. Similarly it is not surprising that they have shown considerable talent in the graphic arts, particularly painting, and many homes and art galleries are adorned with works which by their bold use of color and originality demonstrate in no uncertain terms the existence of a West Indian school of art.

It is in the sphere of literature and drama that we find the law of response and demand operating, for the writer has to seek a wider public than can be found in the West Indies, and the poetry and prose produced are to be found mainly in slim volumes or periodical collections bearing the obvious stamp of local printing and production. Most of the writers, therefore, settle abroad, and although their works are often based on West Indian life and history, they seldom return to their native country. The dramatist, too, finds it difficult to secure an appreciative audience for his work; and the theatre, although there is considerable talent and an increasing number of plays are being written by local authors and performed by local companies, is still at what may not unfairly be described as the amateur dramatic level of a large provincial town.

Nevertheless, during my period of work in the West Indies I have watched what may be described as an intellectual "Operation Bootstrap" spreading throughout these islands and broadening from the small group of the intelligentsia to a wider base which will in time produce a culture that will stand on its own right. This is a society which has not been subjected to what has been described as "a mass culture" and to many of the dubious benefits of this materialistic and technological age, and in my own sphere of work the continuous demands for books on every conceivable subject, particularly by the young people, far outstrip our resources. In the United States and Great Britain a considerable amount of thought is devoted to the problem of attracting people into libraries; here the only bait we need is the book. The remainder of this paper will be devoted to the consideration of the forces within and without the West Indies which are shaping its cultural development.

III

The greatest factor in this development has been the reorientation and extension of the education services, hampered though they are by the ever-present gap between the funds available for this purpose and a rapidly increasing population, 37 per cent of which consists of children under 14 years of age. In the larger colonies every effort is being made to extend the provision of free secondary education, and more significant perhaps is the emphasis which is being placed on technical education in an effort to break down the inherited aversion to any form of activity related to manual labour and to provide technicians for the development programmes which are going forward. The type of material continually in demand in the southern region of our library service in Trinidad, where a technical college has recently been established, is comparable to that of any industrial area in Britain, and it is obvious that the youngsters now growing up will do much to qualify the statement that standards of craftsmanship are low.

The ministries of education are also concerned with the ends as well as the means of their education policy, and it is significant that in Trinidad this ministry has been renamed the Ministry of Education and Culture, and that it takes under its wing library services and a department of culture; more to the point, it is strongly supporting their work. Education extension services and social welfare organizations are also doing valuable work with community groups, particularly in the country districts, and again these activities are reflected throughout these islands by demands for library services which in many cases cannot yet be met. And of course the one thing which has given pride and body to all forms of educational activity in the West Indies has been the establishment of the University College of the West Indies which has brought university education within the reach of many to whom it was hitherto denied.

From the beginning, University College has accepted the responsibility of extending its influence beyond the campus by the establishment of an Extra Mural Department which, under the direction of a senior officer, maintains tutors at strategic points throughout the area, and the latest report of this department indicates that some 7,000 students are enrolled in the various classes organized by these tutors. In most of the libraries one will find these classes going on in the evenings, and the demand created by the interest aroused has been one of the most telling factors in the struggle to establish library services in the smaller islands and (an equally important step) in the recognition of the need of a Regional service to build up a "pool" of specialist material and, by maintaining a Union Catalogue, to organize the interlending of such material between libraries in the area. This is adult education in the true sense of the term; it is also federation in action. An interesting addition to the work of this department has been the appointment of a drama adviser who travels throughout the area working with local groups and organizing drama festivals which bring groups from several islands together.

The existence of the University College has obviously done much to direct and fuse the work of many of the cultural organizations scattered throughout the islands, in the two-way traffic of undergraduates from widely varying backgrounds and social levels gathering to live and to study together and the outward flow of expert assistance and advice from the University departments, together with the returning graduates trained in a West Indian background to work for their own people. The University College motto *Oriens ex occidente lux* appropriately sums up the high sense of mission of its founders, and in keeping with the present spirit of the West Indies, it is pointed out that this is not a quotation from any classical work of literature. It is original.

The other dynamic force which has made the West Indies "culture conscious," if one may use such an expression without offense, is the rapid progress being made towards self-government, which will culminate in 1958 in the establishment of a federation consisting of Barbados, Jamaica, Trinidad, and the Windward and Leeward Islands and, it is anticipated, the achievement of dominion status within the British Commonwealth in the near future. West Indians are now holding the reins of government and occupy the highest posts in the Administration, and the resulting support of all forms of West Indian cultural activity, if not always well conceived or directed, is a healthy and understandable expression of national pride. Moreover, the difficult and protracted negotiations preceding the establishment of federation have brought these islands together as never before, and federation will be ushered in in Trinidad, the federal capital, with a West Indian festival which will include participants from the whole area.

The spirit abroad in the West Indies today can be summed up in the words of one of her leading statesmen, Norman Manley: "But I do know that we have a contribution to make to history. How to make a multi-racial society work with humanity, with self acceptance, with the inner significance of liberty manifest in every sphere—that is a task we have already gone far to master, that is something we will make for the world to admire and, I pray, learn from." This rings true, and its acceptance by those who are working in the West Indies will do much to enable them to place a great many petty irritations and misunderstandings in their proper perspective.

IV

The concluding section of this paper will be devoted to a consideration of the impact of outside agencies working in the

West Indies, which as might be expected from the geographical position of these islands and the ethnic pattern are many and various. Each of the large population groups is served by the cultural agencies of its parent country, such as the office of the Indian Commissioner and L'Alliance Française; and in recent years the increasing interest of the United States in West Indian affairs is reflected by the establishment of the United States Information Service. Although these are British colonies, we find what may appear at first sight to be the unnecessary existence of the United Kingdom Information Office and the British Council, the latter an organization specifically charged with the dissemination of British culture. The Spanish-speaking element naturally looks to Venezuela, whose Department of Culture distributes an impressive and well produced array of publications, such as the quarterly *Revista Nacional de Cultura*. Subjected to this continual barrage of cultural activity, it is not altogether surprising that in some sections of the population there arises from time to time an expression of opinion comparable to that which prompted the University of Oxford Union to pass a resolution "That this house will resist the spread of the American way of life in Great Britain," substituting for "American" whatever form of cultural activity has offended certain susceptibilities.

The task of promoting cultural relations based on mutual respect and trust between the larger powers and countries less advanced politically and economically is one which requires the utmost tact and (what has been sadly lacking in the past in many instances) central organizations which can direct and plan this work with some assurance of continuity. Much of this work is best done in an atmosphere of anonymity with the resultant lack of appreciation and a low rating in the eyes of Treasury officials; moreover, work of this kind always receives the first blast of any financial ill wind, and projects which have taken many years of patient work are often nipped in the bud as they are reaching fruition.

Nevertheless these cultural organizations have made a considerable contribution to the life of the West Indies, not so much, I would make bold to say, in their attempts to "put over" the British, American, or any other way of life, as in their unobtrusive support of local organizations and in the opportunities they have afforded West Indians to follow up the stimulus provided in this way with experience in a wider background overseas. I am quite unrepentant in my opinion that the British and American cultural organizations in this area, which shares with them a common language and fundamentally the same cultural heritage, should concentrate their resources on specific professional and specialist assistance rather than on the maintenance of programmes which relate more closely to the needs of non-English-speaking countries and which often overlap with work already done by local organizations and educational bodies. In other words, without particularly relating it to America, I would subscribe to Eugene Staley's comment that "Communism's most strategic export to under-developed countries is ideas. The tragedy of the world today is that ideas occupy far too prominent a place in the United States' strategic list of prohibited exports."

I would like to justify this sweeping statement by a brief description of the work done by the British Council in the development of library services in these colonies which I think illustrates the principles upon which the statement is based. In 1945 the Council allocated the sum of £80,000 to continue a programme of work initiated by a Carnegie grant and designed to establish free public library services linked by a regional organization throughout the eastern Caribbean. Jamaica by reason of its size and position was dealt with by a similar but separate scheme. Two overseas librarians were attached to the Council, and over a period of seven years they continued the work which had been ably launched by the Canadian librarian in charge of the Carnegie scheme.

This is not going to be a recital of the trials and tribulations of pioneers who can be as boring as the people who insist on discussing in detail their operations; we are concerned only with the way in which this work was done and the results it has

achieved. Today each of these colonies has a free public library
service financed by the government and wholly staffed by West
Indians, many of whom through the Regional Training School
possess the highest international qualifications and are pursuing
this work according to the best standards of professional principles and practice. Here, therefore, is an example of a cultural
programme which has not only achieved its own objectives by
demonstrating the value of a British institution and providing
focal points for its activities throughout the area, but also, by a
programme planned with the cooperation and financial assistance of the governments concerned and therefore keeping pace
with the social and economic development of the area, has made
a valuable and lasting contribution to the cultural development
of the area. Carnegie saw this many years ago when he pointed
out that "a library service does not pauperize: it gives nothing
for nothing; it helps those who help themselves." A recognition
of these principles would, I submit, avoid a good deal of the
misapplication of resources and misunderstanding of motives
which often negate a great many well meaning efforts of this
kind. It is indicative of the happy personal relationships
achieved in work done in this way that the overseas officers often
remain in the service of the local governments to continue it.

The British Government has implemented its policy of assistance leading to economic as well as political independence
by the establishment of the Colonial Development and Welfare
Organization, which has also proceeded along the lines of initial
assistance to projects approved by their advisers in consultation
with the governments concerned, on the clear understanding
that such schemes will eventually have to be maintained from
local revenue. This organization, though not directly concerned
with cultural activities, has done much by planned ten-year
development programmes (£24,000,000 was allocated for the
period 1946-56) to promote many schemes of social and economic development which have helped to raise the standard of
life in these areas.

The British West Indies have also benefited from the work of

the Caribbean Commission, an international organization which
has helped to fill many gaps in accurate statistical information
and research, and whose services as a central clearing house and
information center have, in my opinion, not been fully utilized.
Although it is purely an advisory body, the Commission affords
a *pied à terre* for the activities of international organizations,
such as the World Health Organization and UNESCO, whose
experts have undertaken many useful programmes of work
throughout the area.

Apart from these government-sponsored efforts to assist the
West Indies there are, of course, the overseas business interests
which are taking part in the industrial development of these
islands; and many of the large oil, bauxite, and shipping companies are making generous provision for what might be described as development and welfare programmes of their own.
This is a realistic acceptance of the fact that the efficiency of
these enterprises depends upon the well-being and technical
training of their employees, but many of the officials (and their
wives) go far beyond these terms of reference in their voluntary
work with local organizations and in the promotion of assistance
from similar sources abroad. One can quote as an example the
flood of books which has recently descended upon Trinidad as
a result of a book drive in the United States launched by the
Alcoa Steamship Company.

The mention of shipping reminds one of the tourist trade,
which makes an important contribution to the national income
of the West Indies. I noticed that tourism was originally included in this conference session and subsequently eliminated;
the compilers of the programme may have had the same doubts
as the writer about the relationship between tourism and cultural relations! The average tourist can obviously do little more
than see sights, and he must feel that his contact with the people
of the country consists solely of outstretched hands and exploitation on the one side and the disbursement of dollars on the
other. However there are people I would describe as travelers
rather than tourists, one comes across many of them quietly

pottering around the small islands, who do much to create bonds of friendship and understanding.

V

We have come full circle from the large organizations to the individual, and this is perhaps a fitting conclusion to what has been a personal and limited approach to a subject which touches upon all the problems facing a world whose peoples are being rapidly, perhaps too rapidly, brought together by the wonders of modern science. It may be felt that the tenor of this paper has oversimplified the subject by substituting "human relations" for "cultural relations," but as I have talked to groups of people in many remote places throughout these islands of the Caribbean, I have heard often nagging at the back of my mind the sonorous words of John Donne: "No man is an ilande, intire of itselfe; every man is a peece of the Continent, a part of the maine . . . any mans death diminishes me, because I am involved in Mankinde." The truism that the world is made up of individuals and that its future depends upon the sound judgment and good will of each one of us must be recognized and translated into effective action by all those who are striving to make the world a better place to live in.

Part II

THE DUTCH AREAS

Hans G. Hermans: CONSTITUTIONAL DEVELOPMENT OF THE NETHERLANDS ANTILLES AND SURINAM

THE DUTCH CAME TO AMERICA in the wake of the Spaniards almost a hundred years after the discovery of this "New World" by Columbus, and only because they had been drawn into a war of liberation with Spain. They came to the Spanish colonies because they firmly refused to be treated like a colony themselves by King Philip II and his successors. They came in order to fight Spain in its weakest spots and to safeguard their political independence by safeguarding their economic independence.

I

Conveniently situated at the crossroads of coasting navigation between the various parts of Europe, the Dutch were in an excellent position to organize the transportation of all kinds of merchandise from the Mediterranean to the Baltic Sea, from the Norwegian coast to the ports of the Iberian Peninsula, from Africa to Germany, from Germany to England, and so on, and thus to gain wealth, strength, and fame as the salesmen-shippers of Europe. When under the leadership of William, prince of Orange, better known as William the Silent, they came in 1568 in open revolt against the king of Spain to whom they were subservient and whose tyrannical regime they ever more

53

detested, Spain formally closed its harbors for the Dutch vessels; but as their activities were too advantageous for Spain, the Dutch ships continued to visit Spanish and Portuguese ports with the connivance of the local authorities.

This situation, however, ended abruptly in 1585 when suddenly all the Dutch possessions in Spanish and Portuguese harbors were confiscated and the Dutch sailors were imprisoned. The Dutch then could only get hold of any more "colonial" products by going to the colonies themselves. They knew their way because they had often been there in charter-navigation for the Spaniards. They knew, too, that the colonization of the American continent was too heavy a burden for Spain alone; they had seen with their own eyes how weak and vulnerable the Spanish Empire was, particularly in the Caribbean area with its many, many islands.

At first the Dutch did not want to get a permanent foothold in this area and were satisfied with occasional visits to the Spanish colonies, where they found enough readiness to engage in clandestine business because they paid considerably more for the colonial products than the Spanish mother country. They were confident that with the war ended, the old commercial traffic could be restored. But when a truce of twelve years failed to establish a permanent peace and in 1621 hostilities were resumed, the Dutch decided to establish at least some permanent footholds in the New World. The island of Curaçao (discovered in 1499 by Alonso de Ojeda) after having been a Spanish possession for 135 years was taken by the Dutch in 1634 as a *sedes belli* against Spain. Surinam, at first only a Dutch trading station but afterwards for a long time a British possession, became Dutch permanently in the second Dutch-English war in 1667 when England got New Amsterdam, the later New York.

II

There was no sharp distinction in those days between public law and civil law. Public duties were often entrusted to private organizations; civil contracts often contained regulations of public law. This happened particularly in the field of colonial administration.

The Dutch federal Republic of the Seven Provinces entrusted a private corporation—the West India Company—with the administration of its American "possessions." The West India Company operated with private capital, and its decisions were made by a board of 19 members representing the shareholders in the various participating cities and provinces. This board nominated the governor and the chief magistrates of each colony. These magistrates, together with three or four citizens, formed the council of the colony. This council governed the colony and meantime acted as chief court of justice. The governor got his instructions from the board of the West India Company in Holland, and the board acted freely except in matters of war in which its decision had to be submitted to the chief legislative and executive bodies of the Republic.

A curious fact about this "colonial government" is that it apparently started from two different conceptions of a "colony." The West Indian possessions were treated as "dependencies" to the extent that no major decisions could be taken without the consent of the mother country and that these major decisions were taken by a body primarily interested in profits. On the other hand they were treated as "settlements" in so far as their political institutions were inspired by the political institutions of the mother country, where the city magistrates were also nominated and were responsible both for the administration and for the application of justice. This ambiguous character of the government in the Dutch West Indian possessions repeatedly caused conflicts between people in the colonies and the magistrates at home. Sometimes the board at home blamed the governor for neglecting the commercial interests of the company; sometimes the citizens in the colony complained about the governor and his officers, accusing them of being too eager to make profits and too slack to defend the colonists' rights and their interests.

The West India Company in its original shape existed till 1674; in 1675 a new, reorganized, and much smaller company was established under the same name. This new company did not flourish too well; it had to be supported by government subsidies, and it lingered on until 1791 when its last concession expired. Its shareholders were no more interested in a new concession.

III

After 1792 the Dutch colonies were no longer governed by a private company administering them as a kind of public trustee. Their administration from that year on fell under the direct control of the Dutch government.

At the beginning of this new period, however, the Dutch government, under the spell of the French Revolution and the subsequent domination of Napoleonic France in Europe, was itself subject to a series of internal changes rapidly following each other, each inspired by more or less fundamentally different principles. The idea of the old federal republic of seven sovereign provinces still prevailed for a couple of years, but the Dutch people were fed up with its lack of energy and initiative during the whole of the eighteenth century and wanted to stop the endless mutual deliberations of the provincial governments, their quarrels about privileges and competencies with the resultant weakness and indecisiveness. During the temporary incorporation of the Republic in the French Empire, the bones of these provincial governments were broken; and when, after the fall of Napoleon, the Netherlands regained their freedom, they abandoned the idea of a republic, established a kingdom under the House of Orange-Nassau (in which Belgium was incorporated) and adopted a constitution with as many guarantees as possible against a return of the old provincialism.

This internal constitutional development of the Netherlands was reflected in the development of colonial government. As long as the old institutions of the federal Republic prevailed, the colonies were administered by various boards and councils nominated by the government but in which the cities and the provinces kept their own people and had their own say. Gradually, however, the control of the mother country became more and more concentrated in the hands of a few persons, until the first royal constitution stipulated that the administration of the "colonies and possessions" was an exclusive royal prerogative. The king in fact was not allowed to share his responsibilities for the administration of the colonies either with a private corporation like the West India Company or with the now powerless provinces or even with a parliament in which the Belgians, quite unaccustomed to such an administration and not quite trusted by the Dutch, had too large a voice. The colonial officials were responsible to the king and got their orders from him.

For the time being this autocratic regime worked pretty well, because the first king of the Netherlands, William I, was a broad-minded man who stimulated the economic activity of his own people as well as that of the colonies. As had the West India Company, he charged a council of three officials and three citizens with the internal government of the colonies, and in his instructions to this council, as well as to the governor, he stipulated that they had to take utmost care for the integrity of the civil service, for the application of justice, for the support of the poor, the widows, and the orphans, and for the promotion of economic activity. The instructions to the governor ordered in so many words that the harbor of Curaçao—one of the most beautiful natural harbors in the Western Hemisphere—must be opened for the ships of all friendly nations, that everything had to be done to attract merchants and craftsmen able to increase the islands' wealth, and that agriculture and cattle breeding should be furthered.

IV

During the strong personal reign of King William I the Dutch gradually switched from the idea of provincial autonomy to that of parliamentary democracy, a change in mental attitude which demonstrated itself in the great constitutional reform of 1848 whereby royal power was considerably reduced in favor of parliament.

The father and chief promoter of this constitutional reform, Jan Rudolf Thorbecke, strongly objected to the king's monarchic power in the colonies and secured parliament a share in this power. The people in the colonies, he reasoned, are Dutch citizens. Perhaps the rules of the Dutch government are not all at once applicable to them, but as Dutch citizens they have the full right to be protected by the Dutch parliament. The laws of the colonies had to be subjected to parliament as a guarantee against arbitrariness. Though the constitution still indicated the colonies as "overseas possessions," it is, according to its most renowned commentators, evident that they were after 1848 not considered "possessions."

In accordance with these new constitutional principles, new regulations for Surinam as well as for the Netherlands Antilles were enacted by law in 1865—but these regulations were, curiously enough, not identical for both territories. Surinam got a "colonial parliament" of 13 members, 9 of which were elected by some 800 voters. In the Netherlands Antilles the colonial parliament contained no elected members at all; apart from some senior executives occupying seats by virtue of their offices, its members were appointed by the governor. The Dutch legislative assembly protested against this exceptional position which it considered as inadequate with the relatively high level of education of the whites as well as of the colored people on these islands; but it finally supported the government's proposal because, according to the generally accepted standards of that time—there was no general suffrage in the Netherlands either —the right of voting had to be based on property qualifications, and only a very small group of people—some 200 in a population of 20,000 in Curaçao—could show such qualifications. Nomination by the governor was considered a better guarantee for democracy and against the rule of a few than a system of elections based on 200 voters. Moreover, the government faced the difficulty that another 13,000 people lived on the other islands. In a system of parliamentary elections these people, too, could claim the right to send their own representatives, and this would make regular meetings of the colonial parliament almost impossible as long as communications between the islands were defective. Thus, political institutions in the West Indian territories of the Netherlands after 1865 were not quite similar to the political institutions in the mother country, since they did not all proceed from considerations of "colonialism"; some of them at least were only concessions to local conditions on the islands.

The Regulations of 1865 did not include anything like ministerial responsibility for the colonial parliament. All executive power was concentrated in the hands of the governor, personal representative of the king and responsible only to him. This did not mean that the king could still govern the colonies according to his own pleasure, because the constitutional revision of 1848 in the Netherlands made the cabinet ministers, without whose cooperation the king remained powerless, responsible to the Dutch parliament. Indirectly the governors thus were responsible to the parliament at The Hague. In the stipulations of the law their sole executive responsibility to a monarch might look like sheer colonialism; in fact, however, against the background of the Dutch constitution, it was a responsibility to the elected representatives of the Dutch people for the welfare and the application of law in a part of the Kingdom considered as a settlement of that same people.

The fact that the governor was not formally responsible to the colonial parliament did not mean that this parliament had no power at all. The budget, as well as every bill, had to be subjected to its judgment, and everyone of its members could introduce bills on his own initiative, as well as amendments to the governor's proposals. Generally speaking, the governor could negate its decisions, but in fact he could do so only if the interests of the mother country were evidently at stake, as for instance when the budget of the colony showed a deficit to be supplied by the Netherlands. The islands of the Netherlands Antilles were in fact politically dependent only in so far as they were financially dependent.

During the second half of the nineteenth century many of the highest government executives were local people, descendants of Portuguese-Jewish merchants and of traders, captains, and officials of the West India Company, who a century ago or more had established themselves in Curaçao and formed there an indigenous group of whites with an essentially Dutch culture and with an ability to govern their country equal to the best officials the mother country could provide.

V

Life in the Netherlands Antilles fundamentally changed after 1915 when the Anglo-Dutch Shell Oil Company decided to establish a refinery in Curaçao for the output of its Venezuelan oil concessions. In 1924 Standard Oil of New Jersey followed Shell's example and started a refinery in Aruba. Both these refineries grew rapidly. The Standard refinery in Aruba is at present the world's largest, the Shell refinery in Curaçao closely follows.

Oil created wealth; wealth created financial independence; and financial independence created the desire for complete political self-government. Now that these islands gradually became able to finance their own administration, their own public works, their own schools, their own social provisions, they felt less inclined to accept interference of the mother country in their internal affairs. They did not want to get rid of the mother country; the ties of blood and culture were too strong, and the hard-working leaders of the people were too sober minded not to see that their six islands combined were too small a community ever to realize the status of a sovereign state.

In 1936 the Dutch government revised the Regulation for the Netherlands Antilles. But as this revision was a temporizing attempt to combine a grant of self-government with many elements of the old system—too tightly interwoven with the political institutions of the Netherlands themselves to endure fundamental changes—it led to a rather paradoxical result. The local government indeed got more freedom of decision in local affairs. The ties by which its chief executive, the governor, was bound to the orders and the consent of the government in the mother country were loosened to a certain degree. The governor got a freer hand in local affairs with fewer responsibilities towards the Netherlands. But in the meantime no adequate new responsibilities were created for him within the Netherlands Antilles, as for instance towards the colonial parliament. This grant of self-government for the Netherlands Antilles, though well meant, could easily be interpreted as a grant of self-government to the governor. Thus the situation became more unsatisfactory than before 1936.

This situation could not be very advantageous for the development of real parliamentary traditions. The revision of the Regulation had included the introduction of elections for a majority of the seats in the colonial parliament, and consequently some attempts were made to organize public opinion into political parties. But as none of these parties under the system of the revised Regulation could ever expect a real share in the government by which they could prove their vitality and the ability of their leaders, they could hardly vivify political interest, the very basis of their own existence. In fact they all directed their criticism towards the mother country, seemingly responsible for everything, instead of towards each other. The revision of the Regulation in 1936 was a psychological mistake.

VI

World War II, like a shock therapy, opened the minds of peoples all over the world to new forms of national and international relationships and prepared their readiness to accept solutions never thought possible before and to adapt old institutions venerated by tradition to a completely new situation.

Only six years after the revision of the Regulation of the
Netherlands Antilles, on the anniversity of Pearl Harbor in 1942,
Her Majesty Queen Wilhelmina, deeply moved by the efforts
of both the Netherlands East and West Indies to support the
mother country in its fierce struggle against the German invader,
with the full consent of the Dutch cabinet at that time emigrated
to London, addressed all the peoples of the Dutch Kingdom in a
radio talk in which she made the solemn promise that immediately after the war steps would be taken towards a new partnership
within the Kingdom in which the several countries would "participate with complete self-reliance and freedom of conduct for each
part regarding its internal affairs, but with the readiness to render mutual assistance." Since at that moment the attention of the
Dutch government had to be fully concentrated on the war and
the liberation of the Netherlands, and nobody could predict
how long this war would last, the Queen encouraged all her
subjects to express their thoughts and their wishes regarding the
future status of their country and its internal political structure.

In the Netherlands Antilles, where most people apparently
were interested primarily in the economic consequences of freedom and self-government, only a few people gave their opinions
on the way in which freedom and self-government must be realized. Most people preferred to wait until the end of the war
when the actual position of the Netherlands could be seen more
clearly and the Dutch people could express its opinion, too.

Interest, however, gradually grew. People got rapidly acquainted with the idea of freedom and self-government, and
when the war was over and the Netherlands had overcome the
first heavy difficulties of economic and political reconstruction, the
Netherlands Antilles as well as Surinam were anxious to open the
discussion about self-government and about the reconstruction
of the Kingdom as promised by the queen.

These discussions, started in 1946 and ended in 1954, went
through various phases:

(a) In 1948 a new Regulation was promulgated for the Netherlands Antilles and Surinam both, whereby new political

institutions were established in which self-government was realized as far as the existing prewar constitution of the Netherlands allowed it to go.

(b) In the same year, 1948, a first Round Table Conference was held at The Hague in which various recommendations were made for an enlargement of self-government beyond the limits of the old Dutch constitution.

(c) Again in the same year, 1948, the Dutch parliament accepted a constitutional amendment by which the old constitution was "opened" to the extent that further changes in the internal political structure of the Netherlands Antilles and Surinam, and in the responsibilities of these "overseas territories" towards the mother country, could with a slight difference in parliamentary procedure be realized by law even if they went beyond the limits of the constitution.

(d) In 1949 and 1950 the Regulations of 1948 were revised, again respectively for Surinam and the Netherlands Antilles. Both of these Regulations, later called "State-Regulations," provided complete internal self-government immediately, as allowed by the constitutional amendment of 1948. The provisions on the organization of the Kingdom, however, on which discussions between both overseas territories and the mother country had not been completed, had a provisional, interim character.

(e) In 1952 a new amendment to the Dutch constitution stipulated that the relations between the Netherlands, Surinam, and the Netherlands Antilles should in future be laid down in a charter on which the three countries as equal partners should agree and which should be recognized as constitutional law itself.

(f) In 1954, after various meetings of a new Round Table Conference, an agreement was reached on the content and the wording of the Charter; and in December of that same year its text was signed during a solemn session of the Conference in the Knights Hall at The Hague by the prime ministers of the three partners and by Her Majesty Queen Juliana. With the promulgation of this Charter in the three countries all at once, the reconstruction of the Dutch Kingdom was completed.

VII

The Charter of the Kingdom of the Netherlands is a long
document of 61 paragraphs, but the most important stipulation
is laid down in two lines which contain the principle that the
three partners "manage their own affairs autonomously." With
these five words self-government is anchored in constitutional
law. Each of the three partners can organize its own administration according to its own views without the consent of the
other two.

In fact the political institutions of the Netherlands Antilles
and Surinam are still the same as those laid down in the State
Regulations of 1949 and 1950 because the system created by
these documents, which are recognized now as the internal
constitutions of these "overseas parts of the Kingdom," proved
to be satisfactory for the time being. Except for those stipulations
in these internal constitutions relating to the general principles on which the Kingdom as a whole is built and which cannot be changed except by mutual agreement of the three
partners, the Netherlands Antilles and Surinam are free to
change their internal constitutions by a two-thirds majority
decision of their respective parliaments.

Like the constitution of the mother country, the constitutions
of the Netherlands Antilles and Surinam are based on the principle of a constitutional monarchy. The head of the government
in the Netherlands Antilles, or in Surinam, can do nothing without the cooperation of the local parliament and cabinet, or of the
individual ministers. The ruler is a "constitutional king" who
cannot sign a law which does not get a majority in parliament
and which does not bear the signature of at least one of the
responsible ministers.

The constitutions of both Surinam and the Netherlands
Antilles stipulate that the ruler of the Netherlands is also the
head of government in these countries. Surinam and the Netherlands Antilles thus are kingdoms in their own right—the only
real kingdoms in the Caribbean area.

The King—in point of fact, the Queen—of the Netherlands is represented in each of the two countries by a governor appointed by her, who has of course the same position as the Queen: he has no power without the consent of the local parliament and the signature of the responsible local ministers. He cannot promulgate any law without the consent of parliament and without at least one of his cabinet ministers signing the bill with him. As the head of the government he has no responsibility towards parliament.

Legislative power is vested in a one-chamber parliament of 22 members, all elected by the people of the Netherlands Antilles under universal suffrage of men and women from the age of 23 years on. The members are elected on party lists in a system of proportional representation, with a slight deviation in that each of the islands elects a certain number of members stipulated by law. The island of Curaçao with about 110,000 inhabitants elects 12 members; Aruba with about 60,000 inhabitants, 8 members; Bonaire with about 5,000 inhabitants, 1 member; and the three Windward Islands together with a population of 3,500, also 1 member.

This legislative body has all the usual parliamentary rights. It has the power to vote the budget and every law with or without amendments; every member may propose new bills on his own initiative; parliament may question every cabinet member.

The cabinet consists of five or six ministers and is headed by a Prime Minister who, apart from being chairman, is the equal of each of his colleagues. Each of the ministers is responsible not to the governor, but to parliament. The ministers are nominated by the governor after consultation with parliament.

The courts vested with the judical power are independent of both the legislative and the executive.

VIII

In the old colonial and semi-colonial regimes Curaçao always occupied an exceptional place in the political structure of the

Netherlands Antilles: the position of the admiral's ship in a
fleet of islands, the center of the government. Each of the other
islands had some government of its own, but these island governments had only a very limited scope; they all got rigid instructions from the central government in Curaçao. On the other
hand, the island of Curaçao had no government of its own;
the central authorities administered the island as a side line of
their duties.

This situation was the source of many troubles in Curaçao as
well as in the other islands, particularly in Aruba, since this
island, after the establishment of the world's largest oil refinery
there, became economically and financially self-supporting and
no longer accepted a position of dependence upon its sister island.
The Windward Islands, too, situated some 500 miles from
Curaçao and with an English-speaking population, had their
objections.

To meet this situation the islands got their own separate
governments. Each of them—except the three Windward
Islands, which were bound together into one administrative
unit—got its own legislative body and its own executive council,
both headed by a local governor nominated by the Queen, like
the governor of a province or the mayor of a local community
in the Netherlands.

Administration and finance were divided between the central
government of the Netherlands Antilles as a whole and the island
governments; in fact more than half of the administrative duties
went to the islands.

The relationship between the legislative body and the executive
council in the island governments, as well as their responsibilities,
followed in principle the pattern of a province or local community in the Netherlands, where legislature and executive are
more closely tied together. The local governor of an island is the
actual chairman of the legislative body as well as of the executive
council, and the members of the council may be—and at least
half their number are required to be—members of the legislative
body.

IX

The bulk of the Charter's provisions deal with the construction of the Dutch Kingdom as a whole and the relations between the three kingdom-partners: the Netherlands, Surinam, and the Netherlands Antilles. Generally speaking, the stipulations with regard to the construction of this Kingdom fall under two headings.

(a) *The extension of the Kingdom's responsibilities.* It is generally stipulated that the liabilities and responsibilities of the Kingdom's government are strictly limited to those mentioned in the Charter. In all matters not expressly mentioned in this document, the three partners are free to decide for themselves. Of course this freedom includes the freedom of mutual agreement on matters not mentioned in the Charter and the freedom to declare such matters "kingdom matters." Thus, for instance, the three countries agree about economic coordination. In other matters such as the currency and the monetary system, banking and foreign exchange policy, air-navigation and shipping, and telecommunications, they agreed to consult with each other before taking decisions.

Two groups of kingdom matters are mentioned in the Charter itself. First are those matters which concern the unity and the protection of the interests of the three countries. Under this group the most important matters are foreign relations and defense. Surinam and the Netherlands Antilles have no diplomatic services of their own; they are represented in and by the diplomatic service of the Kingdom as a whole. The Netherlands Antilles are defended by the Dutch navy and they contribute to the costs of this defense. Minor kingdom matters in this group are: the questions of citizenship, the laws about the nationality of ships, and provisions for admission and expulsion of aliens.

The second group of kingdom matters consists of the fundamental principles of justice and administration which are accepted as constitutional law by the Kingdom as a whole. The acceptance of these principles in the constitution and in the judicial and administrative practice of each of the three partners is considered as a kind of "condition of admittance" to the Kingdom. The Charter stipulates: "Each of the countries provides for the realization of the fundamental human rights and freedoms, the rule of law and the soundness of the administration. The guaranteeing of these rights, freedoms, rule of law and the soundness of administration is an affair of the Kingdom."

(b) *The government of the Kingdom as a whole.* The Kingdom as a whole is governed according to the same principles again as the government of each of the three countries. The crown of the Kingdom is by hereditary right to be worn by Her Majesty Queen Juliana, princess of Orange-Nassau, and by her legitimate successors. She is a "constitutional queen" and as such acts only in cooperation with the parliament of the Kingdom and its ministers.

The cabinet of the Kingdom consists of the Dutch cabinet and of two Ministers-plenipotentiary, one nominated by Surinam and one nominated by the Netherlands Antilles. These Ministers-plenipotentiary have their permanent residence at The Hague. Whenever decisions have to be taken on matters regarding the Kingdom as a whole, such decisions can only be taken in a meeting of the kingdom-cabinet of which they are full members. Such decisions are, for instance, proposals of laws valid for the whole Kingdom, the nomination of a governor, the nomination of an attorney general, of the local governors for the islands in the Netherlands Antilles, and so on.

If such decisions require some piece of legislation and consequently the cooperation of the Kingdom's legislative body, the relative proposals are first sent to the parliaments of Surinam and the Netherlands Antilles which may examine them and within a fixed term can submit a report in writing on them before the public discussion in the Kingdom parliament. This "Kingdom parliament" in fact is the Dutch parliament, the States General at The Hague, which contains no members from Surinam or the Netherlands Antilles. If however the Dutch parliament acts as

Kingdom parliament, it follows a special procedure. The provisions of the Charter about this special procedure read as follows:

Before the final vote is taken on any proposal for a Kingdom statute in the Chambers of the States General, the Minister-plenipotentiary of the Country in which the provisions shall apply is given the opportunity to express his opinion on such proposal. If the Minister-plenipotentiary declares himself opposed to the proposal, he may at the same time request the Chamber to postpone the vote till the following meeting. If, after the Minister-plenipotentiary has declared himself opposed to the proposal, the Second Chamber accepts it with a smaller majority than three-fifths of the votes cast, the consideration is postponed and further consultation on the proposal takes place in the Council of Ministers.

Thus Surinam and the Netherlands Antilles have, both together or each separately, a 10 per cent minus 1 vote influence in the Kingdom parliament.

A special procedure has been established further to prevent overruling of the Ministers-plenipotentiary in the Council of Ministers. The Ministers-plenipotentiary have a right to demand a continuance of the relevant discussions if they have serious objections against the preliminary opinion of the Council. The continued discussions are conducted between the Prime Minister, two Netherlands Ministers, a Minister-plenipotentiary, and a Minister to be designated by the country concerned. The ultimate result arrived at in these discussions is binding upon the Council of Ministers.

This solution, different for instance from the solution accepted by France whose former colonies are represented in the parliament in Paris by a number of delegates, was adopted on the urgent request of both Surinam and the Netherlands Antilles themselves. The population of both these countries together is about 400,000. Their own internal constitutions require the establishment of various political bodies which have to be manned by quite a number of able citizens. The very idea of self-government, moreover, also requires that another considerable number of able locally-born officials should be incorporated in the administration of these countries.

A third group of equally able men and women is badly needed in the countries themselves in order to work for the educational, economic, and social welfare of their rapidly growing populations. In order to give them a 10 per cent influence in the Kingdom-parliament, Surinam and the Netherlands Antilles each would have to send a great number of their most able people either permanently or at least for a considerable part of the year to The Hague. Both countries stood firm in their opinion that they could make a better use of their limited man power and thus gave the very first proof of their political maturity and their willingness to use their full strength in making a success of their self-government.

X

Since the first steps to a realization of complete self-government in Surinam and the Netherlands Antilles were taken, almost ten years have elapsed. It is still too early to come to final conclusions about the degree of success regarding the reorganization of the Dutch Kingdom and the establishment of Surinam and the Netherlands Antilles as completely equal and self-governing partners within this new Kingdom. However, some observations on the actual development of autonomy in these "overseas parts of the Kingdom," particularly in the Netherlands Antilles, can already be made.

(a) Democracy can only become a really living system of government if it rests on a widespread interest in the affairs of the community. As far as the Netherlands Antilles are concerned, it may be stated that such a widespread interest seems indeed to be present. The percentage of the male and female population actually going to the polls at the elections, either for the parliament of the country as a whole or for the legislative body of each island, is extremely large; it usually far surpasses 90 per cent,

which is much more than the usual attendance at the elections
in countries of much older democratic standing. Election campaigns are extraordinarily exciting and often reach culminating
points comparable only with a real Caribbean "fiesta."

(b) As in the Netherlands, proportional representation has
led to the development of a multi-party system. The partition
lines between the various parties operating in the Netherlands
Antilles, however, follow quite another pattern than the partition
lines between political parties in the mother country. In the
Netherlands the party system is based on principles of political
theory, partly interwoven with religious principles. Early in the
political development of the Netherlands Antilles an attempt
was made to establish a Catholic party in Curaçao and a
Christian party in Aruba, but although 80 to 90 per cent of the
population are Catholic, this attempt did not lead to success.
There are neither "conservative," "liberal," "socialist," nor
"communist" parties in the Netherlands Antilles. The partition
lines do not run parallel to colour lines, as in Surinam where
the population is sharply divided into a strong group of colored
"creoles" and an equally strong group of "hindustani." Parties
are influenced by quite other elements such as the difference
between town and country, the presence of strong groups of
Dutchmen and of people from Surinam, and last but not least,
elements of personal leadership which make it hard to define
exactly the differences between political platforms. This does
not mean, however, that in the very small communities of the
Netherlands Antilles people are not well aware of these differences for they are exceedingly real.

(c) In a multi-party system a one-party cabinet is an exception; usually the parliamentary majority supporting the cabinet
consists of two or more parties. This almost inevitably leads
either to compromise or to instability. The two full-dress
cabinets, however, by which the Netherlands Antilles have been
governed since 1950 showed a remarkable stability in spite of
the fact that neither of them was backed by an overwhelming
majority. This stability seems to be partly due to the fact that

the backbone of each of these cabinets was a combination of two major parties, one operating only in Curaçao and one operating only in Aruba—two parties which thus could not fight each other in their electoral campaigns.

(d) The reconstructed Kingdom, established within a relatively short space of time, is quite a complicated composition of liabilities and responsibilities. Neither the Netherlands, Surinam, nor the Netherlands Antilles had had any experience with this new political construction, which by its very complexity afforded many possibilities for conflicts. This complicated composition of liabilities and responsibilities, full of difficult situations, had to be handled by people historically acquainted with the idea that authority and more or less absolute power were identical things, and who had to adapt themselves within a short time to the practice of authority with strictly limited powers. It must be stated to their credit, however, that their leaders have up to now shown a remarkable self-restraint. Whenever during the past eight years conflicts arose, a way out was found in sound judgment and deliberation.

(e) Government in these countries is considered a serious business. As in other countries of the world, almost every government measure meets more or less well-founded criticism, and perhaps some of these measures will in the future prove to be failures. But it cannot be denied that the governments of Surinam and the Netherlands Antilles contain hard-working men, completely conscious of their responsibilities towards their own people and trying to find ways towards greater social security and towards economic expansion. In the lower strata of officials, lawyers, teachers, and businessmen, a new generation of capable, interested, self-conscious, hard-working, and patriotic young men is growing up as a real *spes patriae*.

6

J. J. Ochse: ECONOMIC FACTORS IN THE NETHERLANDS ANTILLES AND SURINAM

THE ECONOMIC FACTORS will be described separately for the Netherlands Antilles and for Surinam.

I. The Netherlands Antilles

GEOGRAPHY

The Netherlands Antilles comprise the islands of Aruba, Curaçao, and Bonaire (Leeward Islands), and St. Eustatius, Saba, and part of St. Maarten (Windward Islands). The three Leeward Islands are situated close to the coast of South America. The Windward Islands belong to the completely different group of islands which form the eastern boundary of the Caribbean Sea. When talking about the Netherlands Antilles it is often not realized that they are composed of two groups at a considerable distance from each other. Curaçao, for instance, is 500 miles from St. Maarten. The distinction between "windward" and "leeward" relates to the northeastern trade winds prevailing in the Caribbean Sea: windward are the islands between the Gulf of Paria and Puerto Rico, leeward those between the Gulf of Paria and the Paraguaná Peninsula.

The islands of Curaçao, Aruba, and Bonaire do not have the same geological formation as the north coast of South America.

Their geological development resembles in many respects the other regions of the Antillean area. Characteristic for Curaçao are the handlike inlets of its south shore. The Anna Bay and Schottegat, forming a magnificent natural harbor, are well known. Bullen Bay, Spaanse Water, and Caracas Bay are safe roadsteads where even the biggest ships can bunker. Aruba has no real bays; here the lagoons provide safe anchoring grounds, for instance near Oranjestad and St. Nicolaas where modern harbor installations can be found.

CLIMATE

The Leeward Islands are situated in a region of extreme drought extending from the Orinoco to the mouth of the Magdalena in Colombia. Their climate is a so-called tropical-steppe climate. The average annual precipitation in these three islands amounts to 550 millimeters. Since the evaporation of a water surface is estimated to be 6 millimeters per day, it is not surprising that this very light precipitation in a tropical area causes the country generally to have an arid, and sometimes even a burnt, appearance. The average annual temperature is 27.5° C., with a minimum around 23° and a maximum near 33°. The Windwards are less arid. The average precipitation amounts to 1000 millimeters annually, which is not much for a tropical region.

The water famine of the Leewards prohibits agriculture of any significance. A solution could be found in preventing the small quantity of rain water from flowing down to the sea. Recently several dams which had been neglected have been repaired. New dams are being constructed. Windmills are to be found everywhere; they are characteristic of the scenery of the Leeward Islands.

POPULATION

There are all together 181,100 people living in the Netherlands Antilles. Their distribution over the islands is:

Curaçao	114,700
Aruba	57,400
Bonaire	5,400
St. Eustatius	1,000
Saba	1,100
St. Maarten	1,500
	181,100

The population of the Netherlands Antilles, and especially that of the Leeward Islands, is extremely mixed. The aborigines of pure Indian stock have disappeared. The features of the people of Aruba show the last traces of their Indian ancestry. Apart from the old Netherlands and Portuguese-Israelitic families originally active in commerce and agriculture, Curaçao has a large number of inhabitants of African descent. In more recent times, after the oil industry started attracting workers from the surrounding area, people from Bonaire and from the Windward Islands settled in Curaçao, as did Europeans of various nationalities, North and South Americans, Puerto Ricans, people from the Guianas, from the British West Indies, and even from Madeira. The settlement of the latter groups as a rule had only a temporary character. The prosperity which resulted from the development of the oil industry drew Chinese, Syrians, people from Bombay and, later, Jews from eastern Europe. In Curaçao there are consequently no less that forty different nationalities. In the Windward Islands there are mostly people of African descent, as well as an old, small settlement of Netherlanders, Scotsmen, and Irishmen.

INDUSTRY

Until the beginning of the twentieth century the economy of the Netherlands Antilles was a poor one, with only intermittent periods of improvement. Trade with Venezuela and the surrounding countries was on a limited scale; small quantities of phosphate were exported. The excellent natural port of Willemstad on the island of Curaçao was used as a bunker station but gradually lost its importance. Traffic was fairly heavy, but it did not acquire a truly international character.

For the island of Curaçao conditions changed when in 1916 the Bataafsche Petroleum Maatschappij (Royal Dutch Shell) established a subsidiary, which was subsequently named the Curaçaose Petroleum Industrie Maatschappij (C.P.I.M.). In 1917 a shipping company, the Curaçaose Scheepvaart Maatschappij (C.S.M.), was established, which imports crude oil from Venezuela in tanker ships. Both companies belong to the Royal Dutch Shell group. In a few decades this great enterprise transformed Curaçao from a poor island into an ultramodern center of industry, and Willemstad became an important world port.

For Aruba the upward swing started in 1926 when the American Lago Oil and Transport Company established an oil refinery and a tanker shipping company on that island under the auspices of the Standard Oil of New Jersey group.

The C.P.I.M. and the Lago are among the biggest refineries in the world. Both enterprises process oil from Venezuela; the Lago Company also processes oil from Colombia. The Lago Company in particular has made a specialty of the processing of crude oil for the production of substances of high-octane gasoline. The C.P.I.M. products are more varied; among them lubricating oil is produced in great quantities.

Approximately 300,000 barrels of crude oil are processed on Curaçao every day on a site which is as big as the city of London. On this site there are 850 tanks with a total capacity of 3,700,000 cubic meters. The total length of all pipelines on Curaçao equals 750 kilometers; the central electric plant has a capacity which would be great enough to provide one-quarter of the Netherlands with electric current for domestic purposes. No less than 13,000 employees make their living by working for the C.P.I.M., the C.S.M., and their associate enterprises such as shipbuilding yards, docks, and metal plants.

On Aruba the Lago has an intake of 400,000 barrels of crude oil per day. Owing to intensive mechanization the site is smaller than that of the C.P.I.M. The number of employees is also less large; nevertheless, the 8,000 employees of the Lago, together with their families, constitute half of the Aruban population. Among these employees there are 700 United States citizens. Both companies own hospitals which are among the best equipped in the Caribbean area.

The economic importance of these two oil companies for the Netherlands Antilles can be gauged from the fact that in 1951 the amount of salaries and wages paid out by C.P.I.M. equalled 55,000,000 guilders. If the expenditure on work carried out by local contractors and on local purchases is also taken into account, the total contribution to the wealth of the Netherlands Antilles provided by C.P.I.M. amounts to 74,000,000 guilders, which is equal to twice the amount of currency circulating on Curaçao. The contribution provided by Lago amounts to approximately $25,000,000 (one United States dollar equals two Antilles guilders). It is obvious that the income derived from these two enterprises is of paramount importance to the population, which numbers less than 200,000 persons.

TRADE AND TRAFFIC

One of the reasons why trade and traffic are of great importance to the Antilles is that there are a number of excellent ports which have recently been considerably improved in size as well as in equipment. Furthermore, there is a modern shipbuilding and repairing enterprise on Curaçao which has drydock facilities and gives work to 600 employees.

The airports, of which the two largest are situated on Aruba and on Curaçao, are up to modern standards and provide landing facilities for heavy aircraft. The air safety operations for a large part of the Caribbean area are conducted from these two airports.

The port of Curaçao and that of Aruba each have a heavier port traffic than that of Amsterdam, the largest share in this traffic being taken by the above mentioned oil companies. The port traffic of Curaçao and Aruba jointly is larger than that of the city of New York. Annually 10,000 ships measuring 100,000,000 tons visit these two ports.

Ships from all parts of the world touch at the port of Willem-stad on Curaçao. One of the most important shipping companies contributing to this traffic is the Royal Netherlands Shipping Company (K.N.S.M.), which keeps up regular services with Europe, North America, and most countries of South America. Among the foreign shipping companies whose vessels regularly visit Willemstad, we may mention the American Grace and Alcoa Lines, the British Harrison, Shaw Saville, Royal Mail, and Blue Star Lines, and the Swedish Johnson Line.

The West Indian section of the K. L. M. airlines has services between the Antilles and most of the surrounding countries. It has a staff of 800. Other airlines operating in the Netherlands Antilles are Pan American Airways and Línea Aeropostal Venezolana. St. Maarten, one of the Windward Islands, is a station for one of the lines operated by Air France.

Closely connected with trade and traffic, tourism forms an important source of revenue. Thousands of Americans yearly visit the Antillean ports on pleasure cruises. Local stores are well stocked with products from all over the world and sell at comparatively low prices. For the shipping companies operating the pleasure cruises, the Antillean ports are attractive on account of low port dues and cheap fuel oil. Import duties on alcoholic beverages, perfumes, and other luxury goods are also low. All these factors have combined to earn for Curaçao and Aruba the name of "shopping center of the Caribbean." Efforts are being made to attract still more tourists by building new and comfortable hotels. Since 1947 the central tourist committee has had a representative in New York.

Agriculture, Cattle-breeding, and Mining

The dry climate on the Leeward Islands is not favorable for cattle breeding and agriculture. The Windward Islands have a slightly higher rainfall, but here the lack of transport limits the possibilities for increasing these forms of production. Some improvement was made when a coaster with a refrigerating installation was put into operation in order to keep up a service between the Windward and the Leeward Islands.

Agricultural products are few. From the pods of the divi-divi tree tannic acid is prepared. Aloes are used for the production of aloin, an ingredient of various medicaments. The rind of a special kind of citrus fruit growing on the islands goes into the making of the well-known Curaçao liqueur. These three products are exported in modest quantities. For local consumption a species of sorghum is grown which serves as cattle fodder. Goats are almost the only kind of cattle bred on the islands, especially on Bonaire. Poultry farming is on a very small scale and insufficient to meet local needs.

Of the mining products phosphate is the most important. The Curaçao Mining Company which works the phosphate deposits has 350 employees and exports a quantity of approximately 100,000 tons per annum. On Aruba small deposits of gold have been discovered in a few places.

II. Surinam

GEOGRAPHY

Surinam (Dutch Guiana) is situated on the northeastern coast of the South American continent and is bounded by French Guiana on the east, Brazil on the south, British Guiana on the West, and the Atlantic Ocean on the north. The area is approximately 143,000 square kilometers, and it had in 1953 a population of 240,000, of whom 90,000 live in Paramaribo, the capital.

The country is divided into natural regions: lowlands, savannah, and highland, which are quite different topographically. The northern part of the country consists of lowland, with a width in the east of 25 kilometers and in the west of about 80 kilometers. The soil (clay) is covered with swamps with a layer of humus underneath. Marks of the old seashores are to be seen in the shell and sand ridges, overgrown with tall trees.

Then follows a region, 5 to 6 kilometers wide, of a loamy and
sandy soil, then a slightly undulating region, about 30 kilometers wide. It is mainly savannah, mostly covered with quartz
sand and overgrown with grasses, herbs, shrubs, and lighter
wood. South of this region lies the interior highland, consisting
of hills and mountains, almost entirely overgrown with dense
tropical forests and intersected by streams of all sizes. At the
southern boundary with Brazil there are again savannahs. These,
however, differ in soil and vegetation from the northern ones.

The country is intersected by a number of large rivers running
from south to north. Besides a narrow-gauge railway 135 kilometers in length which runs up to Kabel on the Surinam River,
these rivers are the only entrances to the hinterland. From early
days, therefore, all traffic has been performed by water, as
a result of which the network of roads is still largely underdeveloped. The Surinam Shipping Company maintains regular
passenger and cargo services on the rivers below the rapids,
and also along the coast and to the Caribbean area. International shipping is chiefly by the Royal Netherlands Steamship
Company, Alcoa, and the Surinam Shipping Company.

At present, with government support, attempts are being made
to develop an inland airways system. Besides the normal small
civilian transport planes, helicopters are also used. A number
of airstrips have already been laid out in the interior. The
Zanderij airport is included in the international network of the
K.L.M. and the Pan American Airways.

The climate is tropical and moist, but not very hot, since
the northeast trade wind makes itself felt during the whole year.
In the coastal area the temperature varies on an average from
73° to 88° F. in the course of the day; the annual average is
81° F. only. The mean annual rainfall is about 92 inches for
the period of "moderate rains," from the middle of November
until the middle of February. The period of "moderate drought"
is from the middle of February until the middle of May; the
period of "heavy rains" is from the middle of May until the
middle of August; the period of "severe drought" is from the

middle of August until the middle of November. None of these periods, however, is normally either very dry or very wet. The degree of cloudiness is fairly high and the average humidity is 82 per cent. The climate of the interior is similar, with higher rainfall, but few data are available.

POPULATION

The population is very heterogeneous. The aboriginals were the Indians and of them there are now only approximately 3,700 left in Surinam. The Creoles are descendants of Africans who have, or have not, mixed with other races living in Surinam. The total number of Creoles is approximately 86,000, of whom two-thirds live in Paramaribo. The Creoles not only hold positions in government offices but are also engaged in purely technical occupations and in business. Their language is the Negro-English which had its origin in African and European languages. This Negro-English is used by them when dealing with other groups of the population.

Another important group is that of the Hindustani. When slavery was abolished there was a shortage of labor, and the Hindustani were admitted as contract laborers to Surinam. The first transport arrived in 1873. Immigration continued until 1918 when it was stopped at the request of Great Britain, partly under pressure from the nationalists in the former British India. From 1873 up to and including 1917 about 34,000 Hindustani emigrated to Surinam. When they had terminated their five-year contract, they had the choice of renewing it or requiring a free passage back to their own country. The Surinam government strongly encouraged these industrious and energetic farmers to stay, among other things making agricultural plots available to them. The majority of the Hindustani now make a living in agriculture, especially rice growing. Together with the Indonesians they constitute about 80 per cent of the agrarian population. Although culturally they have strong ties with the country of their forefathers, they are nevertheless out-and-out Surinamians.

Apart from agriculture these people have also found a living in Surinam society as doctors, dentists, technicians, chemists, teachers, etc. They are furthermore to be found in government jobs in the districts, outside Paramaribo, where there is a predominantly Hindustani population. The number of Surinamians of Hindustani descent is 70,000, 15,000 of whom live in Paramaribo. Indonesians, chiefly Javanese, came to Surinam, like the Hindustani, as contract laborers for the plantations. In 1894 the first of them arrived and they came to Surinam until 1939. It should be noted that after the transfer of sovereignty to Indonesia the majority of these immigrants chose Indonesian nationality and consequently lost their right to vote, as a result of which they could not exercise any influence on local politics. In this connection an act was recently passed permitting Indonesians, should they so wish, to regain Dutch nationality by a very simple procedure. At present there are 40,000 Indonesians in Surinam, 4,000 of whom live in Paramaribo.

There are also Chinese, Europeans, and other nationalities living in Surinam. And lastly there are the descendants of the slaves who fled from the plantations during the period of slavery. There are about 22,000 of them living in Surinam.

ECONOMIC CONDITIONS

Plantation farming, which used to be so prosperous, has constantly diminished in importance since the second half of the nineteenth century. The chief causes of this decline should be sought in the drastic shortage of labor and the increased standard of wages closely bound up with it.

In comparison with Southeast Asia the conditions of production in Surinam gradually proved to be so unfavorable that increasing amounts of capital were withdrawn from Surinam. As a result of the opening of the Suez Canal, the cost-price advantages of the Asiatic producers increased considerably, and consequently interest in tropical agriculture was directed more and more to Southeast Asia.

Simultaneously with the decline of the plantations, the first beginnings of small farming were seen, concentrating chiefly on the cultivation of plants such as rice, leguminous plants, and root crops. This was an entirely new form of farming for Surinam where agriculture as a big industry had always produced staple commodities for export, and where little attention had been paid to the inland food supply. Especially after 1900 did small farming manage to gain a constantly more important position in the economic system.

In 1900 the share of small farming in the production was roughly estimated at barely 10 per cent. In 1950 this had increased to about 85 per cent, or Sur. f 11m., as compared to that of plantation farming which was about 15 per cent, or Sur. f 4m.

During and after World War II there were two facts which were of far-reaching importance for the economic structure of Surinam. As the result of increased war production by the bauxite companies, which had become the most important source of prosperity for Surinam since 1930, the national revenue increased to such an extent that it no longer needed the subsidy which it had been receiving from the metropolitan country for decades. Indeed, during a number of years income even exceeded expenditure. The two bauxite companies operating in Surinam, the Surinam Bauxite Company, a Surinam company with mainly American capital and entirely controlled by ALCOA (Aluminum Company of America), and the Billiton Company, together exported (in tons):

1952	3,154,682
1953	3,274,232
1954	3,421,700

Surinam therefore supplies one-fourth of the world production, and consequently is the world's largest supplier of bauxite. The significance of bauxite for Surinam is proved by the fact that about 83 per cent of the export, 30 per cent of the national income, and 50 per cent of the government revenues are derived from the mining of bauxite.

The following figures are of importance regarding agricultural area and production, 1955–56:

COMMODITY	HECTARES CULTIVATED	PRODUCTION* Unit	1955	1956
Rice (rough), paddy	25,000	metric tons	64,526	71,182
Sugar	1,500	do	7,242	7,037
Tubers	520	do	2,341	3,129
Vegetables	290	do	2,468	1,395
Corn	300	do	739	1,263
Peanuts	440	do	419	553
Coffee	2,200	do	473	272
Cacao	1,600	do	130	135
Citrus fruits	1,600	1,000 pieces		
Oranges		do	35,886	39,656
Grapefruit		do	6,336	10,551
Lemons		do	1,844	2,182
Other		do	3,049	3,383
Plantains	960	1,000 bunches	311	306
Bananas			126	218
Coconuts	2,100	1,000 pieces	8,697	9,530

*Paddy production is estimated by a sampling method. For production data on other commodities, extension officers estimate the output of small farmers in the various areas and estate production as reported by the growers.

Following are agricultural exports, 1955–56 (thousands of guilders):

COMMODITY	1955	1956
Rice	2,798	3,428
Cocoa	63	102
Sugar	——	182
Coconuts	53	76
Citrus	336	771
Coffee	802	596
Plantains	24	21
Other	78	51
Total	4,154	5,227

Source: These facts are from the Economic Developments in Surinam, 1956, Part 1, No. 57–58, United States Department of Commerce, Bureau of Foreign Commerce.

Major factors in the 1956 increase in production were: (1) good crop weather in general; (2) increased area under cultivation (1,000 hectares of empoldered—newly recovered—land were distributed to small-scale farmers, the mechanized rice operation at Wageningen was extended by about 5,000 hectares, and about 1,500 additional hectares of other newly empoldered land were brought into cultivation); (3) improved agricultural facilities (storage for rice); (4) more active programs of agricultural education. Two changes took place in agricultural organization in 1956—an Agricultural Marketing Service was set up and three previously independent services (agricultural extension, education, and engineering) were consolidated into a single Agricultural Services unit.

André L. van Assenderp: SOME ASPECTS OF
SOCIETY IN THE NETHERLANDS ANTILLES
AND SURINAM

SOCIETY IN THE CARIBBEAN PARTS of the Kingdom
of the Netherlands is highly composite, without revealing however an attendant complexity of form. Many groups have come
to settle successively and to live together, or rather side by side,
in a neat array of contrasting cultures bent on self-expression and
self-preservation. While this circumstance facilitates study of
any one group, it also compels selectivity in singling out facets
suitable for a discussion like the present limited one.

I have elected to present a cursory survey of the various
population segments in Surinam and the Antilles in their mutual
relationship, in their political expression of social ideals, and in
the process of urbanization in which they are caught.

I. Composition

The Indians are considered to be the original inhabitants; at
least, they were found living there when the Europeans arrived.
In Surinam they belonged to the Carib and Arawak nations;
in Curaçao, Aruba, and Bonaire they were part of the Caiqueto
tribe of the Arawak group. Upon the arrival of the Europeans
the Surinam Indians withdrew into the interior; those of the
Antilles were carried off by the Spaniards and put to work in
the mines of Santo Domingo. Some returned in later times.

86

Organized village life is confined to Surinam. Villages occur only sporadically in the middle of the forest; it is far more common to find them along the rivers and in the savannahs. Never very large, they range in size from a single family to some 150 inhabitants.

Internally there is not too much cohesion. Dwellings are arranged in clusters placed at great intervals. This results from an inborn tendency to avoid trouble and quarrels with one's neighbors. Sometimes a few congenial families desire to isolate themselves from less sympathetic co-villagers; this may then lead to the creation of a twin village some distance away. Even if such twin villages have the joint use of a church and school built in the middle, their social events nevertheless remain unshared.

Apart from being non-social and rather uncommunicative, the Indians have also remained semi-nomadic. Soil exhaustion and the ravages wrought by the parasol ant compel them to move to better locations every five years or so.

The Europeans are first noted in Surinam in 1613 as members of an Amsterdam trading outpost. Very soon afterwards there developed a number of sugar and tobacco plantations. The colonials were largely Hollanders, attached to which there was a fringe of Dutch, British, Italian, and Portuguese Jews.

It is said that by 1800 there were 641 plantations in Surinam, of which more than 450 were engaged in producing sugar, cacao, cotton, indigo, or coffee for export. Pests and adversities caused decline to set in; by 1910 there were only 10 plantations left. Since then there has been some movement in the direction of regeneration of this lost plantation economy. The decline itself has been responsible for the tendency of the European population group to settle in the town of Paramaribo.

In Curaçao the Spanish arrived as early as 1527. In 1634 the Dutch drove them out and also conquered Aruba and Bonaire. Holland turned the islands into a significant commercial center. Curaçao, failing to develop an extensive agriculture, became a central slave market. There was also an influx of white colonists and buccaneers into the islands of Saba and St. Maarten where their descendants are still in evidence. St. Eustatius, finally, was more important in the eighteenth century than Curaçao; it was from there that trade was conducted with the North American revolutionaries. The island settlement was razed by a punitive British raid in 1781, because on 16 November, 1776, the Dutch islanders had been the first in the world officially to salute the new American ensign.

In contrast to Surinam's plantation economy, Curaçao, Aruba, and Bonaire as a group exhibited an early trend to develop first commerce and later industry. This was especially true for Curaçao, because of its geographic availability, splendid harbor, and—today—its favorable air-route location.

People were attracted from all over the world. As a consequence there is quite a polyglot population on Curaçao and Aruba, including Netherlanders, British, Americans, Surinamers, Madeirans, South Americans, Syrians, Poles, Rumanians, Chinese, and arrivals from other Caribbean areas. While on the Windward Islands there exists a certain solidarity among white and colored population segments, the Leeward Islands incline more towards keeping a distance between the two groups.

With the exception of one settlement on Bonaire and certain restricted areas on the Windward Islands, there are no village communities in existence in the Antilles. People just live together in little townships that are mutually isolated.

The Bushnegroes are peculiar to Surinam. They are the descendants of runaway slaves or marrons (Spanish *cimarrón*) who fled into the inhospitable jungle interior. They number around 22,000 at present and live in villages situated exclusively along the rivers. The Bush people, as they prefer to be called, reveal a tendency for settling at points near waterfalls or on island clusters in the middle of a cataract complex. This is probably due to an earlier necessity for seeking protection against animals, raids, and posses. The villages of the *grannans* or chieftains lie far into the upper reaches, well above the large cataracts.

As a general phenomenon, a footpath several hundred feet in length connects the village gate with the river bank; this is a baffle for evil river spirits. Bushnegro villages are always "closed settlements," with the huts in tight proximity, forming a distinct habitation complex. A village is usually formed by one sub-tribe, occupying a stretch of tribal territory "belonging" to that sub-tribe with an unwritten right of disposal.

The village basin is composed of a number of *piecies,* e.g. clusters of dwellings belonging to the members of one *bere* or family community. When the head of a family group dies or when sickness reigns, then the *piecie* is abandoned and a new one built elsewhere.

As is the case with the Indians, twin villages may be formed when internal village relations are getting too taut. Similarly, too, there exists the necessity to move the forage fields around every so often as a result of parasol ant activity. In addition these moves are often inspired because of an almost jealous desire to be undisputed boss of one's own plot of land, without the necessity for joint projects, cooperation, and mutual aid. In this respect the Bushnegro is decidely asocial, or at least deficient in social conscience.

Economically the Bushnegro is almost indispensable for Surinam because he is the only one willing and physically equipped to assure a regular supply of cut timber and forest products.

The Creoles as a population group encompass both the phaenotypical pure Negroes and the negroid-European mixtures that live in the "western" social sphere. They are the descendants of the negro laborers who were imported during the slave era. Numbering approximately 79,000 in 1946, they constituted about 40 per cent of Surinam's population. It is significant that some 60,000 had elected to live in the capital Paramaribo.

The Hindustanis, as the Asian Indians are usually called in Surinam—and I shall refer to them likewise to distinguish them from the Amerindians—came as immigrant laborers in the post-abolition years between 1873 and 1916, as a result of a special agreement between what were then the respective colonial governments concerned. Many of them settled, after expiration of their five-year contract with the plantation, as independent small farmers. Their total number reported for 1946 was almost 58,000, or about 30 per cent of Surinam's population.

The Hindustanis did not band together in "closed villages," as might have been expected. Each one settled near or on his own farm, indifferent as to what others might do or not do. The duration of their mutual contacts had been too short for the forging of lasting personal ties. Besides, they came from differing social classes and from various parts of India; they consequently remained comparative strangers to one another. In selecting their site, the Hindustanis usually chose a location along an existing road or canal, thus initiating the typical ribbon settlements that are such familiar sights today.

The Indonesians were brought into Surinam first as immigrant laborers under contract, later as specially selected colonists. Most of them are Javanese, although there are also a few Sundanese among them. Numbering 35,000 in 1946, they accounted for 12 per cent of Surinam's population. Their settlements are only seldom found along the rivers. The Indonesian prefers dry, sandy soil for his garden crops, located close to the swamps wherein he can develop his rice fields.

There is no trace here, either, of the typical Javanese *desa* or closed village, in spite of attempts to create an atmosphere conducive to such development. The absence of traditional ties with co-villagers, who hail from different parts of Java, and the lack of a magic relationship to the new village soil, account for that. As a result of the independence from the Netherlands achieved by their mother country, many Indonesians in Surinam, having decided to retain their nationality, are now technically foreigners. The fact that in the process they have foregone the right to vote in Surinam elections has caused some second thoughts.

There are further a number of *Chinese, Lebanese,* and *Madeirans* in Surinam, who came down for commercial purposes and consequently settled in centers already in existence.

In the foregoing it can be seen that the societies in both Surinam and the Antilles are far from homogeneous. Not only is there a vast difference between the two territories themselves, but there is even greater diversity internally. As is shown, circumstances make for the presence of convivial groups with a very poorly developed sense of social obligation, which is most extraordinary in view of the comparatively fierce localism that has developed in political aspirations. It is interesting to see how far, and in what way, this egocentrism is reflected in the internal politics of the two territories.

II. Political Life

Both in Surinam and in the Antilles political parties have not yet outgrown the primary development stage. Most of these organizations have been formed since World War II, and close observers are not at all persuaded that the two societies are sufficiently mature for responsible politics.

The Antilles have had the longer experience. There was many years ago a Freedom League, but only for a while. Of the currently existing organizations the Roman Catholic Party is the oldest, dating back to 1937. Next is the Democratic Party founded in 1945. A People's Committee became the forerunner of the National People's Party founded in 1948, favoring home rule for each island and bent upon becoming a single party. This aim was not generally applauded and soon the Catholic People's Party and the Curaçao Independent Party were formed in reaction. On the island of Aruba the so-called "Eman Party," named after its leader, desired secession from the Antilles and independence under the Crown as a separate territory. There are personal parties of this kind on the other islands also.

Surinam witnessed the birth of its first three parties in 1946. They saw the light of life in rapid succession. In May the Muslim Party Surinam came into existence. It favored universal franchise, but for the primary purpose of educating small communities towards self-help and home rule as a basis for eventual regional and national independence. This party recognized that political home rule was not possible for Surinam unless the country were also economically self-supporting. Its sensible initial expectation was that Surinam would become a decentralized territorial unit under central Netherlands authority. Membership in this party is not strictly limited to Muslims; the latter element is largely furnished by Indonesians, but most of the Hindustani members are Hindus.

In August there followed the formation of the Progressive Surinam People's Party, an organization with a Roman Catholic allure. It, too, came out in its initial platform for universal franchise relative to regional decentralization.

In September the National Party Surinam was created, the party of the Creoles, working for assimilation, the gradual introduction of universal franchise, and ultimately for political independence within a Kingdom framework. In 1951 part of the membership seceded with the intention of forming a new Creole party.

It is obvious that all three orientations would, and therefore do, agree upon the need for more and better education, extended and enlarged social welfare programs, and improved economic conditions.

The year 1948 witnessed the emergence of a Negro Political Party, which, however, soon began to show signs of wishing to withdraw from politics again. The many individualistic tendencies in this group impaired the emergence of political ambition.

Speaking generally, in Surinam politics the Hindustani and the Indonesians may be viewed as coming together in an Asian camp. There is a Surinam Hindu Party, but more significant is the organization called the Hindustani-Javanese Political Party; its primary intention was to be a national Surinam party and it published a periodical, *Prakash,* edited in excellent Dutch despite its name.

Two more Asiatic societies emerged in 1950. The Perhimpunan Ahmadya Eslam sponsors both the Islamic way of life and
overall material well-being, and at the same time it looks after
the social interests of its membership. The Perhimpunan Kem-
adjuan Rajat Indonesia wishes to stimulate political interest and
in addition to promote the social and economic interests of its
members.

The Indians and Bushnegroes are as yet unorganized politically. That they are oblivious of politics cannot be said, however;
there was, for example, some concern among the Bushnegroes
over not being represented as a group on the Surinam delegation
to the conference reorganizing the Kingdom of the Netherlands.

In brief it may be stated that the political expression of
Netherlands-Caribbean society reflects the fact that differing
civilizations and cultures, introduced one after the other, are
under pressure to seek harmony and synthesis. They are intent
upon achieving this themselves, but they are prevented because of
the relative poverty and isolation of the country. This isolation is
not so much geographical as it is psychical: each of the separate
cultures (and its sub-cultures) is carried by a comparatively
small group and feels itself threatened somewhat by the others.
Each locks itself away from enriching cross-contact possibilities.

III. Urbanization

There is, however, a counter influence which these territories
share with the rest of their Caribbean environment: the un-
mistakable trend towards urbanization. This term includes
both the trek from rural to urban areas and the movement from
island to island.

This phenomenon is not a sign of sound economic evolution,
because it does not mean that people are attracted by the greater prosperity, better social care, and more varied amusement
possibilities of the cities, but that *they are repelled by the poverty
of the rural areas* and by agrarian unemployment.

In Surinam this trend has resulted in a constant growth of

the town of Paramaribo; in the Antilles a "suction" process attracts people from the other islands, as well as from Surinam, to settle on the island of Curaçao.

From the viewpoint of its effect upon society, the consequence has been for Surinam not only a denudation of the countryside in terms of talent and energy, but the emergence of the Too-Big-City in the sense that relative to its number of inhabitants the *city has too few functions*—there are too few opportunities to make a living.

For Curaçao, prosperous because of its oil industry and commerce and trade, the social consequence of attracting mostly single men has resulted in an excess of them at the expense of the lesser islands. To a certain extent this is also true for Aruba. The employment of these immigrants in industry has stimulated the necessity to provide increasing social legislation. It may possibly be concluded that urbanization of Caribbean society may well efface in the long run some of the contrasts now present among the component groups.

LITERATURE CONSULTED

Dr. J. I. S. Zonneveld and Dr. G. J. Kruÿer, "Nederzettings-en Occupatie vormen in Suriname," *Tÿdschrift van het Kominklÿk Nederlandsch Aardrÿkskundig Genootschap*, Tweede Reeks Dl. LXVIII, 4 (October, 1951), 384.

G. Kruÿer, "Urbanisme in Suriname," *Tÿdschrift van het Kominklÿk Nederlandsch Aardrÿkskundig Genootschap,* Tweede Reeks, Dl. LXVIII, 1 (January, 1951), 31–63.

B. Lambert, "Situation Sociale et Médicale aux Antilles Neerlandaises," *Civilizations, II,* 3 (September, 1952), 407–411.

Numerous articles in the *West-Indische-Gids.*

Part III

THE FRENCH AREAS

Franklin D. Parker: POLITICAL DEVELOPMENT
IN THE FRENCH CARIBBEAN

TO SAY THAT GUADELOUPE with its 12½ isles and
islets, 687 square miles of land, and 229,000 people and Martinique with its one lofty island, 427 square miles of land, and
239,000 persons are overseas departments of the French Republic is a beginning. To say that by virtue of their being overseas departments they have certain rights both to govern their
own affairs and to be represented in the decisions of the whole
Republic and of that still amorphous collection of former French
colonies known as the French Union is a significant next step.
But to describe the constitutional relationships between France
on the one hand and Guadeloupe and Martinique on the other,
which have existed since the adoption of the constitution of
1946, without giving an indication of what had gone before
would be to leave a mistaken impression. The mistake would be
an assumption that the constitution of 1946 had really determined these relationships. The genuine connections between
France and these two *anciennes colonies* can be understood
only through a deeper look into history. This brief treatment
will be facilitated by a series of comparisons with other areas
which have some things, but not all things, in common with
the two we are examining.

I

Second cousin once removed to Guadeloupe and Martinique is the Republic of Haiti, descendant of the eighteenth-century colony of Saint-Domingue. The first and most obvious difference in this case is that Haiti, with its modern French orientation, does not fly the flag of France, while Guadeloupe and Martinique do. The second difference, which goes far toward explaining the first, is that the French carried out a policy in eighteenth-century Guadeloupe and Martinique which they failed to apply so successfully in Saint-Domingue.

Frenchmen first settled Martinique and Guadeloupe proper in 1635, under the auspices of the Company of the Isles of America organized under that name in that same year. For twelve years some of the leaders of this company had been engaged in the occupation of other West Indian islands—including Saint-Christophe, the first, which was soon divided with the British and later ceded to them entirely; Saint-Martin and Saint-Barthélemy, today's overseas dependencies *of* an overseas department (half the first and all the second are ruled from non-adjacent Guadeloupe); and La Tortue, better known to us today as Tortuga, the often undisciplined base from which French influence spread during the rest of the century to the western third of the Spanish island of Santo Domingo.

By the end of the seventeenth century France's three most important colonies in the Caribbean area were Martinique with some 17,000 inhabitants, Guadeloupe with roughly 9,000, and Saint-Domingue with about 8,000. Martinique and Guadeloupe had been developed uninterruptedly for sixty-five years and had become prosperous with sugar and slaves. Saint-Domingue had been formally acquired only three years earlier by the Treaty of Ryswick with Spain at the conclusion of the third of Louis XIV's four wars. About three-fifths of the population of these colonies were Negroes. In the success or failure of France's eighteenth-century policies toward this group lay her ability or inability to hold the three colonies later.

This was not a matter in the eighteenth century of slavery versus abolition. It was instead a question of assimilation versus inundation—assimilation of incoming Africans into the cultural stream, but not into the blood stream, of *la belle France;* and assimilation not thoroughly in an intellectual sense, but rather on the level of language, lay religion, and everyday customs enough so that each African might count himself truly a Frenchman. The inundation was of the French language, French Catholicism, and French manners of living. However, there was such a deluge of imported Africans that assimilation turned out to be quite impossible.

On the eve of the French Revolution, ninety-two years after the Peace of Ryswick, the ratio of whites to Negroes in Martinique and Guadeloupe was roughly one to eight; in Saint-Domingue it had advanced to the rather extreme figure of approximately one to sixteen. If the blacks of Martinique and Guadeloupe, encouraged by their masters and tutors, were learning to consider themselves Frenchmen, many of those in Saint-Domingue were not. The reason was not that the French in Saint-Domingue were trying with any less diligence. It was only that they were bringing in so many Africans that they were defeating their own purposes. Saint-Domingue would soon be Haiti, better described as an African land with a few French characteristics than as a French land with certain African qualities.

When the political storms arose and the mother country itself was wave-tossed from one revolutionary regime to another, Haiti went her own way while Guadeloupe and Martinique remained loyal. There is more than one explanation for this. For seven years and another twelve during the worst of the tempest, Martinique was in effect held for the French by the British. Guadeloupe, which was not similarly affected, was much smaller than Saint-Domingue and hence more easily controlled. Certainly the argument from cultural assimilation alone does not explain why Great Britain in 1783 did not lose her Canadian colonies and retain the other thirteen from New Hampshire to Georgia.

The bloodshed Guadeloupe and Martinique have known during the nineteenth and twentieth centuries came from the conflict of one local class against another, not of the inhabitants (black, brown, or white) struggling against the mother country. The enthusiasm of many Spanish American governments today for the liberation of these areas from colonial rule does not seem to be shared by the people most concerned. Almost twenty years ago the same people maintained allegiance to the French nation, whether Third Republic, Vichy, De Gaulle, or Fourth Republic. The peculiar economic niche which is theirs as long as they are French is doubtless part of the reason for such faithfulness. But a colonial policy assiduously followed by French planters and officials two hundred years ago may be fully as important a determinant.

Second cousins likewise to Guadeloupe and Martinique—and these of the same generation—are the British possessions of the Lesser Antilles, whose first settlement came at about the same time as that of the French islands and whose history, while not the same, has been roughly analogous ever since. The first sugar cane came to Barbados in 1637, the first to Martinique just two years later. After the passage of two centuries the British abolished slavery in 1833, the French permanently only fifteen years later. In purely local matters both the British and the French have moved hesitatingly but surely in more recent years toward permitting local control. The big difference lies in the fact that the British have conceived of their Caribbean constitutionally as an area apart, while the French have moved their Caribbean constitutionally in until today it is an integral part of France.

II

This concept of colonial integration with the mother country was not new in 1946. It was foreign in the eighteenth century to those English-speaking North Americans who when they shouted "No taxation without representation!" were thinking how well they could do without taxation rather than how greatly they craved representation in London. But it was accepted in the eighteenth century by the French who in their first representative assembly after Guadeloupe and Martinique were born discussed the matter and in their second assembly, a few weeks later, voted to receive representatives of the white free men of the islands. This was in 1789—there had been no meeting of a French assembly during the one hundred and seventy-five years previous— and if the French were considerably behind the English in getting a semblance of a modern legislature established, it must be admitted that the white free men of Guadeloupe and Martinique had to wait little longer than those of the mother country to be counted in on the deal. The first mulatto and the first Negro were seated in Paris just five years later by the radical National Convention. France was in fact the first of the European nations to include colonial representatives of any color in her assemblies. Revolutionary Spain twenty-one years later, in the absence of her Bourbon king, followed the French example.

Napoleon brought an end to this first representation of the French Caribbean in France. It was resumed, however, with a widened franchise, during the Revolution of 1848, the deputies now being seldom of pure French descent. After another suspension by the later Bonaparte from 1854 to 1871, Caribbean representation in French parliaments became regular.

It was only natural that the Fourth French Republic should include Guadeloupe and Martinique. It was only a continuation of old practice, slightly modified, for them to be allotted two councilors and three deputies each as their share in the Paris government. It was only incidental that they were allowed also one delegate each in the Assembly of the brand new French Union which includes "metropolitan" France (in Europe), the overseas departments (Guadeloupe, Martinique, French Guiana, and Réunion), the overseas territories, the associated territories, and the associated states. Representation in the French Union with its unilaterally conceived, undemocratic, and largely ineffectual constitutional make-up means next to nothing. There are those who would argue that representation of the four *anciennes colonies* in the parliament of the Fourth French Republic means little more. But when it is remembered that the overseas *territories* are also represented there, so that actually about one out of six persons sitting in France's parliament comes from either Africa or America, it is seen that the French have gone far enough in this matter that one day non-white colonial deputies (assuming a more democratic African representation in time) may hold the balance of power in Paris that the Irish once held between Liberals and Conservatives in London.

First cousins constitutionally speaking to the Caribbean departments of Guadeloupe and Martinique are the twelve over-the-Mediterranean-Sea departments of France in Algeria. These twelve constitute but a small portion of the vast holdings of France in Africa, acquired chiefly in the nineteenth century. Guadeloupe and Martinique, plus the much less populated French Guiana and the tiny isles of Saint-Pierre and Miquelon, are all that are left of the once equally impressive eighteenth-century holdings of France in America. Patriotic Frenchmen find it difficult to concede that one day there may be as little left of the French Empire in Africa as there is now of the French Empire in America. Yet realistic Frenchmen know that at this very time the ties which bind the Algerian departments to the mother country, of which they are supposed to be a part, are most tenuous connections indeed, in imminent danger of becoming as completely severed as those which, theoretically less secure, but yesterday bound Tunisia and Morocco.

Between Guadeloupe and Martinique on the one hand and Algeria on the other there is of course the basic difference that the Moslems of Algeria, with the exception of a few of their intellectual elite, have not come to count themselves as Frenchmen. In religion they are different, in language they are different, in everyday manners there is a gulf between the two populations. But beyond this there is a difference in treatment of the two Caribbean departments and the twelve Algerian, a difference which accounts more than anything else for the determination of Algeria's Moslem leadership to rebel rather than to remain loyal to France's standard. The simple fact is that in Guadeloupe and Martinique neither race nor creed nor color gives one man a constitutional advantage over another, while in Algeria it remains a political disadvantage to be an ordinary Algerian of ordinary Algerian ancestry.

III

The high standard of local democracy which today prevails in Guadeloupe and Martinique has not existed since the beginning, of course, nor yet did it spring into being overnight in 1946. The first local assemblies to include members elected by white residents of the islands were authorized by a decree of 1787, two years before revolution shook up the French Old Regime. More radical legislation of the 1790's abolished slavery and struck down the color line in elections, but maintained a limited franchise which prevented most Negroes in Guadeloupe and Martinique from voting, along with most whites in France. Napoleon reinstituted slavery, and Louis XVIII did away with the local, partly representative councils. The councils came back under Louis Philippe in 1834—in the first election in Martinique, 25 persons of the 750 qualified to vote were non-whites—and in 1848 slavery was made illegal forever. In the year 1870 when Frenchmen at home began to enjoy universal suffrage, the poorest of the poor in Guadeloupe and Martinique received the same voting rights. Many of them, something like a half, do not yet exercise their privilege, but the fact remains that they may when they so choose.

Councils elected by universal suffrage, with one person's vote as important as another's, put Guadeloupe and Martinique far ahead of Algeria in democratic government and ahead also, up to this date, of most of the islands about them. The relationship of council to people, however, is no more important a measure of democracy than the position of the council vis-à-vis the executive. The situation of Guadeloupe and Martinique in this regard is made complex by the determination of the French to include them in France. Until 1946 there were still colonial governors who operated for the Ministry of France Overseas. Now there are prefects acting through the Ministry of the Interior, plus other agents, each dealing with a separate ministry in Paris, just as do similar agents in the departments back home. If one may assume that what is good for the mother country is also good for Guadeloupe and Martinique, one rests his hope for the islands' future on the wisdom of the French to know what is best for themselves. If one believes that occasionally what is good for metropolitan France may be bad for her Caribbean islands, then one finds little solace in their representation in Paris. French Caribbean dissatisfactions in the near future will doubtless focus upon the boundary line which is drawn between national policies laid down in Paris and local policies decided in Basse-Terre and Fort-de-France.

Politics in these two areas since 1945 have run far to the left. When this happens in the Caribbean or elsewhere, there are many who lament the advent of democracies which, as many conceive, make such conditions possible. Yet one may well ponder the fact that the totalitarian dictatorships of today in Asia and eastern Europe in no case came into power because of an overdose of democracy in the country concerned. Where genuine democratic controls prevail, even if the region is among the world's least developed, there need be no fear. In the maintenance of such controls, the existence of a democratic political tradition counts for as much as social and economic betterment, important as are the latter. In matters of government Gaudeloupe and Martinique seem well on the way to developing just such a tradition. It may well tide them over the rough years of socioeconomic adjustment ahead.

Melvin H. Jackson: THE ECONOMY OF THE FRENCH CARIBBEAN

THE FRENCH WEST INDIAN islands of Martinique, Guadeloupe and her dependencies,[1] and the mainland territory of French Guiana, for the first time in their history as colonies or overseas departments, face fundamental changes of outlook and attitudes which must have great implications for the future of those areas. The emergence of the European Economic Community, with its promise of a free market for its participants, is looked upon with a mixture of reserve and extravagant hope.

It is the purpose of this paper, within a limited scope, to examine the background of the islands' economy, its present dilemma, some of the avenues explored for its amelioration, and the possible impacts of the Common Market which has raised such high hopes for the future.

In 1946 the French Caribbean possessions through the provisions of the new constitution promulgated in that year became integrated into the French Republic as departments on an equal footing with the departments of metropolitan France. At a blow the ancient and invidious distinction implied in the word "colony" was replaced by the more dignified term *Département d'outre mer*. Each new department was now represented in the National Assembly and Council of the Re-

1. Marie Galante, Les Saintes, Saint-Barthélemy, and the French portion of the French-Dutch condominium of Saint-Martin.

public (Senate) of France by representatives elected by universal suffrage.[2] This was no mere granting of autonomy within a commonwealth, but a complete integration, social and economic, into the very bosom of the French Republic.

If departmentalization was a sentimental success, the full import of being within the protecting embrace of the French domestic tariff system would be borne home in a very few years after the event. To many of the more thoughtful observers it became apparent that what had actually been effected was the complete and unconditional success of the very system which Colbert had installed in the seventeenth century and which had enjoyed such an indifferent success throughout the eighteenth century. A mercantilism of a variety that could only be dreamed of by the most ardent eighteenth century advocate of that doctrine was a glowing reality. Complete reciprocity of protection was a fact, and with it all came the victory of centralization which French governments had pursued since the days of Louis XIV with a singleness of purpose that is almost unique.[3]

I

The basic plight of the French West Indian islands, in the past as well as today, is economic. It stems from the evils of a monoculture which has characterized the islands since the eighteenth century. Geography, geology, racial and colonial relationships, the system of land tenure, and finally the exigencies of mercantilism in its various guises have all conspired to clamp on the French islands and the Caribbean as a whole a cruel and often vicious economic system.

Once the richest overseas possessions in the world, the islands

2. It should be remarked that the colonies had maintained representatives in the National Assembly since 1871, but it was a representation of a much more limited nature than that under the latest constitution.

3. Herbert Luethy has developed this theme with a great deal of historical insight in *France Against Herself* (New York: Meridian Books, 1956).

plummeted to the position of economic liabilities within the memory of a living man. Their retention in the French Empire was the result of a curious combination of sentimentalism and a proclivity for map coloring.

Traditionally the decline of the French Sugar Islands has been attributed to the abolition of slavery. A cursory examination of the historical facts of the matter show that abolition was merely an anticlimax. The propaganda of the French abolitionist Victor Schoelcher was largely based on the proposition that abolition was the only method of salvaging an already ravaged sugar industry. Actually the Sugar Islands were toppled from their eminence by the introduction of the beetroot sugar extraction process, a process extensively developed during the Napoleonic wars. With the downfall of Napoleon the beetroot sugar industry languished until 1840 when the renewed race for empire revived the strategic importance of European sugar sources. Under the stimulation of a bounty system the beetroot sugar industry flourished, pouring an ever increasing volume of sugar on the markets of the world and driving down the world market prices. Sugar rapidly became one of the most competitive industries in the world, inexorably driving out small and less efficient producers.

The following figures will serve to indicate the course of sugar on the world market from 1840 to 1900:

YEAR	CANE	BEET	TOTAL	% BEET	AVER. PRICE	
	(1000 tons)				PER CWT	
1840	1,100	50	1,150	4.35	s 48	d 0
1860	1,510	389	1,899	20.49	35	0
1880	1,911	1,748	3,659	46.13	20	4
1900	2,850	5,950	8,800	67.61	11	6

From *Encyclopedia Britannica* (11th ed.) Article: "Sugar."

The only cane sugar producers who could face the growing encroachment of the beetroot sugar producers were those who could operate on a large scale, such as those in Cuba, Puerto Rico, Santo Domingo, and the Philippine Islands. The small-

scale producer in the French islands of the Caribbean was driven
to the wall. In order to prevent utter collapse of the island
economy in the face of world competition, the French government had to provide a highly artificial and protected market.
At least the islands would have to assume some of the burden
of government.

The planters who had been the object of government solici-
tude soon transformed themselves into a small and tightly knit
oligopoly that controlled, and still controls, the entire economy
of the islands. For the most part this group was composed of
descendants of the planting aristocracy of the eighteenth century.
Their rule has been perpetuated in Martinique particularly,[4]
where the preponderance of the most productive lands are in
the hands of individuals or in private companies whose stock is
closely held by members of one of the oligopolist families. In
addition to the stranglehold they maintain on the production of
sugar and rum, and besides controlling the only important
capital pool in the island, these families hold most of the major
retail outlets and the lucrative agencies for every variety of product emanating from abroad, from dried codfish to automobiles.

Guadeloupe, so close to and yet so distinctly different from
Martinique, presents an interesting contrast. This island has
always been less aristocratic in its social structure, and its land
holding is more dispersed. The peasant proprietor is more in
evidence, and there is a more vigorous middle-class intelligentsia.
The large sugar operations tend to be in the hands of stock
companies whose major capital derives from France. These
companies, responsible to stockholders, have proved more capable
of adjusting themselves to innovations in plant and agricultural

4. Eugène Revert, *La Martinique* (Paris: Nouvelles Éditions Latines,
1949), pp. 445–450. One of the curious aspects of the French islands lies in
the sharp differences that mark the two islands, although they are only
some 150 miles apart. A clear distinction was made between the two sets
of colonists in the 18th century. *Les Messieurs de la Martinique et les gens
de la Guadeloupe* was the formula then and to a great extent remains so
today.

production. The dispersal of entrepreneurial effort is also noticeable in retail business and among agency holders. They are men
of middle-class business background who are aggressive and
open to new ideas.

The importance of the sugar and rum industries is of fundamental importance to the economic well-being of the islands.
The manner in which they have been handled in the past very
largely accounts for the general economic plight in which the
islands find themselves in our own day. There is little doubt
that the manner in which these industries will be managed in
the future is of vital concern.

At the end of the great days of sugar production, Martinique, Guadeloupe, and the smaller islands fell into a period of
somnolence, scarcely disturbed between 1860 and 1913 save
for an occasional natural cataclysm. The industrial revolution
came to Cuba in 1819 with the first steam-operated sugar mill,
but it scarcely caused a ripple in the French islands, whose sugar
production continued to fluctuate at approximately the same
level. The landowners were satisfied with the returns from a
protected market and saw little reason to invest their funds in
new machinery, or to bother with the introduction of new techniques, or to experiment with new strains to keep abreast of the
harsh outside world of competition.

Between 1860 and 1913 the complacency of the planters
resulted in the slow exhaustion of land and a progressive falling
off of production. During those years Guadeloupe's production
fell by 2,000 tons, and Martinique slipped behind 1,000 tons.
As for French Guiana, it became almost a forgotten land, principally used as a dumping ground for capital criminals and political undesirables ever since 1797.

World War I brought the islands back into the mainstream
of world economy abruptly as sugar prices soared with the
destruction of the European beetroot sugar industry. At the
end of the war the shattered home industries of the beetroot
and the wine growers began to agitate for protection from the
enormously swelled production of sugar and rum from the

islands, and they combined to force the quota system on the colonial producers, to the dismay and outrage of the latter.

But indignation did not last too long among the West Indian producers. Slowly they began to see positive benefits in the quota. The restrictive effect of the system, enacted into law, brought about a rise in price; significant was the fact that quotas for production were limited to those producers who were actually engaged in distilling at the time that the law was passed. Thus the producer was protected with a guaranteed market, and protected as well from new entries into the distilling industry. These latter now had to be content with local markets since they could not export to the French market without owning a quota. In 1934, however, even the local market broke when a surtax was put on it. In that year and the next a renewed brandy-rum war broke out between the metropolitan producers and the colonials; new quotas were imposed, but the colonials knew how to protect themselves. They merely restricted rum output and brought about a rise in prices that served to offset the effect of the new quotas.

To a great extent the story of sugar follows rum, but it should be noted that sugar quotas, imposed after those on rum, never reached such highly restrictive proportions.

The quota system had numerous consequences in both economic and social spheres. The mere owning of a quota was sufficient to insure a guaranteed source of revenue. Because of this, modernization was set back at a time when the need for improvements was pressing. Thus, between the years 1929 and 1946 through a combination of circumstances (quota, depression, and war), machine replacement in the sugar factories had been practically nil. The consequence was to make the French islands the most backward of all the sugar-producing islands in the Caribbean. The depressing effect of the manipulation of the quotas by their owners on island economy emerges from the figures.

Some one hundred and thirty distilleries have been officially listed as holding assigned quotas and as active distillers of rum.

Of these approximately twenty are in full operation. The others range from various stages of ancientness, disrepair, and dilapidation to the stage of not existing at all. The quota owner did not even bother himself with actual production if he did not care to do so. He merely bought the surplusage of the large-scale distiller at non-protected prices and exported them to France under his own quota.

The government has recently moved to end this situation and will confiscate quotas whose owners have not actually manufactured for two consecutive years. The confiscated quotas will be put into a common pool and shared by the active distillers.[5] This tends to give an unpleasant picture, one of protection of entrenched ultra-conservative interests with a cynical disregard for the economic well-being of the islands as a whole.

II

It would be unfair, indeed untrue, to maintain that this is the entire picture. A growing number of progressive planters and producers, many emerging from the ranks of the ruling oligopoly, began making sweeping reappraisals of traditional attitudes and of the system which had prevailed for so long, when the hardships they suffered during World War II emphasized the need to do so; and the French government, pressed financially as well, had to move to lighten the French taxpayer's burden of additional and never-ending deficits from the islands' balance sheet. After the war positive steps were taken when the government announced plans to modernize production with the goal of at least doubling the prewar output of the Antilles.[6]

For nearly twenty years now definite measures have been

5. Chambre de Commerce de la Martinique, *Bulletin Mensuel,* Avril, 1957, pp. 7–9. Copy of a letter from the Secretary of State for Economic Affairs to the Prefect of Martinique, dated Paris, April 4, 1957, referring to a warning issued by the same agency on March 20, 1955.

6. Luc D. Fauvel, *Rapport sur le Développement Industriel dans le Caraïbe* (Port-of-Spain: Caribbean Commission, 1952), p. 112.

taken to step up the inordinately low sugar yield per hectare of cane. Experiments with new strains resulted in the introduction of a Barbadian cane which has gradually replaced the lesser yielding canes in both Martinique and Guadeloupe.

Slowly the more progressive plants modernized. The antiquated steam engines which powered the various stages of cane rendering gave way to electric power. Steam boilers which had deteriorated over the years and had resulted in progressive dropping of steam pressures are in the process of being replaced. Higher boiler pressures have brought an increase in production. The steam locomotives which were a constant fire hazard during harvesting and transportation have given place in the best run plants to diesel locomotives. Even so, the sugar factories have a long way to go before they approach the efficiency of the great plants of Cuba or Puerto Rico. The single line of flow that is still the rule in the French islands renders production extremely hazardous. Should any one stage of the rendering process break down, the entire plant must shut down; and in the production of sugar, time is of the essence, due to the closely integrated relationship between harvesting and rendering.

The following statistics give an insight into the effects of modern plant management on one of the more progressive sugar operations in Martinique. They are interesting because they derive, not from the largest operation, but from one of middle

Year	Cane Ground (metric tons)	Sugar Produced	Render	HA	Acre
1939	38,000	2,500	6.5	4.55	1.8
1955	65,450	5,300	8.1'	5.9	2.4
1956	76,640	5,800	7.7	6.0	2.4
1957	59,850	6,300	9.5	7.3	2.9

Figures supplied by the Usine de la Marin, Marin, Martinique.

size. In this factory the noticeable increase in production of 1957 over 1956 has been due to sweeping modernization. Even with less cane ground the amount of sugar produced was still greater than in 1956. The average yield of cane for this factory in 1957 was of the order of 95 kilos of raw sugar per 1,000 kilos of cane ground. It is well above the Martinique average of 83 kilos[7] in 1956, but well below the yield of sugar in Guadeloupe of 116.726.[8]

The increasing yield of cane illustrated above is not unique, but represents a general trend in the islands. The upward trend in production and yield has focused new attention on the quota system and the problem of handling extra-quota production. The vagaries connected with establishment of the sugar quota, as well as that of rum, has been a source of exasperation to the planters for some time. There seems to be a basic lack of understanding on the part of the quota formulators of the exigencies of cane planting. There are even those who maintain that the quotas are largely arbitrary with little basis in reality.

Sugar yield is hedged about by many imponderables which defy scientific forecasting. It varies from year to year depending on rainfall, its scarcity or superabundance. Over all is the chronic fear of the violent tropical storms that might well wipe out the entire crop of an island. Of recent years the yield of the cane has been of such a nature that surpluses have been accumulating over and above the protected quota. Thus in 1956 with a quota of 75,000 metric tons for Martinique, production amounted to 86,277 tons, compared with the 1955 production of 82,262 tons. The result: an embarassing surplus of 11,276 tons not covered by the quota price.[9] Happily for Martinique, and for Guadeloupe as well, 1956 was a year of exceedingly low beetroot crop yield in France, which allowed the planters and producers to realize a full protected price for their surplus. It was not to be all pure gain, for the surplus so absorbed by France was to be applied against the quotas for 1957.

7. Crédit Martiniquais, Assemblée Générale Ordinaire et Extraordinaire du 25 Fevrier 1957, *Rapport et Résolutions* (Fort-de-France, Martinique). Hereafter cited as Crédit Martiniquais.

8. Crédit Guadeloupéen, Assemblée Générale Ordinaire du 27 Mars 1956, *Rapport et Comptes* (Point-à-Pitre, Guadeloupe). Hereafter cited as Crédit Guadeloupéen.

9. Crédit Martiniquais, 1955 and 1956; Crédit Guadeloupéen, 1956.

An approaching crisis in the quota system is evident in the steadily mounting production figures just noted. The government has had to resort to stopgap subventions to protect planter and producer from losses which would be entailed by selling at world prices, although it has been made clear that the subventions are to be regarded as temporary, ending in 1958. Presumably by this time production will have been stabilized to accord with the quota figures.

For the sugar and rum industries the quota-*cum*-subvention system seems to partake of the character of the wife with or without whom one cannot exist.

The deadening effect of protection on enterprise has had serious repercussions on the social system of the islands. Sugar processing remains a highly seasonal affair. Harvesting and processing the cane crop is compressed into three to four months, scarcely more. During this period of the year employment reaches a peak, but once the harvest-processing is over, the work force is radically reduced. Employment is limited to cleaning the fields, replanting, and cultivation. The factories reduce their staff to a bare minimum for maintenance and machinery overhaul. Some of the less well run operations shut down entirely and reopen just prior to harvest. This means months of idleness for the work force, which may be alleviated by employment on public works, such as roads and bridges, while some seek jobs in other types of seasonal agricultural work. Still others tend their postage-stamp-sized kitchen gardens, or merely collect unemployment insurance which in its turn swells production costs for planter and producer.

Of late years the growth of the banana industry has been increasingly successful in spreading employment through more of the year. Banana cultivation is not a seasonal crop; harvesting, packing, and transport go on constantly. By Central American standards the French West Indian banana output is minuscule. Nevertheless, concentration on a growing European market for tropical fruits shows much promise. The French islands have developed a strain of banana of superior taste and the necessary hardiness to stand the transatlantic passage. The early postwar shortage of air-cooled banana transports is being rectified as more specially constructed vessels are put in service for the carriage of tropical fruit.[10]

The following figures illustrate the growth of the banana industry since it has become significant, in the 1950's.

	MARTINIQUE	GUADELOUPE
	(metric tons)	
1954	61,433	83,588
1955	58,448	71,082
1956	93,362	Hurricane damage

Compiled from annual reports of Crédit Martiniquais, and Crédit Guadeloupéen.

The sharp dip in production in 1955 was the result of the ravages of the banana blight *Cercospora*. Notable work was done to stamp out the disease and to develop preventive sprays by the industry-subsidized Institut des Fruits et Agrumes Coloniaux (IFAC) at its experimental station in Neufchateau, Guadeloupe.[11]

Indications are excellent for a progressive increase in banana output in the future, but on the other hand the French market is rapidly reaching the saturation point.[12] With the expansion of the banana market into Europe, the islands hope to take advantage of the introduction of other tropical fruits as well. At the Neufchateau Experimental Station IFAC is developing strains of avocado and mango suitable for export. It is of interest to note that the strains developed in Florida are much favored.

10. For the metropolitan market, and for the rest of Europe as well, the chief rival to the French islands is the Camerouns.

11. For a description of the fight against *Cercospora,* see *Fruits Guadeloupéens,* No. 5 (Guadeloupe: IFAC, n.d.).

12. France has been importing bananas to the order of 270,000–300,000 tons since 1954. Estimates of the total crop of the entire French Union are as high as 350,000–400,000 tons—a figure that far exceeds the consumption of metropolitan France, which indicates that she will have to tap the general European market to a much greater extent than has hitherto been attempted.

IFAC has made great strides in pineapple cultivation and in fighting the cochineal attacks on the plants. Pineapple juice is rapidly becoming an export of some significance. IFAC has encountered a good deal of apathy in its attempt to foster interest in long-range fruit growing. The constant fear of hurricanes discourages investment of capital which might be wiped out in a day.

Vanilla, once a most profitable and widely cultivated crop, has diminished to the disappearing point with the advent of artificial flavor. Cacao and coffee, however, are making a surprising comeback due to the rise of prices on the world market. Coffee production climbed from 400 metric tons to more than 600 tons between 1954 and 1955, and more planters are bringing the bean back into cultivation.[13]

III

While these agricultural developments hold out hope for breaking the inexorable grip of monoculture, it is generally agreed that the islands must move towards industrialization to provide at least some of their basic needs. Since the heyday of the sugar islands they have been forced to be dependent on imports to feed, clothe, and house their populations. This situation has resulted in a chronic adverse balance of payments which has had to be made up by the mother country, as has been shown.

It has often been suggested that the islands do not make the fullest use of their great sugar crop. The by-product of sugar cane, bagasse, the squeezed-out stalk, has proved to be an amazingly versatile material. Louisiana has been in the forefront of experimentation with bagasse, because in that state natural gas, cheap and plentiful, has replaced bagasse as a fuel with notable efficiency realized in boiler operation and maintenance. The bagasse in turn has been diverted to new uses,

13. Credit Guadeloupéen, 1956, p. 4.

such as the manufacture of building materials, fodder, fertilizer, and plastics.[14] The proximity of the great oil fields of South America to the French islands suggest that conversion to fuel oil might bring comparable results for them as well, if the triple problem of transportation (bagasse being a bulky commodity), capital investment, and the development of other markets can be solved.

The sugar industry may well be developing a new and very important outlet in soap manufacture, although not in the nature of a by-product. The process of combining sugar and fat molecules to obtain sugar ester already accounts for one-fifth of the soap market of the world.[15]

If the development of facilities to convert bagasse into its by-products is unfeasible, there are other areas to develop. Certainly there should be a sufficient market, even of a local nature, for a cement plant to supply the islands' needs and relieve the product of its great transportation costs. Martinique has possibly the only major deposits of pumice this side of Europe. The building booms in Puerto Rico and south Florida have aroused interest in exploiting this natural resource, but the monetary policy of France has discouraged (and still does) foreign investment.

To date exploration for oil has proved unavailing. Professor Lowestein of the University of California has recently completed a geological survey of both Guadeloupe and Martinique, but the results are still undetermined. However, the volcanic nature of the islands' structure seems to preclude oil deposits of a significant size.

One of the most curiously neglected aspects of the islands' economy has been the development of the local fisheries. The present fisheries are primitive. A five-ton vessel would be considered large. Fishing is a coastwise affair, and the catch does

14. Walter Scott, *The Industrial Utilization of the By-Products of Sugar Cane* (Port-of-Spain: Caribbean Commission, 1952), pp. 14–74 *et passim*.
15. *Sugar,* July, 1957, p. 40.

not feed more than 15 or 20 per cent of the island population. Inasmuch as fish is a staple island diet, and has been so for centuries, the catch is peculiarly small. Dried codfish makes up the bulk of the population's diet, and it has to come a long way. From Saint-Pierre and Miquelon the cod is shipped to Brittany where it is processed and packed and shipped out to the islands, with all of the accrued freight and handling charges swelling the market price. Explorations of the Caribbean have indicated that modern fishing vessels with powerful gear, echo-sounding devices, and adequate capacity could make the Caribbean a lucrative fishing ground.[16] With the government ready to contribute toward the building of the fishery industry by setting up storage-plant facilities, it remains curious that entrepreneurs seem reluctant to enter the field. In many parts of the islands it is darkly hinted that "interests" are at work, actively discouraging such a move.

IV

One of the greatest sources of additional revenue to the French islands which remains virtually unexploited is the tourist industry that flourishes especially among the Greater Antilles, the American Virgins, and the British islands generally. To many experienced travellers the breathtaking beauties of Martinique and of the lush countryside of Guadeloupe know no peer in the Antilles. There are some who claim the French islands are more lovely than Jamaica. If there may be some argument about this, French Creole cooking as practised in these French islands should tip the balance. Yet the lack of tourist accommodations is acute. Such hotels as exist are for the most part very poorly run and lacking in tourist appeal. There are notable exceptions in both islands, but their accommodations are extremely limited.

16. Caribbean Commission, *Fisheries in the Caribbean* (Trinidad, 1952), pp. 87–89 *et passim*.

Although it is readily admitted that the tourist trade[17] would bring in valuable revenue and would have a salutary effect on the economy in bringing into existence collateral service industries and would revivify local handicrafts which have nearly vanished, there is an ambivalent attitude discernable. To those most in favor of developing tourism, the reluctance of island capital to invest is clear proof that the great families are not anxious for the introduction of a new industry that would adversely affect their labor market. This allegation is vehemently denied, and the blame is laid in turn on the central government for the crushing tax loads on new enterprise and its stubborn refusal to give such new enterprises necessary concessions.

There are many who do not want to see the entry of Americans on any scale, in the fear that the "restricted" sign will go up to please "race-conscious Americans," a fear that the Communists have been successfully playing upon. This is aggravated by the fear of eventually becoming tributary to the American economic system.

One of the foremost interests working in favor of building tourism for the French islands is Air France. Plans are already under way to inaugurate a direct service from Miami to Guadeloupe and Martinique, using the new jet Caravelles. The fastest service offered now is by Pan American Airways, twice weekly, which necessitates an overnight stop in San Juan. Before such a service is installed by Air France, there will have to be more adequate accommodations in both islands. The Raizet aerodrome at Point-à-Pitre is already being enlarged, and Air

17. Development of tourism in the Caribbean region:

	1951	1955	% INCREASED
Barbados	11,239	14,722	31.4
Curaçao	76,372	113,003	46
Haiti	17,708	55,007	210.6
Puerto Rico	84,967	141,711	66
Trinidad	63,549	76,589	20.5
Virgins	32,436	53,627	69.3

Chambre de Commerce de la Martinique, *op. cit.* p. 33.

France is moving its main base there from Lamentin. This move from Martinique to Guadeloupe has raised a flurry of interest in developing a tourist resort in the vicinity of Vieux Fort, site of the oldest settlements on the island. There is talk of a sixty-room de luxe hotel, but as of the beginning of September, 1957, no actual work was begun. However, that direct action is in the offing is indicated by a survey made of present accommodations of Martinique and Guadeloupe by a representative of the Société Immobilière et Touristique des Départements d'Outre-Mer, an advisory agency attached to the office of the Under-Secretary of State for Economic Affairs in Paris. The agency's function is to make recommendations to help the Caisse Centrale decide on advancing funds to qualified capitalists who might be interested in entering the tourist industry in any of the overseas departments and territories of the French Union.

In its 29th annual report the Crédit Guadeloupéen summed up and expressed the attitude of a growing body of businessmen in the islands as follows:

Tourism seems to us to offer at least a partial means of filling the deficit in our balance of trade. We would be all the more deficient in judgment to continue to neglect this element of invisible export, when consideration is taken of the natural attractions without parallel that Guadeloupe has to offer to tourists whose numbers grow from one year to another. All that would be necessary would be to endow our magnificent beaches, our superb mountain sites, our health giving thermal springs with hotels or inns, not pretentious, but comfortable ones, to see vacationing foreigners come in, in ever increasing numbers.

We cite the example of Haiti to show the importance of tourism on the economic life of a country. Until only a few years ago, Haiti was not as well known as Guadeloupe. Today, tourism brings in more than $25,000,000 per annum.[18]

Whatever the device or combination of devices that might be tried under the existing socio-economic system, they must be

18. Credit Guadeloupéen, 1955, p. 9.

only stopgap. Even the development of the promising tourism can only mitigate the chronic adverse balance that characterizes the economic plight of the overseas departments and weighs so heavily on the taxpayer at large.

V

Although there are growing indications of awareness of an identity with a West Indian heritage among the intelligentsia of the islands, notably in Guadeloupe,[19] it is doubtful whether the islands will, or indeed whether they will ever desire to cut themselves adrift from France, to associate themselves with some type of West Indian confederation of a socialist nature, such as Daniel Guérin proposes, in his controversial *Les Antilles Décolonisées*.[20] To most thoughtful students of the French islands the solution is not in the direction of some such shadowy federation of the Caribbean of the future, but in the nascent realities of the European Economic Community, "The Six," a plan now on the threshold of implementation which has captured the imagination of Europe, if not the world.

On March 25, 1957, France, West Germany, Italy, Belgium, Luxemburg, and the Netherlands signed a treaty which might well mean a new era in the economics of Europe. The treaty calls for the progressive disentegration of tariff barriers and the creation of a free and competitive market for the signatories. This new structure is not to be a mere *zollverein* or customs union on the classic pattern, but a full-blown integration and rationalization of the entire economy of Western Europe.[21] The

19. Michel Leiris, *Contacts de Civilization en Martinique et en Guadeloupe* (Paris: Gallimard, 1955), p. 30.

20. (Paris: Présence Africaine, 1956), *passim*. See especially Chap. 5.

21. On July 9, 1957, five days after the ratification of the Common Market by the West German Parliament, the National Assembly of France voted to ratify the treaties to create the Market, and the Council of the Republic completed the ratification on July 24. At present it is confidently expected that by January 1, 1958, the remaining countries will have completed their ratification and the treaties will go into effect at that time.

treaties themselves are too complex to deal with in this paper, but the importance that they hold for the "colonial" areas is clear. For the first time these areas will have access to a free market in which to sell their produce and buy their necessities. However, it must be noted that the provisions concerning the overseas territories are among the most difficult to construe, and there is a good deal of conjecture as to what the future may really have in store for them.[22]

Under a liberal construction of the treaties, the prospects for the French Antilles and for Guiana look bright. For not only will industrial products benefit from the common market, but agricultural products as well. Customs and quotas will be abolished over a period of fifteen years, although the overseas territories will retain an option of maintaining customs duties on goods coming from The Six to protect their small industries, as long as a preferential status is not granted in favor of the European country to which the overseas territory is politically attached. This privilege is to remain in force for five years, after which time it, too, will be abolished.[23]

The attractiveness of the Common Market for metropolitan France and her overseas departments and territories is obvious. For France the costly burden of maintaining protective markets for her territories would have a foreseeable termination. At the end of five years she would be able to transfer her burden to the entire community of The Six. For the islands the economic necessities of life would be purchased on a free market at competitive prices rather than in the artificially shored-up market within the French tariff system.

While it will certainly be true that the Caribbean islands will be getting less for their main product, the absence of the deterrent of protection and the lobbying of special interests would offset the loss in increased agricultural production for a

22. Carl D. Corse, "The Common Market and the GATT," *Foreign Affairs;* XXXVI (October, 1957), 133–134.

23. See Robert Marjohn, "Prospects for the European Common Market," *Foreign Affairs,* XXXVI (October, 1957), 131–142.

wider market and the widening of Antillean horizons of economic opportunity.

To the objections that have been voiced on the subject of the Common Market, and which will be considered below, the proponents underline the urgency of the situation as it exists today.

Already the integration of the overseas territories into the economy of France has reached the measure of 71 per cent,[24] and the ability to absorb the mounting output, agricultural and mineral, of those areas has reached the saturation point. To this it might be added that the saturation point has been reached in the French capital pool also. Two agencies called for by the treaties, the European Investment Bank and the European Social Fund, hold the promise of a new flow of capital to the islands. The problem of the development of such underdeveloped areas as French Guiana is intimately involved here.

Guiana's immediate and long-range future depends on the attraction of considerable capital to realize her potential, capital which financially-staggered France simply cannot assemble. Guiana produces some gold and diamonds, but not in significant amounts as yet. Bauxite is present in large amounts, but it is of such a low grade that it must await the exhaustion of neighboring and richer deposits, or new processes must be developed.

In spite of widespread optimism, there is also an important sector which feels that the overseas territories should proceed with caution. For example, it is felt that they should have a representative on the Market's council to protect their interests. Most important is the necessity for the European members of The Six to reorientate their present foreign commerce, to substitute the overseas areas of the members of The Six, whose commerce for The Six is now negligible, for their present suppliers of tropical goods.

24. The remainder of the output of the overseas countries is exported outside the French tariff system as follows: European countries, 17 per cent; sterling zone, 7 per cent; dollar zone, 7 per cent. See Chambre de Commerce de la Martinique, *op. cit.*, p. 17.

The most disturbing part of the new community treaties is the emphasis on the rationalization of the industry of The Six, which contemplates relocation of industry and migrations of labor within the borders of the Market community. To many this would seem to indicate that the industry so desirable for the overseas territories would be in effect stifled by the very nature of the Market community. If this eventuality should happen, say those who are unfriendly or reserved about the plan, as it would certainly seem from the expressed aspirations, would not the tropical areas be in the same or even worse position than before? Would they not be merely members of another *pacte coloniale* under a more grandiose name?[25]

Whatever decisions may be made in the near future, one thing seems to be certain. The economic future of the French West Indies is not fated to continue indefinitely in the grip of an eighteenth-century mercantilism, call it by any name that you will. Far-reaching changes are in the making, and it is hoped that they will redound to the profit of these beautiful islands and their fine people.

25. See the arguments for and against, presented in Chambre de Commerce de la Martinique, *op. cit.,* pp. 16–21.

Carl L. Lokke: SOCIETY IN THE
FRENCH CARIBBEAN

No SOCIETY can be understood apart from its history.
This is particularly true of the French Caribbean, above all of
French Guiana. These three overseas departments, parts of the
French Union, are remnants of a once vast empire in the
Western Hemisphere.

This empire began as a gleam in the eye of that doughty
monarch, King Francis I. When Francis ascended the French
throne, the newly discovered lands beyond the western horizon
were neatly divided between Spain and Portugal. No less an
authority than the Pope had settled the matter. But Francis did
not consider it settled; he sent out exploring expeditions anyway. In reply to a protest from the Emperor Charles V he was
very plain. The sun, he declared, shone for him, too.[1] Where was
the clause in Adam's will that excluded him from a share in the
New World beyond the seas?

The heads of other northern powers had similar ideas. In due
course they broke the monopoly of Spain and Portugal and
carved out empires in the Americas. The various parts of the
French Caribbean under discussion were acquired in the seven-

1. W. Adolphe Roberts, *The French in the West Indies* (Indianapolis,
1942), p. 13; J. Saintoyant, *La colonisation française sous l'Ancien Régime
du XVᵉ siècle à 1789* (Paris, 1929), I, 32.

teenth century. The French established a post in what is now
French Guiana as early as 1604—that is, three years before the
English founded Jamestown. They began to colonize both
Martinique and Guadeloupe in 1635. In 1648, a momentous
year in the history of modern Europe, the French divided with
the Dutch the little island of St. Martin. This amicable arrangement has persisted uninterrupted to the present day. The French
part falls under the jurisdiction of Guadeloupe.

1

The foundations of the present racially complex society in
these areas were laid early. Normandy furnished the largest
contingent of settlers from France; other settlers came from
Brittany, southwest France, the region around Paris, and also
from Holland. Their coming was not welcome to the native
Caribs who resisted stoutly but in vain. A few survivors among
them were assimilated into the society of their conquerors. Some
colonists, lacking perhaps the patience to await the arrival of
brides from France, married Carib women.[2] From such unions
certain families today are proud to trace their descent. One is
reminded of the First Families of Virginia who are proud to
have the blood of Pocahontas in their veins.

Soon Africa, not voluntarily, contributed to the population of
the islands. With the cultivation of the sugar cane and other
tropical products, it became profitable to obtain Negro slaves
to do the work. These were brought from the African littoral
extending from Senegal to the Gold Coast, even as far south as
Angola. By the end of the seventeenth century the slaves outnumbered the whites in both Martinique and Guadeloupe. In
1699 Martinique had 6,252 whites and 8,916 slaves; Guadeloupe
had 3,921 whites and 6,185 slaves.[3]

The juxtaposition of the two races led to miscegenation.
This evil the royal government early undertook to curb by pro-

2. Eugène Revert, *La France d'Amérique* (Paris, 1949), pp. 52–53.
3. *Ibid.*, p. 60.

visions of the Black Code of 1685.[4] A married master who had
a child by a female slave lost mother and child, and paid a
fine to boot. An unmarried master in the same situation was
required to marry the mother in the Church, thus setting her
free. In the insouciance of the tropics, however, these injunctions
were honored more in the breach than in the observance. The
mixed population of the islands continued to grow with or
without benefit of ceremony.

But the total population under the Old Regime did not grow
by natural increase. It sank whenever immigration ceased. This
situation with respect to the Negro population has been commonly attributed to slavery. In any case the emacipation of the
slaves in 1848 brought in its train a different trend, from
natural increase or from new immigration. According to Victor
Schoelcher, in 1847 Guadeloupe had 93,000 slaves and Martinique 74,000.[5] As these people when freed had no stomach
to continue plantation labor and the owners had none to see
their holdings go down in ruin, the latter undertook to bring
in plantation hands from outside. Between 1852 and 1887 they
introduced 78,800 Asiatics (77,000 Hindus, 1,300 Chinese, and
500 Annamites) and 16,000 Africans. Traces of the Hindu immigration may be still be observed.

Thus the population of the two islands is considerably more
mixed than it was in the eighteenth century. The European
element in this melting pot has lost ground numerically. Deaths
in the past exceeded births in certain periods. But other reasons
form more dramatic explanations of the decline. During the
French Revolution the white planters in Guadeloupe were
decimated. Their compeers on the neighboring island seem to
have suffered no major losses until the disaster of May 8, 1902.
On that day an eruption of Mount Pelée destroyed the largest
city, St. Pierre, with its 30,000 inhabitants; in a twinkling one-

---

4. The text of the Black Code is found in Isambert, *Recueil général des
anciennes lois françaises,* XIX, 494–504.

5. Revert, p. 61.

half of Martinique's white population was wiped out. Thenceforth, each island had about the same number of whites, that is between 4,000 and 5,000.[6] Martinique had more in the seventeenth century.

But despite earthquakes, hurricanes, and volcanic eruptions, the population has steadily grown. Contributing causes are the program of tropical hygiene, the fight against leprosy and syphilis, and the checking of infant mortality. According to the census of 1954 Martinique had 239,130 inhabitants and Guadeloupe 229,120.[7] Both islands, embracing together (including Guadeloupe's dependencies) an area equal to that of Rhode Island, have long been regarded as overpopulated.

II

In the case of French Guiana, with its population of 27,863, the contrary situation exists. This area, comparable in size to the state of Indiana, has always been underpopulated, during slavery times and since. French Guiana is the Cinderella of the three Guianas, in fact of the French Caribbean. Its poor name and indifferent success are attributed to its climate and to the former penal settlement there.

Actually the climate which averages about 80 degrees Fahrenheit differs little from that in the other Guianas. Nor does it differ much from the climate of Martinique and Guadeloupe, though the humidity no doubt is higher (about 90).

In this connection it is interesting to compare the views of two Americans two centuries apart. Edward Bancroft of Massachusetts spent three years in Dutch Guiana in the 1760's. In his published *Essay on the Natural History of Guiana* (1769), he sounded the praises of the country.[8] The heat, he wrote, was

6. *Ibid.*

7. Institut National de la Statistique et des Études Économiques, *Recensement de 1954: Population des Départements d'Outre-Mer* (Paris, 1954), p. 3.

8. See quotations from this book in the *Annual Register, 1769* (3rd Ed., London, 1779), pp. 272–282.

not excessive because of the trade winds by day and the land breezes by night, and the climate bore favorable comparison with that in the salubrious island of Barbados. In contemplating the "perpetual uninterrupted summer" in Guiana, Bancroft felt impelled to quote as description Alexander Pope's glowing couplets:

> Stern winter smiles on that auspicious clime,
> The fields are florid with unfading prime;
> From the bleak pole no winds inclement blow,
> Mould the round hail, or flake the fleecy snow.

Ernie Pyle, a famous correspondent of World War II, visited Cayenne in the fall of 1938. The sending of the last shipload of convicts from France to this penal colony seems to have provided the incentive for his trip. Pyle published a series of seven articles on his observations there, one for each day he was compelled to stay, as the Pan American plane stopped at Cayenne but once a week.[9] In reply to the question whether it was "unbearably hot" in French Guiana, he had this to say: "In Cayenne it is very hot, but I don't find it quite as bad as the summer heat in Washington, D.C."

Guiana's bad reputation with respect to climate stems undoubtedly from Choiseul's ill-starred colonizing venture on the Kourou River. This venture took place right after the Seven Years' War, in the same decade that young Bancroft wrote his *Essay*. Thousands of colonists fell victims to disease and privation. Forty years later the Abbé de Pradt declared that the memory of the Kourou disaster hung over the languishing colony like a kind of funeral crepe.[10] Nor did it help the reputation of the colony when in the late 1790's the Revolutionaries sent to French Guiana a number of political exiles. Notable among them was Barbé-Marbois, the man who later sold

9. *Washington Daily News,* Dec. 29, 30, 1938; Jan. 2, 4, 5, 7, 9, 1939; Lee G. Miller, *The Story of Ernie Pyle* (New York, 1950), pp. 103–104.

10. M. de Pradt, *Les trois âges des colonies, ou de leur état passé, présent et à venir* (Paris, 1801–1802), I, 153.

Louisiana to the United States. (His hostess in Guiana taught her parrot to say: *Déporté sans jugement.*)[11]

Guiana's 13,000 slaves, like those in the islands, were emancipated in 1848. The result was the same. Work on the plantations ceased. The owners, like their countrymen in Martinique and Guadeloupe, undertook to meet this situation by gradually bringing in workers from Africa and India (1,520 Negroes and 8,471 Hindus).[12] Relief seemed in prospect, too, when the French government in the mid-1850's sent to Guiana several thousand lesser criminals. It wished to provide these unfortunates, after they had served their terms, with an opportunity to get a fresh start in an undeveloped country. To the planters the convicts were a potential source of labor. These expectations were realized, however, in very small degree. The convicts, like the new colonists a century before, did not flourish on the unfamiliar Guiana coast. In the face of poor food and lodging, and hard labor, these Europeans also perished by the hundreds from tropical fevers and diseases. As if this were not enough to sound the agricultural knell of the colony, gold was discovered in the 1850's in the hinterland. Energetic, able-bodied men went there in quest of quick fortunes in the mines. Gold became and has remained the chief product of French Guiana. Foodstuffs were imported; they still are.

In time all sorts of convicts were sent to this penal colony, not only from France but from various parts of the French Empire. They seem to have numbered several thousand in 1938. Ernie Pyle divided them into three classes: (1) *Déportés,* the men deported for treason or some military dereliction in World War I; (2) *Transportés,* the one-crime men, such as murderers, robbers, forgers, swindlers; and (3) *Relégués,* the habitual, incorrigible criminals—that is, what he called "the skunks and the lice and the rats of French humanity." Now Pyle was as honest a

11. E. Wilson Lyon, *The Man Who Sold Louisiana; the Career of François Barbé-Marbois* (Norman, Oklahoma, 1942), p. 108.

12. Revert, p. 222.

journalist as ever slipped paper into a typewriter. The authorities did not permit him to visit the prisons in person. But his romantic notions about the fine qualities of the convicts in Guiana, he was free to say, did not stand up in the face of the *libérés* he saw and the things he heard in Cayenne. Most of them were confirmed criminals, no good in France or in Cayenne. The tragedy of Dreyfus on Devil's Island had given the world the wrong impression. At the same time Pyle had no kind words for the penal system or the secrecy observed by the authorities about it. In contrast to the situation a century before, he wrote, the colony had "entirely gone to pot."

If this Scripps-Howard reporter gave the penal colony a "bad press," he had plenty of precedent to follow. The colony probably never had a good press after Zola exposed before the civilized world the injustice done to Dreyfus. In 1899 this condemned, later vindicated, army captain was brought back to France after spending four years on Devil's Island. When he died in 1935 the press told the whole story afresh. The *New York Times,* a newspaper with "All the News That's Fit to Print," gave it space on the front page.[13] But other news in the 1930's also kept Devil's Island and French Guiana unfavorably and fairly frequently in the public eye. A glance at the index to the *Times* reveals a number of items about the escapes, sometimes the futile attempts to escape, of convicts from the colony.[14] Other items discussed the sending to this accursed region of new shiploads of condemned men: 973 convicts on one ship in 1935, 1,000 in 1938.[15]

Then the war came. It brought the collapse of the Third Republic, and some new ideas. The Fourth Republic raised the Caribbean colonies to the status of overseas departments in the

13. *New York Times,* July 13, 1935.

14. *Ibid.* (Index), July 8, 31, Aug. 17, Oct. 16, 1933; July 24, Nov. 7, 10, 1934; Aug. 3, 9, 1936; Feb. 21, July 8, Oct. 17, 24, Dec. 5, 1937; Feb. 1, Mar. 26, Apr. 3, 5, May 4, Aug. 25, 26, Sept. 9, 1940.

15. *Ibid.* (Index), Sept. 8, Nov. 24, 1935; Oct. 26, Nov. 15, 21, 22, 23, 27, 1938.

new French Union. Also, in 1946, it abolished the transportation
of convicts to Guiana. By that time the penal population there
had sunk to 1,543 men. These men were gradually brought
back to France: the repatriation process seems now to have
been entirely completed.[16]

With the convicts gone, will French Guiana experience a
rebirth? How long will it take to eradicate a century-old stain?
Will agriculture flourish again as it did under slave labor a
hundred years ago?

Everyone seems to agree that French Guiana will never
amount to anything, never develop a wholesome society, unless
it can, like the other Guianas, attract large numbers of immigrants to exploit the land, the forests, and the mines. This it
has never been able to do in a big way. In view of the over-
population of Martinique and Guadeloupe and the underpopu-
lation of Guiana, one wonders why the islanders have not
flocked to the mainland department. Apart from the greater
opportunities in a comparable climate and under the same flag,
they would escape the constant menace of hurricanes and volcanic eruptions. After the disastrous eruption of Mount Pelée in
1902, a group of people did migrate from Martinique to
Guiana. They founded the village of Montjoly a few miles
from Cayenne.[17] Some of them did well in trade and gold
contraband. Many died, however, and others returned to their
native island. On the whole the experience of these settlers did
not encourage others to follow their example. In fact the role
of pioneer makes no appeal to these islanders; they do not occupy
uncultivated land in their own territory. Curiously, not even
the gold mines in the interior inflamed their imagination or any
desire to get rich quickly. It was otherwise with their neighbor

16. *Ibid.* (Index), Apr. 11, 1946; Apr. 22, Aug. 24, 1947; Mar. 10,
1951. There is mention of 100 convicts still at St. Laurent as late as 1953.
See Pierre Denoyer, "Ce qui reste, aux îles de Salut de l'ancien 'Enfer du
Bagne.' L'île du Diable va-t-elle devenir un centre touristique?" *France
Illustration*, Jan. 24, 1953.

17. Revert, p. 249.

islanders. Of the 1,500 people connected with the Guiana mines in 1944, it is estimated that 70 per cent came from the British Antilles.

Under young Robert Vignon, the first prefect under the departmental system, an effort was made to settle in Guiana a group of Displaced Persons from Europe.[18] Sixty-five families were recruited in the French and British zones in Germany. The French government made a contract with each family, agreeing to furnish it a fixed salary for two years and necessary facilities for getting established. In the selection of the families an effort was made, it appears, to engage mechanics, builders, and farmers. National origin did not matter. These assembled immigrants formed in truth a veritable Tower of Babel—Poles, Hungarians, Yugoslavs, Czechs, Slovaks, and Ukrainians. Their knowledge of French was slight.

The new settlers arrived in two groups, in July and in November, 1949. To the natives they must have seemed like a harbinger of better days to come, for only two years before the first group of Guiana convicts, some 500 men, had been returned to France. Such Europeans were welcome. They established a village at St. Jean on the Maroni River.

For a time, of course, disillusionment seized these new arrivals. In Europe they had longed for liberty; in Guiana they did not know what to do with it. Confronted with the facts of heat and humidity, they could not, like Alexander Pope at a distance, rejoice over this "auspicious clime," lacking "winds inclement," hail, or snow. They longed for snow at Christmas and said so. The matter of obtaining customary food, too, was crucial. Cries went up, "No meat!" "No potatoes!"

Most of these immigrants gradually adjusted themselves. They set to work to build houses and roads. Each family kept its own garden for growing radishes, green beans, bananas, pineapples, mangoes, and other foodstuffs. Fishing provided another means of support. Those individuals, mostly unmarried, who had no

18. Pierre Denoyer, "Un nouvel mode de colonisation: l'expérience de Saint-Jean du Maroni," *France Illustration*, Apr. 12, 1952.

taste for this way of life, were transferred to other activities in
St. Laurent and Cayenne. The undertaking at St. Jean suggests
the Matanuska Valley project in Alaska in 1934.

III

No society can be strong and purposeful if disease is rampant
within it. The several parts of the French Caribbean have all
suffered from the ravages of tropical diseases. According to the
Martinique death statistics for the period 1931 to 1946 the
average life expectancy for men and women was $39\frac{1}{4}$ years;
women of course outlived men by more than five years.[19] In the
last decade or so serious efforts have been made to improve the
health situation. For example, malaria used to be a serious
menace in French Guiana; most of the population was afflicted
with it. The Pasteur Institute, which was established in Cayenne
in 1940, identified 164 species of mosquito and then conducted
a vast DDT spraying campaign along the coast and in the
interior to eradicate this pest. According to Dr. Floch, the
Director, in an article published in 1956, the malaria rate has
decreased by 98.8 per cent.[20] In Guadeloupe plans are afoot
to build a large new leprosarium near Pointe Noire; it will take
the place of the old, antiquated one in Désirade.[21] Two years
ago a sum of money was voted for the extension and improvement of the Lamentin Hospital in Martinique.[22] The authorities
appear to recognize that production is connected closely with
health.

Public elementary and secondary school education is provided
in the three areas.[23] Guiana is distinctive in having a private
school for leprous children. As the leading department in the
Caribbean, Martinique maintains in addition to two *lycées* (one

19. Revert, p. 65.
20. H. Floch, "French Guiana: Malarial Control," *The Caribbean,* IX
(July, 1956), 270–271, 276.
21. Dr. Pennec, "The New Leprosarium at Pointe Noire, Guadeloupe,"
The Caribbean, X (April, 1957), 222–225.
22. "Funds Granted for Hospital," *The Caribbean,* IX (August, 1955), 24.
23. See statistics given in *Annuaire statistique de l'Union française, 1949–
1954* (Fascicule I, Paris, 1956), pp. 31, 34, 44.

each for boys and girls) a law school and a technical school. The bent of the inhabitants for law and politics is reflected perhaps in the fact that the law school has one-half as many students as the other.

In 1957 the United States maintains six consulates in the British Caribbean, three in the Netherlands Caribbean, and only one in the French Caribbean (Fort-de-France, Martinique). If the French Caribbean experiences a real rejuvenation, this distribution of posts may change. (A century ago the United States maintained one consulate each in Guadeloupe, Martinique, and French Guiana.) Martinique in particular offers inducements to the tourist. Described as an "island of flowers and beautiful scenery," it is said to resemble a crumpled piece of paper.[24] One of the attractions is the annual carnival extending from January 11 through Shrove Tuesday. The first date is selected in commemoration of the disastrous earthquake of January 11, 1839, which destroyed the city of Fort-de-France.[25] On Ash Wednesday the people bury Vaval, the King of the Carnival. For tourists of a pugnacious turn of mind there are cock fights and fights between a mongoose and a snake. Félix Rose-Rosette, the mayor of Fort-de-France, writes of the latter encounter: "Ce combat, original et fort captivant, mérite l'attention du touriste."[26]

IV

But whether the future smiles or frowns upon Martinique and the other French areas, they are likely to carry on. Their history is already long. Among the records of the Department

24. Maurice Nicolas, "Martinique, Sidelights on Tourism," *The Caribbean*, IX (July, 1956), 267–268, 275.

25. According to the United States Consul at Saint Pierre, scarcely seven out of 10,000 buildings in Fort Royal (Fort-de-France) were left undamaged. Payton Gay to Secretary of State, Feb. 7, 1839. Consular Dispatches, St. Pierre, Martinique, Vol. 2 (National Archives).

26. *La Martinique* (Paris, [1953]), p. 75.

of State in the National Archives, one finds a dispatch from the
United States Consul in Martinique, dated August 18, 1903.
After discussing a recent cyclone in which sixty lives were reported lost, the Consul commented as follows: "In a short time
Nature and Man will make Martinique again blossom as the
rose. Reconstruction is already under way. Soon the places of
ruin will be the abode of sunshine, and the Martiniquan, poor
and rich alike, will begin again and then settle down and await
the next chapter of sorrows."

Part IV

THE UNITED STATES AREA:
PUERTO RICO

11

Arturo Morales Carrión: THE HISTORICAL ROOTS
AND POLITICAL SIGNIFICANCE OF PUERTO RICO

THE COMMONWEALTH OF PUERTO RICO is today
the object of considerable interest to students of political science,
as well as to people from many lands eager to find an answer
to the twin problems of colonialism and insufficient economic
development. Thousands of visitors have gone to Puerto Rico in
recent years to examine at close range the island's experience.
It is a novel, dramatic, and momentous experience. In the realm
of human thought and action it far surpasses the very modest
bounds of geographical space within which this human drama
is played.

This paper does not aim at portraying the manifold government activities now underway in Puerto Rico. It is mainly
concerned with the historical growth of the commonwealth idea
and its success within the last generation. Notwithstanding the
obvious difficulties of finding a historical perspective for contemporary events, it seeks to broaden the view of Puerto Rico's
recent political evolution. It is essentially interpretative, and not
informative. Needless to say, it is not an official version, but the
considered thought of a student of the island's history.

The paper sets forth the author's basic personal conviction that
the commonwealth status of Puerto Rico was not an improvisa-
tion. It was not a hurried formula, thought up overnight to do
away with the thorny status question. Political solutions thus

139

conceived tend to be flimsy historical structures. They are easily swept aside by the winds of expediency. All basic political innovations must eminently suit the environment from where they spring and must respond to fundamental historical urgings. If they are to change a people's future, the change must accommodate itself to a complex of intellectual trends and stubborn social and economic realities.

The Commonwealth of Puerto Rico is an experiment deeply responsive to these fundamental tenets. Since it involves an original relationship between two cultures and two traditions, between a highly industrialized nation and a typical society in process of development from an agrarian status, between a world power and a small nationality, no explanation of its past, present, and future can be offered without taking into account the climate of opinion in both countries.

The paper, therefore, traces certain currents of thinking in the United States concerning Puerto Rico's status, as well as certain trends in the island, throughout the first half of the century. It is hoped that the result will show a merging of the two streams of thought, as Puerto Rican inventiveness and initiative since 1940 found in Washington—and in American public opinion in general—a receptive climate for its aspirations.

Let us, then, consider first the United States background.

I. The United States Background

The Honorable Earl Warren, Chief Justice of the United States Supreme Court, was the ranking guest of honor in San Juan on February 4, 1956, when the Commonwealth's Supreme Court proudly inaugurated its new building. In his address he referred to the institutions of the Commonwealth of Puerto Rico as follows:

In the sense that our American system is not static—in the sense that it is not an end but the means to an end—in the sense that it is an organism intended to grow and expand to meet varying conditions and times in a large country—in the sense that every governmental effort of ours is an experiment—so the new institutions of the Commonwealth of Puerto Rico represent an experiment—the newest experiment and perhaps the most notable of American governmental experiments in our lifetimes.[1]

Behind those words lay more than half a century of relations between Puerto Rico and the United States. If the expansionists of 1898, led by Theodore Roosevelt, Admiral Alfred T. Mahan, and Senator Henry Cabot Lodge, had been told at the time that Puerto Rico's institutional life would some day evoke such strong admiration from the Chief Justice of the United States, they would have been very much surprised.

In the doctrine of "Manifest Destiny," so popular at the end of the nineteenth century, Puerto Rico was to be the Malta of an American Mediterranean, a rampart of great strategic value zealously guarding the new United States sphere of influence. This basic concern led to the military invasion of the island. To it may be added the proud conviction, so popular among United States leaders at that time, that the United States had the moral duty to bring the blessings of liberty to the erstwhile remnants of the Spanish colonial empire. Upon disembarking in Puerto Rico, General Nelson A. Miles eloquently expressed this feeling in his proclamation dated July 28, 1898:

We have not come to make war upon the people of a country that for centuries has been oppressed, but, on the contrary, to bring you protection, not only to yourselves but to your property, to promote your prosperity, and to bestow upon you the immunities and blessings of the liberal institutions of our Government. . . . This is not a war of devastation, but one to give to all within the control of its military and naval forces the advantages and blessings of enlightened civilization.[2]

1. "Address by the Honorable Earl Warren, Chief Justice of the United States Supreme Court, at the dedication of the new Supreme Court Building of the Commonwealth of Puerto Rico, San Juan, Saturday, February 4, 1956." Press release.

2. Office of Puerto Rico, *Documents on the Constitutional History of Puerto Rico* (Washington, n.d.), p. 55.

It was relatively easy for the United States to put Puerto Rico's strategic facilities to good and immediate advantage. But translating the doctrine of Manifest Destiny into institutional norms and practices well adapted to the mores of an island society reared through the centuries in the Spanish way of life was a different and more difficult task. There soon began an intense, dramatic, and at times pathetic story of trial and error, of inter-cultural friction and adaptation, a story which sometimes seemed to lead into blind alleys of frustration and misunderstanding.

Under the law of nations Puerto Rico was a conquered land. It became a possession of the United States government, a part of the federal domain, lying outside the Union's continental limits. It was natural to apply past experience in regard to territories conquered by federal arms. The military were to be in control until Congress determined the form of civil government that the conquered territory should have.

But the military governors were well aware that their responsibility was not limited to the affairs of war. There were engrossing problems of government and administration which required a clear policy. Brigadier General George W. Davis, the last military governor, who possessed much insight into the perplexing issues involved, properly thought that military administration in Puerto Rico should conform to the basic constitutional principle "that the people themselves are to make and enforce their own laws." He looked forward to Puerto Rico repeating in its evolution the traditional pattern of other United States territories. "The changes that have already been made," he wrote in a circular dated August 15, 1899,

and those now intended, should supply for the island, until otherwise provided by Congress, a form of government resembling, as respects the superior branches, the Territorial form heretofore applied in the United States to those portions of the national domain in a transition stage or one preparatory to full statehood and membership in the National Union.[3]

3. *Ibid.*, pp. 59–60.

The enactment of civil government by Congress in May, 1900, under the Foraker Act, did not clarify, however, the basic goal of Puerto Rico's political evolution. No promise or declaration was made regarding statehood. While the debates on the Act certainly expressed United States interest in retaining Puerto Rico within its political system, there was also a growing awareness that the island posed a problem different from that of the mainland territories. This was manifested in the handling of three basic elements in the relationship of Puerto Rico with the United States: citizenship, taxation, and trade.

In the original bill United States citizenship was to be granted to the people of Puerto Rico, together with free trade. The bill had substantially all the provisions which were usual in the acts organizing United States territories. But the Administration had a change of heart when the question arose of providing revenues for the local government. It was decided that a tariff of 15 per cent should be collected on all merchandise coming into the United States from Puerto Rico, and vice versa. The duties thus collected were to be placed at the disposal of the President to be used for the benefit of Puerto Rico until the new civil government and its legislative assembly enacted and put into operation a local system of taxation. Free trade would then be decreed by the President.

The proposed tariff was a temporary measure, but it led to eliminating the provision that granted United States citizenship to the islanders. Senator Foraker, the Administration spokesman, thought that it was inconsistent with the constitutional provisions regarding uniform taxation. The Administration's *volte face* came under heavy fire from the Democratic minority. A long, intense, and at times bitter debate took place. Many constitutional precedents as well as judicial decisions were quoted. Some Republicans joined with the Democrats in denouncing the change of policy, but the party line held firm and the bill was finally passed with 40 yeas and 31 nays, 16 Senators not voting.[4]

4. For the final debate on the bill, see *Congressional Record, Fifty-Sixth Congress, First Session*, XXXIII, 3667–3698.

The Foraker Act was regarded as a temporary measure "to provide revenues and civil government for Puerto Rico." It was essentially a compromise between the desire to do away with military government and the lack of a clear, coherent policy as to the future status of Puerto Rico. It was realistic and far-sighted in its economic provisions, which took cognizance of the basic fact that Puerto Rico presented problems and circumstances quite different from those of the mainland territories and therefore required special treatment by Congress. The provision regarding free trade after a local system of taxation had been established and the decision that all collections of duties and taxes in Puerto Rico under the Act were to be paid into the treasury of Puerto Rico instead of the treasury of the United States were a landmark in the relationships between the island and the American Union. Also, the provision (Section 14) which made inapplicable in Puerto Rico all United States internal revenue laws.

The Act failed, however, in the question of citizenship and political rights. In effect it created a body politic under the name "The People of Puerto Rico," composed of citizens of Puerto Rico who were entitled to the protection of the United States (Section 7). But nothing was said regarding the granting of United States citizenship, and The People of Puerto Rico thus established had indeed very limited rights.

The Governor and his cabinet, as well as the Supreme Court, were appointed by the President. The top executive officials, the Governor excepted, plus five other persons of good repute, were to form an Executive Council which would act as an upper house. Only in the lower chamber, the House of Delegates, could the popular will express itself. The result was a paternalistic government, taking its cue from Washington and doing away with the basic American doctrines of separation of powers and government by consent.

While providing a secure foundation for the island's development in the economic sphere, the Act was doomed to failure in the political. The denial of citizenship left many Americans with a bad conscience. The status of Puerto Rico became a puzzle. The United States Supreme Court, when asked for an interpretation, judged in Downes v. Bidwell, in 1901:

. . . that whilst in an international sense Puerto Rico was not a foreign country, since it was subject to the sovereignty of and was owned by the United States, it was foreign to the United States in a domestic sense, because the island had not been incorporated into the United States, but was merely appurtenant thereto as a possession.[5]

No wonder that Chief Justice Fuller, in a dissenting opinion, considered that Puerto Rico was left "like a disembodied shade in an intermediate state of ambiguous existence."[6]

Under the Foraker Act the basic question of citizenship constantly troubled relations between Puerto Rico and the United States. Would the granting of United States citizenship involve the promise of eventual statehood? The Republican Administration, at first under Theodore Roosevelt and later under William H. Taft, came to separate the two considerations. Roosevelt saw clearly that citizenship should not be denied to the people of Puerto Rico. On December 3, 1906 in his message to the Fifty-ninth Congress, second session, he asked that United States citizenship "be conferred on the citizens of Porto Rico." A year later he reiterated this demand and in 1908 again insisted on his recommendation.[7]

No action was taken by Congress in spite of several bills introduced to that effect. The question dragged on for many years. A growing sore spot in the United States administration of Puerto Rico, it also began to embarrass the United States in its relations with Latin America.

5. Downes v. Bidwell, 182 U.S. 244, 341.
6. Ibid., 372.
7. Roosevelt's messages are quoted in *Hearing before the Committee on Pacific Island and Porto Rico, United States Senate, Sixty-Second Congress, Second Session on H. R. 20048, An Act declaring that all citizens of Porto Rico and certain natives permanently residing in said island shall be citizens of the United States,* May 7, 1912, pp. 26–27.

As early as the Theodore Roosevelt Administration, the possibility of using Puerto Ricans in diplomatic missions abroad had been considered. President Roosevelt appointed the Puerto Rican delegate to Congress, Señor Tulio Larrínaga, as a member of the American delegation to the Pan American Congress held in 1906 in Brazil. But Señor Larrínaga was not an American citizen. Roosevelt used this situation to put pressure on the citizenship bill. On March 26, 1906, he informed Senator Foraker of Larrínaga's designation and added: "It will be a real misfortune not to have the citizenship bill for Porto Rico pass in this session prior to his going there."[8]

The embarrassment grew over the years. In 1911 Secretary of War Henry L. Stimson traveled through Puerto Rico and the West Indies. He returned convinced of the need of reshaping the political relationships between the island and the United States, for the sake of American foreign policy. On May 7, 1912, Stimson appeared before the Senate to support a citizenship bill for Puerto Rico. His testimony is of remarkable importance as evidence of a new type of thinking in the United States regarding Puerto Rico.

After praising Puerto Rican loyalty, Stimson added:

Last summer I traveled through the West Indies and saw a good many Latin-American peoples, and I found that when they would speak to me frankly they regarded this attitude of the United States toward Porto Rico as an evidence that we regarded not only the people there, but Latin-American peoples in general, as of a different class from ourselves, and of an inferior class. And therefore not only in respect to our political relations with Porto Rico itself, but to our diplomatic relations with other countries of the same blood, it seems to be a very deep-seated sore and irritation.[9]

He spoke of the need of obtaining "that sympathetic relation with the island which must be the foundation of a satisfactory

8. *Ibid.,* pp. 26–27.
9. *Ibid.,* p. 4.

government." The solution did not lie in ultimate statehood, which Stimson observed "would not be of benefit to either Porto Rico or the United States." A way had to be found which should avoid a position of drifting, and he insisted that "our attitude toward Porto Rico and the relation of the two communities being deemed to be permanent should be definitely formulated as far ahead as we can."

The young Republican statesman favored a frank expression of views on the subject by the different branches of the government. He advanced his own personal views with remarkable clarity: "I see myself," he said,

no inconsistency in the grant of American citizenship to Porto Rico; no inconsistency between that and the ultimate ideal that Porto Rico shall have practically an independent local self-government. I think that is what most of the people of the United States would prefer to have them do—that is, a relation where they exercise supervision over their own affairs, over their own fiscal and local self-government; with the link of American citizenship between the two countries as a tie, and in general such relations between the United States and Porto Rico as subsists, and as has been found perfectly workable in the case of the various self-governing portions of the territory of Great Britain— Australia, for instance, and Canada, to the mother country.[10]

Under persistent interrogation, Stimson further clarified his stand. Puerto Rico's economic position was dependent upon the United States tariff on sugar. A change in the tariff could ruin the island. He envisaged a strong Puerto Rican demand for representation in the Congress. The answer, again, was not statehood. The answer was to give Puerto Rico "the same local tariff power and the same autonomy in regard to its commercial relations" enjoyed by the great self-governing colonies of England. Stimson remarked:

It is only fair to state now that I believe that anyone dealing with the problem of citizenship should also face frankly the prob-

10. *Ibid.,* p. 5.

lem that Porto Rico must eventually be given self-government, even to the extent of making their own tariff. Of course, we can expect reciprocal trade relations with the United States to be established simultaneously with and as a condition to such tariff autonomy.[11]

This was rather bold thinking for his day. Congressional opinion was not ready for such views. Stimson, however, influenced the Administration's stand on Puerto Rico. In his annual message to Congress, December 6, 1912, President Taft again recommended citizenship for Puerto Ricans, while rejecting statehood as the ultimate form of relation between the island and the United States. And Taft, following Stimson, added:

I believe that the aim to be striven for is the fullest possible allowance of legal and fiscal self-government, with American citizenship as the bond between us; in other words, a relation analogous to the present relation between Great Britain and such self-governing colonies as Canada and Australia. This would conduce to the fullest and most self-sustaining development of Porto Rico, while at the same time it would grant her the economic and political benefits of being under the American flag.[12]

By 1916, under the Wilson administration, the time was ripe for a change in Puerto Rico's organic law. The change was made feasible by persistent Puerto Rican demands, in and outside of Congress, which had given rise to pre-independence feeling in the island and were backed by pressure from American liberal opinion. Under the leadership of Congressmen William A. Jones and Horace M. Towner, and of the able Puerto Rican Commissioner, Luis Muñoz Rivera, a bill was introduced in the House to provide civil government for Puerto Rico. Congressman Towner opened the debate on May 6, 1916, with the House sitting as a Committee of the Whole. It was obvious, from his statement, that the Administration hoped that the grant-

11. *Ibid.*, p. 8.

12. "Message of the President of the United States on Fiscal, Judicial, Military and Insular Affairs," December 6, 1912, p. 15.

ing of United States citizenship, together with political reforms, would lay the foundation of a better understanding between Puerto Rico and the United States and would check separatist sentiments. But Towner was looking farther into the future, and the concluding sentences in his statement were endowed with a unique prophetic quality:

As nearly all the essential concessions looking to a larger measure of self-government for the Island are granted in this bill, which if passed will constitute their new Constitution, it is confidently believed that the dream and desire for independence will not be longer indulged or cherished and that Puerto Rico may become a great and prosperous self-governing Commonwealth, which, if not independent, will maintain its association and because it will be mutually beneficial to Puerto Rico and to the United States to continue it. I venture the prediction that the next constitution of government for Puerto Rico that will be formulated will not be drawn in Washington but it will be formulated in San Juan by the people of Puerto Rico and sanctioned and approved by the United States. (Applause.) As the present constitution of Canada was formulated at Ottawa, as the present constitution of Australia was drawn at Melbourne, and as the constitutions of those great self-governing Commonwealths were approved without change by the Parliament at London, so will the future constitution of Puerto Rico be drawn by their own people and approved by the Congress of the United States.[13]

However, while it was a substantial advance over the Foraker Act, the Jones Act fell considerably short of those expectations. United States citizenship was granted to all citizens of Puerto Rico, the Executive Council was stripped of its legislative functions, and the area of local self-government was increased with an elected Senate. But the Governor continued to be appointed by the President, together with key members of the Insular Cab-

13. *Congressional Record Containing the Proceedings and Debates of the First Session of the Sixty-Fourth Congress of the United States of America,* LIII, 7469.

inet and the judges of the Supreme Court. The new constitution to which Towner referred continued to be a mere organic act, a law Congress could amend at will. "Congress," as Resident Commissioner Antonio Fernós Isern has written, "continued to be an absolute sovereign over the people and the territory of Puerto Rico, albeit a benevolent sovereign."[14]

The vision of a self-governing commonwealth, associated with the United States by the link of a common citizenship, was indeed buried in the distant future. Its realization required favorable historical circumstances and a wide and bold use of constitutional inventiveness. Under the Jones Act, as ruled by the Supreme Court, Puerto Rico continued to be an unincorporated territory.[15] Unincorporation left the field of Congressional creativeness quite open. With great lucidity a young legal counsellor working then in the War Department, Felix Frankfurter, had defined the bounds of the problem in 1914 with these words:

The form of the relationship between the United States and an unincorporated territory is solely a problem of statesmanship. History suggests a great diversity of relationships between a central government and a dependent territory. The present day shows a great variety in actual operation. One of the great demands upon inventive statesmanship is to help evolve new kinds of relationship so as to combine the advantages of local self-government with those of a confederated union. Luckily, our Constitution has left this field of invention open. The decisions in the Insular Cases mean this, if they mean anything: that there is nothing in the Constitution to hamper the responsibility of Congress in working out, step by step, forms of government for our insular possessions responsive to the largest needs and capac-

14. For a useful discussion of Puerto Rico's political evolution see Antonio Fernós Isern, "From Colony to Commonwealth," *The Annals of The American Academy of Political and Social Science,* Philadelphia, CCLXXXV (Jan., 1953), 16–22.

15. See Balzac v. People of Puerto Rico, 258 U.S. 298. It is interesting to note that William Howard Taft, then Chief Justice, delivered the opinion of the court.

ities of their inhabitants and ascertained by the best wisdom of Congress.[16]

After the First World War there was, however, scant sentiment in the Congress or the Administration in favor of a basic revision of the political relationships of Puerto Rico with the United States, although Towner, who occupied the governorship from 1923 to 1929, as well as his successor Theodore Roosevelt, Jr., believed in broadening the basis of self-government for the island.

Their efforts coincided with the emergence of a Puerto Rican school of jurists who, through careful analysis of constitutional doctrines, were to put forth the idea of an "associated free state" as the proper desideratum.

These efforts led nowhere because of insular, as well as mainland, conditions. But the idea was for the first time set forth in legal form and actually reached the Congress in 1922 in the so-called "Campbell Bill," drafted by the eminent Puerto Rican lawyer, Miguel Guerra Mondragón. This was a bill "to declare the purpose of the people of the United States as to the political status of the people of Porto Rico, and to provide an autonomous government for the said island, creating the Associated Free State of Porto Rico."[17] The bill retained the basic provisions of the Jones Act regarding free trade with the United States and Puerto Rico's exemption from the United States internal revenue laws (Section 9). It provided for a Resident Commissioner of the United States, appointed by the President, with the advice and consent of the United States Senate, who would act as adviser to the government of Puerto Rico and would represent the President. The Resident Commissioner was invested with ample powers: he could call upon the armed forces in case of rebellion or invasion, could suspend the privilege of habeas corpus, could

16. Quoted in Miguel Guerra Mondragón, "La Fórmula de la Comunidad," *Revista de Derecho, Legislación y Jurisprudencia del Colegio de Abogados de Puerto Rico,* Vol. VIII, Núm. III, p. 232.

17. Introduced as H.R.9995, Sixty-seventh Congress, second session.

place the island under martial law and suspend the entering into effect of any law approved by the legislature of Puerto Rico which, in his opinion, might be antagonistic to the sovereign rights of the United States, pending the President's final decision.

The bill also provided for a governor elected by the Legislature to head the executive department, as well as the militia (Section 13). It is interesting to note that the principle of parliamentary responsibility was included. The Governor, for instance, could select as heads of the various executive departments elected members of the Senate and House of Representatives. Another significant feature of the bill was that, while the Presidential veto over insular legislation was eliminated, the Congress of the United States reserved the power and authority to annul unilaterally all Puerto Rican laws. The election was contemplated of two Resident Commissioners to the United States, instead of one as under the Jones Act. The Legislature could not create or abolish any department without the consent of the President. The execution of United States laws relating to immigration, tariffs, and customs, and the regulations governing them, according to Section 39, were to be effected in Puerto Rico through officials appointed by the Governor and with the advice and consent of the island's Senate.

The judicial power was also reserved to Puerto Rico's authority. The governor, under Section 40, was to appoint the Supreme Court judges, and all judgments rendered by the Court were to be final, except in case of the interpretation of a constitutional provision or of a law enacted by the Congress of the United States.

The Campbell Bill, had it been enacted, would have been a significant landmark in Puerto Rico's constitutional development. From the standpoint of complete self-government, or "home rule," it had, however, certain obvious drawbacks. No allowance was made for an expression of Puerto Rico's popular sentiment regarding the new form of government. It would have been a unilateral act of Congress, still an organic act decreed from afar and not the product of democratic self-determination.

Furthermore, it is difficult to see how, under the bill, the duality of executive power, so delicately distributed between the United States Resident Commissioner and an elective governor, could have worked harmoniously.

The urge to find a flexible formula for self-government, which would avoid both statehood and complete independence, also haunted Governor Theodore Roosevelt, Jr. Few governors realized as he did the full significance of the United States' stewardship over the island. Few governors understood, as he did, Puerto Rico's unique position in hemispheric affairs. Few governors felt, as he did, the pressing need to bring economic alleviation, educational opportunities, and better health to the thousands of *jíbaros,* or peasants, who formed the backbone of the island's population, the core of its culture and traditions.

As Stimson and Towner before him, Theodore Roosevelt, Jr., looked for a solution, patterned after the British experience with dominion status, that would be beneficial to both countries. He was sensitive to the fact that Puerto Rico had a collective personality of its own and was deeply respectful of the cultural values involved. He wrote regarding dominion status:

To begin with, to gain such an end there would be no reason to continue the hopeless drive to remodel all Puerto Ricans so that they should become similar in language, habits and thoughts to continental Americans. Second, a financial status which contemplated an economic condition only sufficiently good to maintain her own internal government was far more imaginable than one where the island would have to contribute toward the maintenance of the federal government. A dominion status also could carry the same advantages as statehood as far as trade relations are concerned. The tariff barriers would not be raised against Puerto Rican products, and, therefore, her major industries, which are now entirely dependent on markets within the United States, would not be destroyed. Lastly, the pride of her people would be satisfied on realizing self-government within their own borders.[18]

18. Theodore Roosevelt, Jr., *Colonial Policies of the United States* (New York, 1937), pp. 117–118.

This goal, which he saw "far in the future," coincided also with United States interests and its need of hemispheric unity. Roosevelt popularized the conception of Puerto Rico as "a connecting link" between the Americas, and as "a show window looking south." In due time, Puerto Ricans, with their Latin American culture and background and their acquaintance with United States methods of thought, would be ideally suited, in his opinion, for the chores of industry, banking, and diplomacy.[19]

In the early thirties this was but a dream. The times were tense and troubled. Conditions in Puerto Rico became well-nigh desperate. Frustration and discontent were rife. Creative political thought and action, in the United States, in Puerto Rico, and elsewhere had to seek primarily a way out of the economic chaos, an improvised remedy to the misery and grief created by the depression. Out of this bitter human test, further aggravated by the turmoil of the Second World War, there was to emerge the new pattern of relationships between the island and the United States. It was both bold and realistic, an innovation in the American constitutional tradition, and yet quite responsive to a peculiar historical circumstance. It was novel in its process and techniques, but conformed also to a tradition, a trend of thought that had gradually developed in both countries among sensible and experienced men, who had failed, nevertheless, to rally and orient public opinion to their way of thinking.

II. The Puerto Rican Background

Let us now summarize the historical background of the commonwealth status as regards Puerto Rico. As in most countries under colonial rule, the search for freedom in Puerto Rico has been closely linked with a change in status. Colonialism, it is generally admitted, does not merely subsist under a colonial status. Countries enjoying full sovereignty on paper may suffer from colonialism in their economic life, their political action, or their intellectual outlook. Colonialism among other things is a condition in which basic policies involving a people's economic

19. *Ibid.,* p. 119.

existence, political organization, or cultural and spiritual life are dictated from afar, by a power remote and different, and implemented by local representatives of that power not directly responsible to the people. But colonialism can also be a willingness to accept a psychological inferiority in exchange for a certain modicum of local power or economic gain, an acquiescence in surrendering to a distant government or social or economic group the basic responsibility of shaping a country's destiny, without properly consulting the popular will.

Colonialism can even be benevolent and respectful to a high degree of individual rights. But it puzzles the mind and festers the spirit. It is a force of inhibition or a spur to bitter protest and frustration. Where it does not create social conflict, it creates a persistent embarrassment between the governing and the governed, an impossibility of friendly, constructive communication.

Thus, the fight against colonialism is a fight along two fronts: the external front of the status, so obviously visible; and the internal psychological front, the inner front of the mind where colonialism thrives among the subtle forces governing human and collective behavior. On those two fronts the fight has been waged for over four generations in Puerto Rico.

Puerto Rico's political conscience was a product of nineteenth-century liberalism and the growth of the democratic ideal throughout the Western World. The island, however, did not embark upon the experiment of total separation from Spain leading to political anarchy and *caudillismo,* as did the other Hispanic countries of the New World. It did not seek, like Cuba, an armed solution in the *manigua.* The fight against colonialism was essentially civil. It aimed at autonomy and self-government, undoubtedly influenced by the British colonial experience with Canada and Australia. Its slogan was "the maximum decentralization of power compatible with national union."[20] This ideal

20. For a short history of Puerto Rico's political thinking during this era see the author's *Ojeada al Proceso Histórico* (San Juan, 1950); also Antonio J. Colorado and Lidio Cruz Monclova, *Noticia y Pulso del Movimiento Político Puertorriqueño (1808–1898–1952)* (Mexico City, 1955).

was to a considerable extent embodied in the Spanish Autonomous Charter of 1897, approved unilaterally by the Spanish courts but with substantial Puerto Rican support.

History did not give the latter Charter a fair chance to prove its worth. Its effectiveness is now only a matter of conjecture and speculation. But psychologically the Charter was a significant conquest of political rights, since it put, to a high degree, local matters in local hands and provided for Puerto Rican representation in the Spanish parliament and in all treaty-making affecting the island's interests. The question for all thoughtful Puerto Ricans at the end of the Spanish-American War was whether under United States rule a similar self-respecting status could be found. Statehood loomed as the evident solution. All parties accepted it, only to find disillusionment under the Foraker Act. Not that statehood sentiment died after 1900. It continued as a minority ideal through the rough and tumble of the island's political life. It still animates an important segment of public opinion, despite Congressional indifference and the fact that it does no longer find a niche in party platforms in the United States.

With statehood seemingly unattainable, it was no wonder that pro-independence feeling grew, particularly among the intellectual classes. In view of the deficiencies of the Foraker Act, the sentiment spread until a climate of political opinion was created. A classic debate developed between the two solutions of statehood and independence. It was difficult to think of a third way. The colony was the all-pervading reality, no matter how benevolent Washington's rule, how tolerant and respectful of individual rights.

The Puerto Rican leader of the generation at the turn of the century was Luis Muñoz Rivera. He had labored for autonomy under Spain, and after 1898 he had to accommodate his thinking and actions to a new set of relationships, to a new understanding of the cultural values, the mores, the peculiar idiosyncrasies of the rising giant from the north. He was a man sorely tried by history. In his later years, as he fought within Congress to broaden the basis of government, he came to believe in "home rule" as an intermediate practical step. In his writings, lectures, and speeches he referred to the British experience with Canada and Australia and set it up as an example that the United States could follow, if statehood was not feasible.[21]

Muñoz Rivera died in 1916. A year later the Jones Act came into effect. A new period began under new insular leadership and within a changed political relationship. But the classic debate persisted. When the United States Supreme Court made clear that the Jones Act did not mean incorporation within the Union, some Puerto Ricans who were careful students of American constitutional history began to search for a new formula. One of them, the eminent jurist Luis Muñoz Morales, published in 1921 a book of lectures, *El Status Político de Puerto Rico,* favoring the establishment of an "unincorporated state," a constitutional innovation yet compatible, in his view, with the rulings of the Supreme Court. Muñoz Morales thought that Congress could grant to Puerto Rico the same type of government enjoyed by the federated states, with the right to elect a governor, to appoint the judges of the Supreme Court, and including the surrendering of Congressional power to annul all local laws. He also favored the continuance of the privilege that Puerto Rico had of receiving all custom duties, internal revenues, and income taxes. Within this category of an unincorporated state Puerto Rico would enjoy the same self-government as any of the incorporated states. It would be deprived of voting representatives in Congress, but in return would not share other burdens. Muñoz Morales believed, as Stimson before him, that the island should be granted the tariff-making power, provided that no harm be done to commerce with the United States. He envisaged the coming into being of this new relation through an act of Congress approved by the representatives of the people of Puerto Rico or through an act of the Legislative Assembly of Puerto Rico approved by the Congress.[22] It is interesting to note that

21. See his *Campañas Políticas* (Madrid, 1925), II, 248; also III, 268 ff.
22. Luis Muñoz Morales, *El Status Político de Puerto Rico* (San Juan, 1921), pp. 86–90.

the distinguished jurist even considered the changed symbolism of the United States flag. In a territory or possession the flag is a symbol of absolute United States sovereignty, and so also evidence of a relationship of political dependence and subordination. But in an unincorporated state it would be the symbol of a fraternity and compact rather than of domination and power.[23]

This new approach made some headway within the Unionist party, then dominant in the legislature. It seemed to coincide on many points with the views that men like Towner held in the States. For a time in 1922 it looked as if a meeting of the minds would come about. The Unionist party platform, traditionally in favor of independence through evolutionary self-government, was changed to accommodate the new school of thought.

Political leadership of the Unionist forces after Muñoz Rivera's death had fallen into the hands of a vibrant, emotional, and well-meaning man, Antonio R. Barceló. In 1921 and 1922 a historic correspondence took place between Barceló and Towner. In spite of his pro-independence feelings, Barceló was ready to support a formula:

. . . by virtue of which we declare that we aspire—as all worthy peoples throughout History—to be free and to be the masters of our country in the present as well as in the future, aspiring at the same time, in order better to insure freedom in our country, that between it and the people of the United States there should exist a noble association of a permanent and undestructible character.[24]

Barceló made clear that the new association did not imply the classical form of statehood. He felt that ethnic, linguistic, and historical differences were opposed to this solution. Puerto Rico

23. *Ibid.,* p. 91.

24. " . . . una fórmula en virtud de la cual declaramos que aspiramos— como todos los pueblos dignos a través de la Historia—a ser libres y dueños de nuestra patria, a que entre ella y el pueblo de Estados Unidos exista una noble asociación de carácter permanente e indestructible . . . ." Antonio R. Barceló to Hon. Horace M. Towner, February 28, 1922. The writer owns a photostat copy of this letter obtained from one of Barceló's close associates, the late Andrés Rodríguez.

should be a state, but a distinct kind of state. "We understand," he wrote,

that instead of becoming an Incorporated Territory [Puerto Rico] should become a Free State, not as a member of the Confederation [sic] of, but in association with, the United States.[25]

The Campbell Bill, embodying the concept of this free associated state, had been drafted by a capable Puerto Rican lawyer, Miguel Guerra Mondragón, after a long conference with Barceló and the Speaker of the House, Phillip Campbell. The British Parliamentary Act on Irish Home Rule served as inspiration. The bill was supported by an Assembly of the Unionist party. But it came to naught. The Administration wavered in its support, while in Puerto Rico the whole idea became enmeshed in the classical debate between the "perfectionists" who wanted either statehood or independence.[26]

It fell into the background of Puerto Rican politics, only to be kept alive by a reduced group of jurists and writers or by political leaders who, having believed in either of the classical formulas, became impatient or disillusioned with both.

Works like *Puerto Rico ante el Derecho de Gentes* (1928) by Senator Juan B. Soto or *El Futuro Status Político de Puerto Rico* (1937) by the former leader of the Republican or Statehood party, José Tous Soto, clearly showed that in spite of its historical

25. " . . . pero este nuestro, que es distinto, nosotros entendemos que en vez de llegar a convertirse en Territorio Incorporado, debe llegar a ser Estado Libre, no como miembro de la Confederación de, sino en Asociación con, los Estados Unidos." *Ibid.*

26. See the story in Miguel Guerra Mondragón, *op. cit.*, pp. 233–234. On April 2, 1928, the leaders of the Legislative Assembly, Antonio R. Barceló and José Tous Soto, sent an extensive letter to the Puerto Rican Resident Commissioner, Félix Córdova Dávila, reinstating the case for self-government under an associated free state. This was in reply to a letter by President Calvin Coolidge in defense of American rule over the island. See *Carta dirigida por los señores Antonio R. Barceló, Presidente del Senado, y José Tous Soto, Presidente de la Cámara de Representantes, al Comisionado Residente de Puerto Rico en Washington, Hon. Félix Córdova Dávila, contestando la carta del Presidente de los Estados Unidos al Hon. Horace M. Towner, Gobernador de Puerto Rico*, n.d., pp. 40–42.

adversity self-government under a basic concept of association was far from joining the niche of academic curiosities. Soto favored the adoption by Congress of a resolution authorizing the people of Puerto Rico to establish their own constitution patterned after American democratic principles, and stipulating that once a constitutional government was set up the island should enter into a permanent treaty with the United States, thus forming a union within which "each people would enjoy complete independence and sovereignty, with respect to the administration and government of their internal affairs; constituting one international state in every matter dealing with their foreign relations." All foreign affairs related to Puerto Rico were to be handled by an Under Secretary of State in Washington, who would at the same time be Secretary of State of Puerto Rico. Soto further advocated the right of the island to enter into commercial treaties, and that no commercial treaty entered into by the United States would be valid in Puerto Rico unless ratified by the insular Senate.[27]

Tous Soto also agreed with the idea of a constitution which, enacted by Puerto Rico, would change it into an associated free state. He favored, however, not a treaty, but a curious constitutional amendment that would admit associated free states into the Union subject to the following basic differences: senators and representatives from the associated free states would only vote on matters related to their respective states; on the other hand, legislation adopted by Congress, without their votes, could only apply locally if sanctioned by the legislatures of the associated free states. "We would be," Tous Soto wrote, "associated with the federation, without being within the federation. Our association would not be with the states, but with the Union of States."[28]

The decade of 1930–40, a decade of stress and strain through-

27. Juan B. Soto, *Puerto Rico ante el Derecho de Gentes* (San Juan, 1928), pp. 93 ff.

28. José Tous Soto, *El Futuro Status Político de Puerto Rico* (Ponce, 1937), pp. 70–82.

out the world, also left its scars in Puerto Rico. Economic difficulties aggravated by the depression and the explosive population growth led to a period of unrest such as the island had never before experienced under American rule. The New Deal Administration under Franklin Delano Roosevelt took an active and sympathetic interest in the island's social and economic ills. Rehabilitation programs were formulated, aid was extended, but everything seemed to bog down in a hopeless morass. The Administration was bedeviled by the status question, the old dichotomy sharpened by the gravity of the economic situation. The classical political solutions, so vehemently debated, had more than ever an air of unreality around them, in view of the urgent task of attending to the growing misery and want.

III. The Achievement Period

It was at this distressing juncture that a basic reorientation took place in Puerto Rico's political and economic thought. The Popular Democratic party was founded under the dynamic leadership of Luis Muñoz Marín. Its immediate objective was the implementation of a program of social and economic reform. The status question could wait. It did not become an issue in the elections of 1940 in which the party, almost bankrupt, hardly known among the urban leaders, squeezed through to a surprising victory.

A new era began, of far reaching consequences. This is not the place to retell the story of the amazing transformation that took place in the island. Governor Muñoz Marín has aptly summarized it in the following words:

A people that had been floundering in hopelessness began swimming towards the shore. Hope, indeed, became one of the natural resources of the people, and dedication to the salvation of the country an attitude not too unusual. Voters stopped selling their votes. Compliance with political pledges began to be something that could be really demanded of successful candidates for office. And there began to be a feeling that there was strength in the people that made hardship a training for abolishing hardship, rather than an illustration of the need to bow to ineluctable fate. The idea that something could be done by workers and businessmen and farmers and political leaders and teachers besides waving for help from a raft lost at sea began to catch on.[29]

The dramatic surge forward was aided by Washington's sympathetic understanding and support. Under the governorship of Rexford Guy Tugwell a tacit partnership was created to tackle the island's principal economic ills. Friends began to appear in both United States parties. Many of the things done were quite unorthodox. Many an eyebrow was raised, but the program marched on.

On the status question Tugwell spoke with a boldness and clarity unheard of from previous governors. He was a staunch believer in self-determination, although he felt that Puerto Rico's future depended on closer, rather than looser, ties with the United States. He minced no words: "This moral problem," he said on July 4, 1942,

of the United States in Puerto Rico is surely as hard a one as ever confronted a nation. To put Puerto Rico outside the tariff and quota walls of the nation would bring quick ruin. To keep Puerto Rico inside without a clear showing of desire would always stand as a reproach to democratic professions. Sooner or later Puerto Ricans must be allowed to choose and must accept the responsibilities of choosing for themselves.[30]

Tugwell saw his role as that of the last appointed governor. He favored an elective governorship as a much needed step, and also a basic revision of the organic act. To him the act had become substantially a treaty. "The Congress in all justice ought

29. Luis Muñoz Marín, "Puerto Rico and the U. S., Their Future Together," *Foreign Affairs*, July, 1954, p. 543. See for this period, Earl P. Hanson, *Transformation, the Story of Modern Puerto Rico* (New York, 1955).

30. R. G. Tugwell, *Puerto Rican Papers* (San Juan, 1945), p. 96.

to recognize that this is so and ought not to make changes in it unilaterally—that is, without consent of the Puerto Rican People. . . ," he wrote in 1944.[31]

When the Second World War was over, the process that led to the commonwealth status really began. The first step was the appointment in 1946 of Jesús T. Piñero as Governor of Puerto Rico. Piñero had been elected Resident Commissioner in 1944. He commanded, therefore, full popular support. A further step was taken when in 1947 the Jones Act was amended to permit the election of the governor and liberalize the executive branch by making all members of the cabinet appointees of the governor, with the advice and consent of the Puerto Rican Senate.

It was only natural that Luis Muñoz Marín should be the first elected governor. He had led the party to victory and reform, and by 1946, ably supported by the party leadership, he was already searching with boldness, imagination, and clarity for a formula to surpass and discard the old political dichotomy between statehood and independence.

With the election of Muñoz responsible government was a fact. But legally the status still bore a colonial imprint. Puerto Rico was still a creature of Congress, which could unilaterally annul all of the island's laws.

The basic breakthrough occurred in 1950. In March of that year Resident Commissioner Antonio Fernós Isern, wise in the ways of Congress, introduced a bill to provide for the organization of a government by the people of Puerto Rico under a constitution of their own adoption. On July 3, 1950, Public Law 600 was approved. In its first article the law stated: "That, fully recognizing the principle of consent, this Act is now adopted in the nature of a compact so that the people of Puerto Rico may organize a government pursuant to a constitution of their own adoption."

There were two basic features in the new Congressional legis-

31. *Ibid.*, p. 193.

lation. The part of the former organic act which referred to
the *modus operandi* of the federal government in Puerto Rico
and the relationships between the government and people of
Puerto Rico and those of the United States continued upon
approval of the Puerto Rican voters and, according to the
principle of compact, as a Statute of Puerto Rican-Federal Relations. Puerto Ricans retained their American citizenship, free
trade was assured with the mainland, as well as exemption
from payment of United States internal revenues to the insular
treasury when paid on Puerto Rican products brought to the
continent, the refund of custom dues collected in Puerto Rico
on foreign imports, the position of the Resident Commissioner in
Congress, the Federal District Court in Puerto Rico, and other
provisions defining the role of federal jurisdiction in the island,
similar to the states.

The novel aspect of the legislation dealt with the mechanics
through which the compact was to be implemented by Puerto
Rico and the United States. Public Law 600—it should be
stressed—was no ordinary law of Congress. The act could only
take effect if approved by the people of Puerto Rico in an
island-wide referendum. Upon approval of the act by a majority
of the voters participating in such referendum, Public Law 600
provided that the legislature of Puerto Rico was authorized to
call a constitutional convention to draft a constitution. The said
constitution—according to the law—had to provide a republican
form of government and include a bill of rights.

A period of intense political and constitutional activity in
Puerto Rico was ushered in by the approval of Public Law 600.
There was first the referendum on June 4, 1951, in which 65
per cent of the 777,675 qualified voters of Puerto Rico participated and 76.5 per cent of those voting approved the act. On
August 27 of the same year, 92 delegates were elected to the
constitutional convention, representing three of the four parties
of the island. Only the Independentists—a small minority—
abstained.

The convention met in September, 1951, and concluded its

painstaking work in February, 1952. An official English and an official Spanish version of the constitution were adopted, and wide publicity was given to the document throughout the island. On March 3, 1952, nearly 375,000 voters accepted the constitution, with only 83,000 rejections. The President transmitted the document to the Congress of the United States, which ratified it promptly. On July 25, exactly 54 years after American troops had landed on the island, the Commonwealth of Puerto Rico was proclaimed in an impressive ceremony attended by distinguished guests from most countries of the Americas.

Thus, the Commonwealth of Puerto Rico was born on July 25, 1952, as a new form of political association, in response to a long historical urge for self-determination in Puerto Rico, and in keeping with the wisdom and democratic idealism of American constitutional theories and practices.[32]

The Commonwealth of Puerto Rico was baptized in Spanish as *Estado Libre Asociado de Puerto Rico,* the "Associated Free State of Puerto Rico." The old name was retaken, but the substance of the political relationship to which it referred went in many aspects much farther than had the Campbell Bill. The solemn establishment of the principle of compact gave to the new relationship a basis of mutual consent. As Governor Muñoz Marín, the Commonwealth's foremost spokesman, has written:

The most significant aspect of the new status lies in the recognition that the arrangement is indeed founded on the principle of consent, expressed by a compact in the form of an Act of Congress subject to the approval of the people of Puerto Rico at the polls. Another basic characteristic is the concept of association as distinguished from the historical idea of union, so far as states are concerned, and of possession, so far as unincorporated territories are concerned. It embodies association with the United States, not union among the states. These are the characteristics

32. For a summary of the constitutional process see the section "Political Development" in *The Annals. . .* , already quoted, pp. 1–47. Also A. Fernós Isern, *Puerto Rico Libre y Federado* (San Juan, 1951). The above paragraphs have been taken from the author's pamphlet *Puerto Rico: Self Determination in Practice* (San Juan, 1953), pp. 8–10.

that clear the status of the former colonial character of "territory" or "possession."[33]

Externally the meaning of the relationship was tested in a long debate at the United Nations in 1953. Was Puerto Rico under its new status a non-self-governing territory or a self-governing political entity? If non-self-governing, the United States had to continue reporting on the island under Article 73(e) of the Charter. The result was a victory for a liberal democratic interpretation of the Commonwealth status.

The General Assembly of the United Nations in a resolution adopted in November, 1953, expressed the opinion "that it stems from the documentation provided that the association of the Commonwealth of Puerto Rico with the United States of America has been established as mutually agreed association" and further recognized that under the compact "the people of the Commonwealth of Puerto Rico have been invested with attributes of political sovereignty which clearly identify the status of self-government attained by the Puerto Rican people as an autonomous political entity."[34]

Shortly before the voting, President Eisenhower, through Ambassador Henry Cabot Lodge, had sent a message to the Assembly which deeply honored United States respect for the principle of self-determination. "I am authorized," Ambassador Cabot Lodge stated

to say on behalf of the President that if, at any time, the Legislative Assembly of Puerto Rico adopts a resolution in favour of more complete or even absolute independence, he will immediately thereafter recommend to Congress that such independence be granted. The President also wishes me to say that, in this event, he would welcome Puerto Rico's adherence to the Rio Pact and the United Nations Charter.[35]

33. Luis Muñoz Marín, "Puerto Rico and the U. S., Their Future Together," *Foreign Affairs,* July, 1954, pp. 546–547.

34. United Nations Document A/C.4/L.300.

35. Taken from the *Provisional Verbatim Record of the Four Hundred and Fifty-Ninth Meeting,* November 27, 1953.

To these two momentous declarations, which clarified Puerto Rico's status before the world, the Commonwealth Legislative Assembly replied with a resolution that reflected the dominant political sentiment in the island. In view of the President's message, the Legislative Assembly thought it proper to set forth the principles "which must inspire the development of the Commonwealth within the bonds of association and affection that link it with the United States of America." These principles involved: (1) a rejection of separation; (2) an assertion that the commonwealth status "is a status in itself which fulfills the highest ideals of freedom and human dignity and which is dynamic in its potentialities for growth"; (3) a reaffirmation of the Commonwealth as an instrument to further freedom and democracy as well as human rights; and (4) the declaration that common citizenship and common defense were the essential bases of the association. It added these significant words:

We consider that the development of the Commonwealth idea shall be realized through changes, mutually agreed upon, directed toward eliminating those functions of the federal government which experience shows are unnecessary to the concept of free association and for that reason impair its deep and full significance.

Regarding Puerto Rico's role in the New World—an old consideration which had been in the minds of several statesmen in the United States and the island—the resolution affirmed:

Puerto Rico, a vivid example of the potentialities of the creative coexistence of the two great cultures of America, has an exalted mission of service to the ideals of understanding and brotherhood which actuate the foreign policy of the United States and of other countries of the Western Hemisphere. The Commonwealth should consequently participate more intensively in international activities and organizations, the better to serve the principle of inter-American solidarity.[36]

36. Puerto Rico House of Representatives: Concurrent Resolution 21, January 18, 1954.

IV. The Future Outlook

The compact between the United States and Puerto Rico is not, of course, a perfect document. Within the Statute of Puerto Rican-Federal Relations there are areas of authority still awaiting further clarification, and it is hoped that in the coming years greater Puerto Rican participation in the making of all applicable laws will be achieved through an appropriate formula. Experience as well as wise and prudent leadership will dictate such changes as may be deemed necessary.

The principle of growth and improvement has been succinctly stated by Governor Muñoz:

All that restricts the authority of Puerto Rico in Puerto Rico without any appreciable advantage to the Union and without being essential to the principle of association through common citizenship, should be in some proper manner at some proper time—there need not be a great hurry about it—removed from the compact. . . .

And he has added:

The significant values are: That suitable participation by the citizens in the approval of the laws that they must obey cannot for a very prolonged period be considered covered by the generic consent given in a referendum. . . .[37]

Future action on the growth of the Commonwealth status may conform to the following pattern which Governor Muñoz has outlined:

Perhaps a more promising manner of seeking for the actual shape of the future arrangements would be by not thinking in terms of applicable or inapplicable federal legislation, but in terms of federal functions essential to the principle of association and to the facts of common citizenship, such as defense, including defense against subversives, currency, wage standards, political international relations. As regards non-political inter-

37. "Speech delivered by Governor Luis Muñoz Marín at the University of Kansas City, April 23, 1955," Press Release, pp. 6–7.

national relations the Commonwealth should probably acquire the right of accession or non-accession to economic treaties affecting the interests of its citizens as it had under the Spanish Charter of Autonomy of 1897. The manner of operation of each federal function probably could be established with greater pertinence and realism in an ad-hoc drafting of the Federal Relations Act. This procedure I am confident would prove more satisfactory than an agreement that certain kinds of federal laws, the subject matter of which justifies their application, should receive the a priori approval of their unformulated language.[38]

It is obvious, therefore, that the commonwealth status as conceived by its founders is no midway station. It is an organic status with a capability of growth within its scope and context. It is rooted in basic democratic principles and undeniable realities. It is eminently suited to the island's environment and its geographic and cultural position. It responds to a yearning for freedom which has the experience of history behind it. Those who helped create it in recent years, whether in Puerto Rico or in the United States, are rightfully proud of their work. But recognition must also be given to leaders of former times who looked forward to a day when Puerto Rico would be a useful and significant partner of the United States in the struggle to make democracy a living force. Thus, the future of the Commonwealth of Puerto Rico is nurtured with the vision of men from several generations who with prudence and foresight labored for the removal of the onus of colonialism from another land of the Western World.

38. *Ibid.*, p. 8.

12

Cándido Oliveras: THE ECONOMY OF
PUERTO RICO

BEFORE DISCUSSING THE DEVELOPMENT of the
Puerto Rican economy during the last few years, it is important
that the unique characteristics of the relationship between the
Commonwealth of Puerto Rico and the United States be
noted. The special political relationship with the United States
results in: (1) access to United States markets on a duty-free
basis of Puerto Rican products; (2) the refund of United
States excise taxes and customs duties to the Commonwealth
government; (3) exemption of all Puerto Rican residents from
federal taxes; (4) substantial expenditures by the federal government in the island, including direct operational disbursements,
contributions to joint projects with the Commonwealth government, and transfer payments to individuals and businesses;
(5) common citizenship with the United States, which has
made possible large-scale migration to the mainland; and
(6) inclusion in the United States monetary system, which
makes possible the free flow of abundant capital resources.

These characteristics of the special relationship are both
positive and negative from the standpoint of economic growth.
A major part of the economic programs and legislation which
have been introduced to accelerate economic development attempts to strengthen the positive forces and contain the negative impacts of the relationship.

170

While access to the United States markets on a duty-free basis is a definite asset, it was necessary to attract the types of industries which would utilize such advantages. Until World War II Puerto Rican agricultural products tended to be the principal source of trade with the United States. It was not until such techniques as tax exemption, factory buildings at low rentals, and other incentives were adopted that the potential advantage of being within the United States tariff walls was fully realized and manufacturing for United States consumption expanded.

With a local market of only 2,270,000 persons it is difficult to establish manufacturing plants of efficient size oriented toward local consumption which can compete with production from the mainland.

There is no question that expenditures by the federal government in Puerto Rico for goods and services, as well as transfer payments primarily to veterans, have been beneficial. However, since a major part of these expenditures were related to defense activity, the possibility of reduced troop strength has always been a "sword of Damocles" over the Puerto Rican economy.

While the free movement of peoples between Puerto Rico and the United States has been a decisive factor in stabilizing the population and preventing increased unemployment, there is a danger that the Puerto Rican economy may lose portions of the better educated and more skilled segments of its labor force, just when the opportunity for a major step forward in economic development becomes possible.

I

The economy of Puerto Rico during the last decade has attained a high rate of growth in the volume of total output and income. Total real output as measured by the gross product in constant dollars increased 69 per cent, an average annual rate of 5.4 per cent. There has been a corresponding increment in payrolls and most other types of income flowing to individuals.

Total personal income went up to $1,064 million in 1957, or $468 per capita in today's prices. Real personal income per capita rose by 70 per cent. Reflecting the rising flow of consumer income, total personal consumption continued its expanding trend with an advance from $651 million in 1947 to $1,021 million in 1957. The gain in real terms was approximately 57 per cent during this ten-year period.

This rapid improvement in the levels of income and in the standard of living of the people of Puerto Rico was accomplished by changing the structure of the economy so that the preponderance of employment in the low-wage sector has been shifted to the high-wage sector. The principal difference between the two sectors is the amount of equipment and technology to which the worker has access and his ability to utilize them.

The change in structure of the Puerto Rican economy is revealed by the net commonwealth income generated in individual industries and by the income of the labor force by industries. Perhaps the most significant development in the industrial complex of Puerto Rico has been the increase in the relative importance of manufacturing in terms of net income. Manufacturing accounted for 15 per cent of the total ten years ago, and has since been increasing steadily until in 1957 the proportion was 21 per cent. The year 1956 may be considered a turning point in the development of Puerto Rico's economy, since the income generated in the manufacturing sector surpassed that of agriculture for the first time.

The volume of agricultural production has shown no substantial increase during the last decade. Ten years ago agriculture contributed about one-fourth of the total net income. Currently agriculture accounts for less than one-sixth of the total income produced. The total value of farm production for fiscal year 1956, the latest year not seriously affected by adverse weather conditions, was placed at about $221 million, an increase of only 19 per cent over 1947. Some sectors, notably milk, coffee, beef, and vegetables, showed increases, but these were partially offset by declines in legumes, fruits, and other minor crops. Income from sugar cane has been subject to ups and downs during the last ten years, but is now at about the same level as ten years ago.

Net income generated in manufacturing advanced about 16 per cent during each of the last two fiscal years. If the agriculturally based manufacturing industries, namely, sugar milling and tobacco stemming, are excluded, the annual rate of increase in net income was about 22 per cent. The movement away from agriculturally based industries is not a new phenomenon, but has been taking place for some time.

In recent years the growth in manufacturing industries in Puerto Rico can be attributed to the factories promoted under the Economic Development Program. As of June, 1957, there were 455 new plants in operation under this program, and because of the great acceleration during the last fiscal year in the rate of promotion, the number of plants to be in operation by June, 1958, is estimated at 570. New industries account at present for about 50 per cent of the total employment in manufacturing. These new firms are oriented toward the export market. In the 1930's the sugar mills were the only significant establishments which produced for the United States market. Now Puerto Rico is attracting manufacturing establishments on the basis of advantageous geographical location and political association and, in addition, on the basis of a rapidly growing local market and a rapidly developing skilled labor force.

As a consequence Puerto Rico is taking on the character of an international trading economy as revealed by the percentage of its gross product which it exports and imports in the form of goods and services. Ten years ago 48 per cent of the gross product was exported. Today 58 per cent of the gross product is exported. Purchases from the rest of the world amounted to 69 per cent of gross product a decade ago. Today such purchases amount to 75 per cent of the gross product.

In addition, there is some evidence that indicates that Puerto Rican manufacturing is entering a second stage of diversification. In underdeveloped areas manufacturing activities usually tend to be closely associated with agriculture and relatively simple apparel manufacturing, such as home needlework. During the first stage of diversification and development, apparel activity expands, shifting gradually from the homes to factories. Apparel output may exceed domestic needs, and a large export market may develop. The main strength of this development rests upon the previous skills created by the home industries and the existence of relatively low wages. The home needlework industry may continue to flourish for a time, and agriculturally based industries may expand somewhat as a few new products are added.

The second stage of growth involves the manufacture of new products which depend less on low labor costs and which tend to utilize higher capital investment. The attraction of these industries to the developing area may be in terms of earnings on investment rather than in terms of a differential in costs of production. Thus, incentives such as tax exemption may prove to be more important than extremely low wages.

The construction industry has been one of the most dynamic sectors of the Puerto Rican economy during the last decade. Construction value put-in-place amounted to $1,056 million during the decade ending in 1957. Housing construction during this ten-year period has been valued at $386 million, or about one-third of the total. Most of the financing of this construction was obtained abroad, primarily loans guaranteed by the Federal Housing and the Public Housing Administrations. Up to 1957 the public housing authorities in Puerto Rico have provided roughly 20,500 dwelling units with an estimated value of about $100 million.

Construction of productive types of facilities, such as industrial plants, generating stations, and the like, registered the greatest rate of expansion. For the period 1948 to 1957, inclusive, non-residential construction was valued at $670 million, of which $190 million was performed by the private sector and $480 million by the government sector in power plants, aqueducts, sewers, roads, and schools.

The role of the commonwealth government in the economic

activity of Puerto Rico has been consistently expanded during the last decade. The net income originated by the commonwealth and local governments more than doubled during this period reaching a level of $133 million in 1957. On the other hand, the federal government activities in Puerto Rico have fluctuated significantly as a result of expansions and curtailment of defense programs. This sector contributed 7 per cent of the total net income of Puerto Rico, or $75 million, and is not expected to grow.

The substantial progress registered in the primary sectors of the economy was also reflected in the supporting sectors of the economy, such as trade, public utilities, finance, and services. The net income originated in these other sectors expanded from $253 million ten years ago to $466 million in 1957, an increase of 84 per cent.

II

Within the last decade the natural increase in the population of Puerto Rico was reduced from 64,300 to 59,200 in 1957 as the result of a drop in the crude birth rate from 42.2 to 32.9 per thousand while the death rate declined from 12.5 to 7.0 per thousand. The high level of migration to the United States mainland, of approximately 46,000 per year as an average for the last ten years, has maintained the population almost stable at a level of about 2,250,000. While there was a slight increase in the population of labor-force age, participation rates declined, with the net effect that the labor force was reduced by approximately 3 per cent to a level of 636,000 in 1957. During this same period employment also declined by 4 per cent, and unemployment still stands at the high level of 84,000, or 13 per cent of the labor force. Considering that during 1951 the average annual unemployment reached a peak of 110,000, the present level represents substantial improvement.

Adjustments in the composition of the labor force which reflect the changing industrial structure are moving in the direction to be ultimately expected. While it is difficult to say whether the withdrawals from the labor force are a result of lack of employment opportunities or of shifting to better spheres of employment, it is apparent that the rather drastic changes which have been occurring in particular sectors since 1951 have not resulted in increased unemployment, as unemployment dropped by 26,000 during the last six years.

Further evidence exists for believing that the withdrawals from the labor force in certain sectors of the economy have not been entirely the result of job disappearance. Shifts to better jobs or migration and retirement are suggested by the reduction in the number of self-employed and unpaid family workers in agriculture from 90,000 to 62,000 in six years. Decreases in wage and salaried employment, which were heavy in sugar cultivation (27,000), domestic servants (15,000), and home needlework (32,000) during the last six years, were almost offset by increases in wage and salaried workers in manufacturing, construction, trade, government, and professional services.

In 1957 the average compensation of workers in the industries which reported decreased employment was $671 compared with $2,116 for the industries which showed increased employment. Quality of the jobs apparently improved as measured both in terms of number of weeks worked a year and in terms of the number of hours worked per week. This is a tendency which seems to have been accelerating in recent years. The improvement in job quality has been accompanied by an overall shift of the labor force out of agricultural jobs and into nonagricultural jobs.

If the human resources available to the low-wage sector are reduced, the utilization of tools and other aids for improving productivity will become worth while. As a result wages paid to the remaining employees in the low-wage sector will continue to rise until they meet the prevailing rate in the high-wage sector. The speed with which this equilibrium will be accomplished depends upon the ability of the high-wage sector to grow. In any economy the ability to expand output in the high-wage sector by adding new units or by transforming selected parts of the low-wage sector, through the addition of capital equipment or other means of increasing productivity, depends upon the growth of effective demand for the output. Increased mechanization should only take place when justified by demand and when wages are rising as the result of a shift in structure of the economy, thus making increased mechanization desirable from the standpoint of operating costs.

One of the most urgent problems confronting the commonwealth government in the next few years is the expansion of the public school system so that the entire school population can be accommodated and the drop-out rates for all levels of education be reduced. Even if this is accomplished, it is believed that Puerto Rico will fall somewhat short of providing the number of sufficiently educated workers that its growing economy might otherwise absorb. This circumstance indicates that the development of human resources may prove to be the most crucial problem in the achievement of the desired rates of economic development. Therefore, continued attention must be given to devising ways of upgrading the educational standards of the labor force. Such measures may include not only the improvement of the present educational system, but a major expansion of adult education programs.

III

The most significant economic development in Puerto Rico during the last decade was the extremely high level of investment. During the last few years investment rates in Puerto Rico reached levels which are typical of advanced industrial nations with potentials and resources for the investment of capital goods.

Investment in fixed capital goods, such as new construction, machinery, and equipment, during 1957 amounted to $262 million, or 21 per cent of the total output of the economy. For the period 1948 to 1957, inclusive, fixed investment in Puerto Rico amounted to about $1,600 million. Approximately

40 per cent of these funds was obtained from investment sources in the United States.

The principal sources of local savings are the funds generated by the government, depreciation reserves, and undistributed corporation profits. It is becoming apparent that the higher level of industrial activity is beginning to supply a large proportion of the funds required to meet the investment needs of the economy.

Although the overall rate of investment is important, the ability of an economy to grow depends upon the composition of the investment. During this last decade Puerto Rico invested in plant, machinery, and equipment approximately $960 million. The government public authorities, namely, the Water Resources Authority, the Aqueduct and Sewer Authority, and the Industrial Development Company, contributed greatly to this high rate of capital formation.

The growth in output, particularly the long-term average growth, will be determined chiefly by the rate at which existing technology, machinery and equipment, and managerial skills can be combined with the economy's progressive and expanding labor force. Output gains from year to year appear to be directly related to the rates of investment.

IV

The substantial progress in Puerto Rico during the last decade and the significant changes registered in the structure of the economy have provided the basis for very optimistic economic projections over the longer range. The principal goal for the economic planning of the island for the next 20 years is to reach a minimum family income of $2,000 per year. To achieve this objective, the total production of goods and services in Puerto Rico is expected to increase to $3,800 million in 1955 prices, and the net income to rise to $3,200 million by 1975.

Analyzing the structural interrelations among the different industrial sectors, that is, the effects that the primary sector of the economy of Puerto Rico—manufacturing, agriculture, construction, and government—have upon the secondary sector, it was calculated that to reach a level of net income of $3,200 million in 1975, it is necessary that the net income of the primary sector achieve a level of $2,200 million. The balance will be originated in the secondary sectors.

Through detailed studies the potentialities of development of each sector have been estimated. To attain the needed increase in net income of $1,600 million in the primary sector, manufacturing income would have to rise by $1,200 million between 1957 and 1975. This, of course, requires an enormous expansion in factory production, but recent rates of growth of this sector are in accordance with this goal.

Although this probable rate of growth entails an average annual rate of increase of about 6 per cent, it is expected that the level of employment will not rise at that same rate. Productivity will register a substantial increase, not only as a result of productivity changes within each sector, but also as a consequence of the expected change in industrial composition with a stronger participation of those industries characterized by higher productivity.

With these increments in output and productivity of each of the specific sectors, the economy will require a level of employment of about 800,000 in 1975. A continued decline in employment is expected in agriculture, home needlework, and household services, but these contractions will be more than offset by substantial increases in manufacturing and other sectors. It is estimated that in 1975 the labor force will be just slightly higher than the available employment opportunities.

The attainment of these production, income, and employment goals would mean an average annual family income of $5,400. At the same time practically every family in Puerto Rico will have an income of $2,000, an achievement which was realized in the United States only within the last few years.

Petroamérica Pagán de Colón: PUERTO RICAN
SOCIETY IN TRANSITION

ALL HUMAN SOCIETIES ARE CONSTANTLY in transition—more rapidly at some times than at others—and are best understood through the dynamics of social change. When social changes are so slow as to resemble social stagnation, the inhibiting agent has often been the institution of colonialism. Because colonialism is today everywhere moribund, the world is experiencing the greatest and most widespread social change in its history. But one cannot expect that change to take place without resistance, internal friction, and constant questioning on the part of the society in transition.

In 1940 Puerto Rico had an election that amounted to a revolution against the institution of economic colonialism. It resulted in an explosive release of individual and social energies for the improvement of the life of the people. Our achievements since 1940, in the political and economic fields, in the increase of production, in family income, in education, public health, housing, agriculture, and rural electrification, have attracted world attention. Modest as they are when measured by world standards, those achievements are to us a source of invigorating pride; for they are truly enormous when compared with our opportunities for achievement. We have set ourselves the goals of abolishing poverty in our society and of strengthening democ-

180

racy as a way of life. But it is easier to set such goals than to envisage or plan the structure and mores of our changing society as it nears them.

Puerto Rico's modern society is an outgrowth of that which developed slowly during nearly four centuries of Spanish rule. Many of the social institutions established then still survive, though some in modified and rapidly changing form, and some anachronistically. But we remain a Spanish-speaking people with a Spanish heritage, which makes us essentially a Latin American community of United States citizens. Even if we wanted to, we could not jettison that heritage without losing the pride and substance of identity which adds so much to the vigor of our current transformation.

I. Puerto Rican Society, 1508 to 1898

The old, patriarchal society, with overtones of feudalism, which developed between 1508, when Ponce de León arrived in Puerto Rico with the first group of Spanish settlers, and 1898, when Puerto Rico was ceded to the United States as a result of the Spanish-American War, shaped itself in part in response to three interrelated socially-limiting factors: (1) lack of opportunity for self-government and so also for concerted social action toward the general improvement of life; (2) widespread poverty; and (3) relative isolation from the world, its trade, its ferments, its ever-changing ideas. All three, together, undoubtedly had much to do with making ours a close-knit, more or less homogeneous society which resembled those of Latin America elsewhere, but avoided the extremes found in countries more liberally endowed with exploitable natural resources.

Arturo Morales Carrión[1] has pointed out that slavery never attained the wide base in Puerto Rico that it did in neighboring countries, and that Puerto Rico's society, during the first few centuries after settlement, consisted largely of two groups: (1)

1. "Orígenes de las Relaciones entre los Estados Unidos y Puerto Rico: 1700–1815," *Historia*, II, 1 (1952).

the Spanish hierarchy of government and church officials, military men, and businessmen, who made San Juan their headquarters and who were mainly oriented toward the great Spanish Empire in which Puerto Rico was insignificant economically but tremendously significant in its strategic position; and (2) the Puerto Ricans themselves, a more or less rural people which slowly forged its own characteristics and became passionately devoted to Puerto Rico's soil and landscape. This group lived largely by subsistence agriculture and—"disdainful of metropolitan commands," in the words of Morales Carrión—by abundant smuggling that reached all the way to the United States and the thirteen colonies preceding them.

More or less between these two groups was a class of privileged landowners, created largely by royal grants, from which various segments of Puerto Rico's modern upper class were eventually to emerge. They cultivated coffee and some sugar cane and raised cattle, but never grew very rich. In the early days they were assigned Indians under the institution of *repartimiento*. Later they owned slaves, but never very many.

With time, several other distinct groups emerged. One was that of the artisans and independent workers, mainly urban, who were organized in guilds reminiscent of medieval days. The other were the *agregados,* landless rural workers who were tied to various landowners by a series of obligations, mostly personal and informal.

During the so-called "Age of Revolution" in the Americas, which began with the wars that led to the establishment of the United States and ended with the establishment of the twenty Latin American republics, Puerto Rico experienced a sudden, enormous expansion in its population—from 45,000 in 1765 to 156,000 in 1800. This was caused by the influx of settlers from elsewhere—men who remained loyal to the twin idea of Crown and Church, Frenchmen from Haiti, French and Spanish settlers from North America who were unhappy over the Louisiana Purchase, Royalists from Venezuela and Colombia, followed by Corsicans and Frenchmen from Europe after Napoleon's fall.

They came with capital, and they finally settled the crown lands in the island's mountainous interior which had long been a haven for Indians.

The rural society that developed through those centuries was one that owed its essential placidity in part to the relatively equitable distribution of land. When the United States took over in Puerto Rico, the average size of farms was twelve acres, and over 90 per cent of the farms were worked by their owners. Though there were some fairly large estates, especially on the coastal plain and in the coffee mountains, latifundia to the extent that it had developed in many other Latin American countries after the Spanish conquest was unknown.

An outstanding and important characteristic of Puerto Rican society was, and still is, the lack of racial prejudice and discrimination—except in certain upper-class social circles. In Puerto Rico—with that exception—race or color is never a cause for discrimination, and every man and woman is judged on his own merits. As Vincenzo Petrullo[2] remarked in commenting on Puerto Rican society: "We in America are so accustomed to thinking in terms of race prejudice or tolerance that it is difficult to imagine a people which is not color-conscious. The Puerto Ricans are almost such a people."

Needless to say, this attitude toward race, with its attendant general democracy and kindliness in all human relations, leads to bewilderment and distress on the part of many of the thousands of Puerto Ricans who today come to the States, as permanent residents or as temporary agricultural workers, and who find it difficult to adjust to new and more competitive ways.

During Spanish colonial days our society could be classified as being, on the whole, quite paternalistic. The "little man" gave allegiance and work to the *patrón,* and the latter gave protection and help in return. Even today our rural *jíbaros* solicit the intervention of a "third party" when they need something.

2. *Puerto Rican Paradox* (Philadelphia: University of Pennsylvania Press, 1947), p. 21.

(For example, a person wishing to file a claim for social security may ask someone whom he believes to have influence to accompany him to the social security office.) This use of the third party is, of course, the symbolic continuation of the relationship with the *patrón* of former times. One of our present government's most important activities is that of community education, which leads rural communities toward analyzing, and acting upon, their own problems.

One of the traditional characteristics of Puerto Rican society has always been a close-knit and far-flung family structure, which has served in part as a social defense against poverty. Blood relationship, no matter how tenuous, has been the valid basis for intra-family assistance. That strong family sense still prevails, although today it is necessarily breaking down under the impact of industrialization, the phenomenal growth of our cities, the broadening and strengthening of the wage system, and the government's expansion of social welfare programs.

In the individual family the man was supreme. The place of women was in the home, as homemakers and child bearers, and in the church. This began to change with the influence of United States patterns. Today more and more women, qualified by education and social consciousness, take important positions in government, education, and business. At the lower levels, thousands of women have become the principal breadwinners by taking jobs in industry while their husbands still remain seasonal agricultural workers or small farmers or are performing other jobs in the modern Puerto Rican economy.

While we have always been, and still are, a predominantly Catholic country, the organized church has had a somewhat less mandatory influence in shaping our social structure than elsewhere in Latin America.

Under Spanish rule education was rudimentary and church controlled, and reached relatively few. When Puerto Rico became a part of the United States, over 80 per cent of our people were illiterate; today well over 80 per cent are literate. There was no normal school to train teachers until 1902, no university until 1903. Sons of the well-to-do went to Europe or the United States to study. The better classes trained their children to become doctors, lawyers, or other professionals, and manual work or craft was considered only for the poor. That attitude has completely changed—which is a strong boost for our present direction of rapid social and economic development.

II. Puerto Rican Society, 1898 to 1940

Our first great social upheaval came with the advent of the United States as the governing power. Latifundia then showed itself in Puerto Rico for the first time. United States capital poured into the sugar regions and came to dominate the sugar business, which became our most important industry and in time led to a typical one-crop economy. A few Puerto Rican planters became wealthy, helped by the sugar companies who wanted powerful friends in our society. As a result of the rising prices of sugar after World War I, Puerto Rican millionaires appeared on the scene for the first time in the early 1920's. Many small planters, however, were forced by economic pressure to sell their lands and were pauperized.

Thousands of cane cutters, working at abysmally low wages for five months per year and unemployed the rest of the time, became our largest single labor force. Some companies treated them better, and more paternally, than did others, but there was an enormous difference between corporation paternalism and the human relationship of *patrón* and worker that had preceded it. During the first four decades of the twentieth century, we developed a landless rural proletariat—workers in a semi-industrialized rural sweatshop, subject much more than ever before to the vicissitudes of world markets and the varying morality of large corporations.

The four decades preceding 1940 saw the introduction of many technical and social innovations. The power for their control for the public good, however, remained in Washington. On paper we had a degree of self-government that was notable as colonial affairs went in those days. In practice it didn't work in a system in which the ultimate power remained in the hands of an appointed, continental governor who could veto laws and control patronage, and in which the United States Congress set policies and could at any time override the actions of Puerto Rico's legislature. It was not until 1952, twelve years after the democratically revolutionary 1940 election, that we attained the commonwealth status in which we are today completely self-governing in our internal affairs and policies and in free association with the United States.

Prior to 1940, politics pervaded all phases of our life, but was largely a partisan struggle. One of the most striking features of our modern society is the sudden, dedicated political consciousness of our people, who in every election dedicate their votes to basic issues rather than immediate gain. In his 1940 campaign Muñoz Marín, as head of the newly formed Popular Democratic party, taught our people not to sell their votes but to use them for the improvement of their lives. Our new, but deep-rooted political morality, under which it is today virtually as impossible to buy a vote as it was less than twenty years ago to win a *jíbaro* vote without buying it, is perhaps the most important single aspect of our modern social revolution.

III.   Puerto Rican Society Today

The years since 1940, when we began to exercise an ever-growing control over our own affairs, have been marked by a series of drastic social changes to which our people must today adjust. The fact that such adjustments take time, and are often made with difficulty, is common to all societies in rapid transition.

Average family incomes have risen from $660 per year in 1940 to $2400 today;[3] our government's goal is to create, as soon as possible, a *minimum* family income of $2000.

An agricultural economy in 1940, Puerto Rico has now

3. Puerto Rico Planning Board.

arrived at the point where, in 1956, total income from manufacturing had outstripped that from agriculture.

The growth of the cities, with their new problems in housing and social adjustments, has continued and has steadily accelerated. The race between the growth of slums and their elimination through government housing efforts continues year after year.

A new middle class has sprung up and is growing rapidly. A new class of professionals lives side by side with newly created entrepreneurs and distributors who use new and modern means for moving goods. The former urban guild workers are replaced by trained, skilled workers, many organized in unions, with rising incomes and standards of living. Many members of that middle class are now living in new urban developments, watching TV, shopping in *supermercados,* and as rapidly as possible acquiring all the modern gadgets, as do their counterparts in the United States.

Today Puerto Rico is spending proportionately more money on education than any country in the world, except Israel. This year we have succeeded in bringing practically every child of school age into school, and the Department of Education is directing its efforts to retaining them in school for the greatest number of years possible. Nor are the educational facilities limited to children of school age. In marked contrast to the attitude existing at the turn of the century, there is enormous demand for all kinds of vocational education and training from elementary level to advanced college work. There are from 50,000 to 60,000 young men and women and adults enrolled in vocational programs, and the number is growing as new courses of instruction are offered. This universal education system in which Puerto Rico is now engaged will have two immediate results. It will strengthen the democratic process and the democratic forces in our society, and it will lead to better employment and better incomes for the workers. Education, improved income, radio and television, membership in the United States armed forces and participation in such wars as the Korean, greatly improved internal and external transportation facilities, the migration to the mainland which is so marked a feature of our modern life—all of these have combined to eliminate our former isolation from the world. In varying degrees, and often against much understandable resistance, the ideas and concepts so spread form a powerful force for change in our present society.

Our changing ways of life are breaking down the old paternalistic system and the formerly close family unit. They are also reflected in the demographic field. The birth rate has gone down from about 43 per thousand in 1947 to about 34.7 per thousand today. Our new vigor, however, is also reflected dramatically in new conditions of public health. The death rate has dropped from 18 per thousand in 1940 to 7 per thousand today. The fact that almost 35 Puerto Ricans are born for every 7 who die, plus the fact that those who live now have a life expectancy of 68 years as compared to 46 years in 1940, creates urgent social, economic, and political realities that we must face, and are facing, realistically.

Such are a few of the social forces which are giving direction and shape to modern Puerto Rico. We are constantly trying to measure and evaluate the dynamics involved and to take a measure of their worth; but by the time the social scientist has tested his tools and published his findings, conditions are so changed as to make his report dated. The aspirations of a people elude statistical analysis, being dynamic, not static. Eugenio Fernández Méndez, in his essay "Reflexiones sobre 50 Años de Cambio Cultural,"[4] said when speaking of the writers of the period: "The big question of all of these writers is ¿Qué somos? ¿Cómo somos? and the more fundamental question, ¿A dónde vamos?"—"Who are we? What are we? Where are we going?"

Today we know who we are and what we are. We also have a good idea of where we want to go and have charted tentative plans for the achievement of our goals. As Puerto Ricans we

4. *Historia*, V, 2 (October, 1955).

feel a humble pride in what we have accomplished, a recognition of the size and complexity of the problems ahead, and faith in our ability to achieve somewhat the measure of our dream. We have gone a long stretch on the *Jalda Arriba*, the long, hard, upward road that symbolizes the spirit of our Operation Bootstrap. We know where we are going, and that realization is the one outstanding, most important psychological attribute of modern Puerto Rican society.

BIBLIOGRAPHY

Díaz Soler, Luis M. *Historia de la Esclavitud Negra en Puerto Rico: 1493-1890*. Río Piedras: University of Puerto Rico Press, 1953.

Fernández Méndez, Eugenio. "Reflexiones sobre 50 Años de Cambio Cultural en Puerto Rico," *Historia*, V, 2 (October, 1955).

Morales Carrión, Arturo. "Orígenes de las Relaciones entre los Estados Unidos y Puerto Rico: 1700-1815," *Historia*, II, 1 (1952).

Osuna, Juan José. *A History of Education in Puerto Rico*. Río Piedras: University of Puerto Rico Press, 1949.

Petrullo, Vincenzo. *Puerto Rican Paradox*. Philadelphia: University of Pennsylvania Press, 1947.

Stycos, J. Mayone. *Family and Fertility in Puerto Rico*. New York: Columbia University Press, 1955.

Part V

SOME GENERAL
CONSIDERATIONS

Frederic W. Ganzert: TRADE TRENDS
AND PROSPECTS

IN THE INTEREST OF CLARITY, each of the separate
areas will be examined in turn: the British, French, and Dutch
areas, and for the United States, Puerto Rico.

I. The British Areas

At the end of 1954 studies made by the Research Branch of
the Central Secretariat of the Caribbean Commission revealed
that with respect to the countries served by the Commission the
balance of trade had been consistently and increasingly unfavorable to the area as a whole and, with the exception of oil and
bauxite, to individual countries. Not only was the export trade
of the area dependent upon the metropolitan and Canadian
markets, but there was an increasing imbalance of trade with the
respective metropolitan countries, a debit balance with Canada
in all but a few British territories, and a consistent debit balance
with the United States. Moreover, foodstuffs were customarily
imported in large quantities from a number of countries which
were negligible as markets for the area, and the export trade was
dominated by a limited number of commodities, notably oil,
bauxite, and sugar with its by-products. Finally, intra-Caribbean
trade was insignificant.[1]

1. Caribbean Commission, "The Nature and Direction of Caribbean
Trade," *Caribbean Economic Review*, VI (December, 1954), 26.

These trade patterns have not changed in the last three years, except for an increase in the volume of trade. There has also been an increase in intra-Caribbean trade, especially between Trinidad, British Guiana, Jamaica, the French Departments, and the Netherland countries, Trinidad serving as the hub of this increased trade among the Caribbean areas.[2]

Normally, except in 1953 and 1954, the British Caribbean region as a whole has had an adverse balance of trade with the United Kingdom, but with Canada the balance has been generally favorable. With the United States there has been a sizeable import surplus. The United Kingdom is still the chief customer of this area, taking 39.7 per cent of exports in 1956, in comparison with 16.6 per cent taken by Canada and 10.1 per cent by the United States.[3] Although the United Kingdom buys a considerable portion of Trinidad's oil and natural asphalt, there is not so much dependence upon the metropolitan country as a market for petroleum products. If individual commodities are considered, Britain is a more important buyer than the percentage would indicate: for example, the British market alone absorbs the important secondary crop of bananas; and the citrus industry is almost entirely dependent upon the British market. Britain also takes the larger share of sugar exports, which are divided between it and Canada.[4]

The import side of the picture shows the United Kingdom still the main supplier of textiles, chemicals, machinery, manufactures, and motor vehicles; and Canada the chief purveyor of foodstuffs. The United States furnishes mining equipment, machinery, metal products, and grains. Total import figures for 1956 show the following percentages: United Kingdom, 39.7; United States, 10.1; and Canada, 16.6.[5] With reference

2. Eric Akan, Administrative Officer, Central Secretariat, Caribbean Commission, Letter to the author, November 13, 1957.
3. Great Britain, Central Office of Information, *The West Indies, a Nation in the Making* (London, 1957), p. 53.
4. Marianne Cellner, "Trade Relations and Prospects," *The Statist,* special issue—*A Survey of the British Caribbean* (London, September, 1956) p. 19. (References to this issue will be designated *"The Statist."*)
5. Great Britain, Central Office of Information, *op. cit.,* p. 53.

to imports, the proportion received from various suppliers varies with the territory concerned. The case of Trinidad, whose chief industry is refining crude oil imported from Venezuela, is exceptional in that more than one-quarter of its imports are from the Andean republic, which ranks second to the United Kingdom as a supplier. To Jamaica the United States supplied in 1955 nearly 21 per cent of the colony's imports, a higher proportion than for the Caribbean as a whole. Jamaica and Trinidad have become increasingly larger purchasers of United States agricultural products. Jamaica ranks next to the Netherlands Antilles as a consumer of American farm products, taking in 1955 wheat flour valued at $3.1 million or 62 per cent of its total supply. Trinidad's flour imports from the United States in recent years have ranged from 1 to 5 per cent of its total. In 1955 the United States portion increased to 16 per cent, as bulk purchases ended and subsidization of flour imports opened the market to American flour. In the British Caribbean as a whole, imports from the United States would be greater were it not for the tightening of exchange restrictions in 1949. Since 1951 a token import scheme has been in operation, and the region's trade with the dollar area has been liberalized very gradually. In British Guiana, Great Britain has a larger share of the import trade than in any other area of the British Caribbean, about 48 per cent; but in British Honduras the United States enjoys a large share of the import market. The value and direction of external trade are shown in Tables 1 and 2.[6]

The growing trade in local products among Britain's Caribbean territories indicates a trend away from previous economic ties. Stimulation has been given this trade by the recent growth of intra-Caribbean shipping services, almost non-existent before 1955.[7]

6. *Ibid.*

7. The First National City Bank of New York, "The British Caribbean, an Emerging Federation," *Foreign Information Service* pamphlet (New York, September, 1956), p. 6. The foregoing, as well as other publications and unpublished memoranda, was made available to the author through the courtesy of Mr. William K. Hora, assistant cashier.

TABLE 1

BRITISH CARIBBEAN AREAS
VALUE OF EXTERNAL TRADE
(In millions of pounds sterling)

	IMPORTS (C.I.F.)		EXPORTS (F.O.B.)	
	1948	1956	1948	1956
Barbados	6.35	12.7	3.05	7.47
British Guiana	10.0	20.9	7.71	19.8
British Honduras	2.0	3.99	1.53	2.49
Jamaica	19.9	58.3	11.5	38.8
Leeward Islands	1.89	4.71	1.46	3.44
Trinidad	27.5	62.8	27.6	68.9
Windward Islands	3.7	6.65	1.90	4.04
Total	71.34	170.05	54.75	145.34

TABLE 2

BRITISH CARIBBEAN AREAS
DIRECTION OF EXTERNAL TRADE
(In percentages)

	IMPORTS			EXPORTS		
	1936–38	1948	1956	1936–38	1948	1956
United Kingdom	38.0	34.5	37.3	44.0	43.6	39.7
Other Sterling Areas*	11.7	9.3	10.5	7.1	8.6	9.7
United States	18.1	18.2	16.7	9.8	6.2	10.1
Canada	14.9	21.3	10.9	21.6	17.1	16.6
Central and South America	4.3	11.3	11.4	1.2	7.6	3.0
Others	11.6	4.7	11.7	11.4	7.8	12.7
Unclassified	1.4	0.7	1.4	4.8	9.2	8.1
Total	100.0	100.0	100.0	100.0	100.0	100.0

*Including trade between colonial territories in the West Indies group.

The rice trade between Britain and Jamaica, Trinidad, Barbados, and the Leeward and Windward Islands, which began
when British Guiana replaced Burma as a supplier of rice during
World War II, has been increasing in volume as the mainland

territory has expanded its production of the cereal. In 1955 the total value of this trade was BWI $12,031,000.[8]

Timber plays an important part in intra-regional trade, the largest proportion consisting of pitch-pine exports from British Honduras to Jamaica.[9]

Trinidad supplies coconut products to the Windward and Leeward Islands and raw material to Jamaica under the Oils and Fats Agreement of 1947, which forbids the shipment of coconuts or coconut products outside the British Caribbean area until after local needs have been met. Trinidad also exports fresh citrus fruits to British Guiana, Barbados, and some of the other Caribbean islands.

Exports of petroleum and petroleum products from Trinidad to other territories of the British Caribbean in 1955 totaled BWI $12,428,000. Trinidad also furnished cement valued at BWI $2,217,000. Other products featured in intra-British Caribbean trade are rum from Barbados, margarine from Barbados and Trinidad, medicinal and pharmaceutical products from British Guiana, laundry soap from Trinidad and Barbados, biscuits from Barbados and Trinidad, and printed cotton fabrics from Trinidad.[10]

Some assistance in closing the gap betweeen exports and imports in the British Caribbean has been given by the United Kingdom government through the Colonial Development and Welfare Funds grants, which in the ten years ending in March, 1955, aggregated almost $100 million.[11]

Further aid is also derived from the Commonwealth Sugar Agreement of 1957, which enables the British Caribbean sugar

8. A. G. Sanderson, "The Caribbean, a Growing Market for U. S. Farm Products," *Foreign Agriculture,* XX (Washington: U. S. Department of Agriculture, June, 1957), 4.

9. Great Britain, Central Office of Information, "Progress in British Guiana," *Overseas Information Service Document No. R. 3635* (London, June, 1957), pp. 7 f and 12.

10. Regional Economic Committee of the British West Indies, British Guiana, and British Honduras, "Intra-Regional Trade of the British Caribbean for 1955," *Bulletin No. 57* (Barbados, April 8, 1957), Table III.

11. First National City Bank, p. 5.

growers to get for approximately 70 per cent of their crop a price per ton which is equivalent to that which the sugar growers of Puerto Rico and Hawaii obtain for every ton of their respective crops. The agreement, which will continue until the end of 1963, allows the West Indies and Guiana an annual export quota of 900,000 tons of raw sugar, of which 670,000 tons will be purchased by the United Kingdom at negotiated prices.[12]

The mining of bauxite in Jamaica and British Guiana, which is entirely in the hands of North American companies, has served to bring in outside funds and to increase exports from the British Caribbean area. In Jamaica the three mining companies, whose investment has trebled in four years, are Reynold's Jamaica Mines, Ltd., and Kaiser Bauxite Company—both American— and Alumina Jamaica, Ltd., a subsidiary of Aluminum Ltd., of Canada. By 1959 annual production of bauxite in Jamaica will reach 6 million tons, in addition to 720,000 tons of alumina produced on the island. The $100 million investment of 1953 will next year represent the investment of one company alone, Alumina Jamaica.[13]

The Canadian company produces alumina locally and supplies distant smelters at Kitimat and in Scandinavia. The two American companies export the raw ore to nearby Gulf ports for processing in the United States. Shipments of bauxite from Jamaica to the United States in 1956 showed an increase of 18 per cent over 1955 and comprised 45 per cent of the total United States imports.[14]

The petroleum exports of Trinidad are one of the mainstays of the British Caribbean area, making Trinidad the most prosperous colony and replacing sugar as the largest single export commodity. Although the oil industry in Trinidad employs fewer workers than the sugar industry, it accounts for over 77 per cent

12. Barclay's Bank D.C.O., *Jamaica, an Economic Survey* (London, April, 1957), p. 4.
13. Anon., "Mining in Jamaica Means More and More Bauxite," *Engineering and Mining Journal*, CLVIII (September, 1957), 97.
14. U. S. Department of the Interior, "Bauxite in 1956," *Mineral Market Reports*, MMS. No. 2683, September 20, 1957, p. 8.

of the value of all domestic exports. During 1952 a new company, a subsidiary of a large American producer, entered the Trinidad oil scene, and in 1955 the Texas Company bought out the Trinidad Oil Company at a reported figure of $176,400,-000, a major addition to the dollar pool of the sterling area. The advent of Texas in Trinidad is expected to provide the increased capital which in the future will be urgently required for new drilling or for building up refining, should unavailability of locally mined petroleum force the Trinidad oil business to direct its chief efforts toward refining imported crude oil.

The revival of the banana industry, which declined during World War II, is an example of the success of efforts toward agricultural diversification which have been undertaken in the British Caribbean area, particularly in Jamaica. In 1955 bananas to the value of more than £20 million were imported into the United Kingdom. Over half of them were from the West Indies, which supplied more than 13 million stems or bunches. The bulk came from Jamaica, which until 1953 had a long term contract with the British Ministry of Food for the export of at least 85 per cent of the crop at a price negotiated annually. The Jamaican government has since concluded twelve-year agreements with two marketing companies for the transport and distribution of bananas in the United Kingdom. Efforts are also being made in Trinidad[15] to increase the acreage devoted to banana culture and to introduce disease-resistant banana strains suitable for the soil of Trinidad and Tobago.

In recent years Jamaica has become a substantial producer of cocoa, by Caribbean standards; and Dominica, St. Lucia, and more recently British Honduras and St. Vincent have started cocoa cultivation, using clones produced at the cocoa research station at the Imperial College of Tropical Agriculture.[16]

Production of citrus fruit is steadily increasing in Jamaica and in Trinidad. Grapefruit is an important export of British Hon-

15. Barclay's Bank D.C.O., *Trinidad, an Economic Survey* (London, January, 1957), pp. 10 f.
16. Anon., "Agriculture," *The Statist,* p. 35.

duras, and limes of Dominica. Most of Jamaica's citrus and citrus products are sold to the United Kingdom or other members of the sterling area. New Zealand is the most important market for Jamaica's fresh oranges.[17]

In industrial development the greatest advance has been made in Jamaica and Trinidad, which have most of the factories of the area. Although Jamaica has tried to industrialize itself by the use of protective tariffs and import licensing, Trinidad has given cotton spinning, weaving and dyeing, and shirt manufacturing more moderate safeguards against competition from Hong Kong and India. The most widespread and popular incentive to industry throughout the British Caribbean area, however, has been the tax concession. All the colonies provide inducement to new industries ranging from the privilege of duty-free importation of building materials and plant equipment to extensive income tax concessions.[18]

Most of the factories process local agricultural products and industrial raw materials. Since World War II Jamaica has added textile and knitwear industries and now manufactures cement, garments, shoes, storage batteries, furniture, and wall board. Local enterprises also prepare fruit juice concentrates and breakfast foods. Trinidad has much the same industries, but also produces essential oils, chemicals, rubber goods, plastics, and stockfeeds.[19]

Tourist spending in the British Caribbean area is one of the most important sources of dollars, and efforts are being made steadily to increase this lucrative business by providing up-to-date hotels and satisfactory services. The United States Department of Commerce estimates that the gross receipts from tourism in all the West Indian islands in 1955 were $107 million, exclusive of transport receipts by British and foreign lines. Jamaica

17. U. S. Department of Agriculture, "Citrus Industry of British Honduras, Jamaica, Trinidad," *Foreign Agricultural Report No. 88* (Washington, April, 1956), *passim.*
18. A. A. Shenfield, "Industrialization and Opportunities for British Capital in the British West Indies," *The Statist,* pp. 25 f.
19. First National City Bank, p. 4.

received $7 million of this total, thereby making up its normal trade deficit for the period.[20]

It is estimated that Barbados is earning annually not less than BWI $7 million from the tourist trade. The government of that colony recently enacted legislation under which capital expenditure for hotel construction can be offset against profits for income-tax purposes over the following seven years.

Attracted by the equable climate and varied scenery, more than 127,000 tourists, mostly Americans and Canadians, visited Jamaica during the fiscal year which ended March 31, 1956. The number of tourists visiting Trinidad and Tobago in 1956 was approximately 80,000, compared with 65,000 the previous year. Development of tourism in Jamaica is encouraged by the Hotel Aids Law, which allows concessions in the form of duty-free imports of building materials and hotel equipment and also permits the hotel proprietor in each of any five years of an eight-year period to set off against income arising from a hotel, for the purposes of income tax, one-fifth of the capital expenditure.[21]

New hotels are being built in Tobago, which is rapidly becoming a popular resort for visitors from the United Kingdom and the United States. American film companies are also beginning to use the island as a location for making pictures.

In the opinion of some authorities the economic pull of North America is growing stronger in the British Caribbean and will continue in that direction after federation. The shipments of bauxite to the United States and Canada and the growth of the tourist trade have already brought about a shift which will become intensified after the formation of a customs union, which is expected to follow federation. A customs union should stimulate the market for local manufactures, and the increased demand should create a need for further investment of North American capital. The large labor surplus offers opportunities similar to those already used by the manufacturers in Puerto Rico.[22]

20. Louis S. Law, "Tourism," *The Statist*, p. 71.
21. Barclay's Bank, *Jamaica, an Economic Survey*, p. 14.
22. First National City Bank, p. 6.

On the eve of British West Indian federation serious thought
is being given in Canada to the problem of strengthening economic ties with the British Caribbean area by government loans
or grants, by outright investment, or trade promotion. Although
since World War II Canada has been the second most important market for British West Indian products, after Great Britain, the volume of exports of agricultural commodities has fallen
off, and Canadians regard the trade volume with this area comparatively small. The gap left by declining agricultural exports
has been filled by exports of bauxite and aluminum, the products of Canadian investment. West Indian leaders think that a
greater effort should be made to stimulate not only the sale of
agricultural commodities already being shipped to the Canadian
market, but to promote the sale of new products which may be
required by altered tastes and technological change. Advantages
possessed by Canada over the United States are the assurance of
preferential tariff treatment and a tradition of shipping service.[23]

The late Professor C. G. Beasley, sometime economic advisor
to the Development and Welfare Organization for the West
Indies, believed that even after federation the effective marketing
of many West Indian products would continue to be closely
bound up with relations with the United Kingdom. In his opinion the following obstacles would prevent any break in close economic relations with the United Kingdom:

(1) the geographical handicap that the small production
units are dispersed and internal shipping facilities restricted, and
assembling, handling, standardization, and shipping are costly;

(2) the handicap of size—the home market is small
though very varied in its demands;

(3) for the most part, British Caribbean products form
an insignificant proportion of world production, and the bargaining power of the region in world markets is therefore limited.[24]

23. Charles J. Burgess, "Trade Relations Between the British West Indies
and Canada," *The Statist*, pp. 21 f.
24. C. G. Beasley, "Prospects and Obstacles to Economic Development,"
The Statist, p. 15.

Although the United States enjoys certain advantages over Canada in competition for trade with members of the British West Indies Federation, and although some increase in American exports may be expected, certain obstacles to any revolutionary change in trade direction are seen by trade analysts of the Bureau of Foreign Commerce of the United States Department of Commerce. First, the American market would not be capable of absorbing primary British West Indian agricultural products like sugar and bananas. Sugar would be barred from the United States by traditional American tariff legislation, and bananas could not meet the competition of established suppliers in Central America and elsewhere in Latin America. Without a market in the United States for these and similar tropical products, the British West Indies Federation could not obtain the dollar exchange necessary for any wide expansion of purchases in the United States. Because of this situation it is believed that the new federation must look to the United Kingdom, Canada, and other areas in the British Commonwealth as outlets for their principal exports.[25]

II. The Dutch Areas

For years the foreign trade of the Netherlands Antilles has been dominated by petroleum, obtained mostly from Venezuela, but also in a small amount from Colombia. Refining is carried on by the Curaçao Petroleum Industry Company (C.P.I.M.), a subsidiary of the Royal Dutch Shell Group, and in Aruba by the Lago Oil and Transport Co., an affiliate of the Standard Oil Company of New Jersey. About 87 per cent of the total imports of the Netherlands Antilles in 1956 was crude petroleum, and the exports of the same commodity in that year were about 99 per cent of the total. The United States share of the total trade of the Netherlands Caribbean area increased from $75 mil-

25. U. S. Department of Commerce, "Progress of the British West Indies Federation and Possible Effects on United States Trade," *Memo.*, October, 1957. Courtesy of Dr. George Wythe, Director, Bureau of Foreign Commerce.

lion in the period 1937-39 to $174 million in 1948-50.[26] In 1956 total trade between the Netherlands Antilles and the United States was valued at $316.5 million, representing exports to the United States of $236.5 million and imports from the United States of $80 million.[27]

Official export statistics published by the government of the Netherlands Antilles show that in both 1955 and 1956 the United States was the leading taker of exports, followed by the United Kingdom; whereas, the Netherlands ranked sixth—after Brazil, Argentina, and Canada.[28]

As a source of imports to the Netherlands Antilles for the same two years Venezuela led, with the United States second. In 1955 the United Kingdom ranked third, and the Netherlands just slightly ahead of Colombia in virtually a tie for fourth place. The following year the Netherlands still occupied fourth place, whereas Colombia had dropped back to fifth. The fluctuations are shown in Tables 3 and 4.[29]

Before World War II imports of the Netherlands colonies from Europe, especially from the Netherlands, were proportionately higher than from the United States, but during the conflict most supplies came from the United States. Netherlands Antilles officials maintain today that regardless of the fact that trade with the United States according to absolute figures appears larger than trade with Europe, the trend is now away from the United States and back toward Europe, and that for the last two years there has been a decline in imports from the United States. The decline is attributed to the higher prices of United States merchandise and the vigorous trade promotion efforts of Dutch and British trade commissioners.

26. Caribbean Commission, *op. cit.*, p. 10.

27. U. S. Department of Commerce, *Quarterly Summary of Foreign Commerce of the United States,* January-December 1956 (Washington, June, 1957), p. 2.

28. Netherlands Antilles, Government Information Service, *The Netherlands Antilles* (Curaçao, November, 1957), p. 35.

29. *Ibid.*

TABLE 3

NETHERLANDS ANTILLES IMPORTS

COUNTRY OF ORIGIN	1955	1956
(In millions of N.A. guilders $1 U.S. = 1.905 N.A. guilders)		
Venezuela	1,220	1,227
United States	120	151
Colombia	55	61
United Kingdom	60	74
The Netherlands	56	67
Trinidad	11	16
West Germany	5	8
Rest of the world	39	52
Total	1,566	1,656

TABLE 4

NETHERLANDS ANTILLES EXPORTS

COUNTRY OF DESTINATION	1955	1956
(In millions of N.A. guilders)		
United States	389	420
United Kingdom	150	183
Brazil	127	93
Argentina	70	91
Canada	63	73
The Netherlands	58	65
Cuba	46	61
Panama and Canal Zone	34	37
Rest of the world	567	562
Total	1,504	1,585

The statistics in Tables 5 and 6 are furnished by the government of the Netherlands Antilles:[30]

30. Director, Department of Social and Economic Affairs, Government of the Netherlands Antilles, Letter to the author, November 21, 1957.

TABLE 5

NETHERLANDS ANTILLES IMPORTS
(In 1,000 N.A. guilders)

	1946	1951	1956
The Netherlands	4,308	37,290	44,095
Europe (excluding the Netherlands)	25,165	26,740	55,288
United States	59,916	103,501	87,901
Other	28,525	26,203	26,199
Total	117,914	193,734	213,483

TABLE 6

NETHERLANDS ANTILLES EXPORTS
Exclusive of petroleum
(In 1,000 N.A. guilders)

	1946	1951	1956
The Netherlands	1,744	1,476	2,557
Europe (excluding the Netherlands)	593	503	5,436
United States	1,950	3,426	5,247
Other	12,706	18,548	4,360
Total	16,993	23,953	17,600

Exports in addition to petroleum are phosphate (to Canada), aloes (to the United Kingdom), dry salted goat skins (to the United States), shipchandling; and perfumes, watches, jewelry, and other luxury products (to tourists).

The Netherlands Antilles are the largest market in the Caribbean possessions for United States farm products, in 1955 their imports of United States wheat flour aggregating a half-million dollars. Fresh poultry was a close second to flour and rice, and citrus fruits were important. Canada was the second supplier of flour.

Netherlands Antilles authorities have for some time realized the need for freeing the islands from dependence upon a single industry and have made plans for diversification. The efforts to diversify were given an impetus by the enactment of legislation in Venezuela requiring the refining in Venezuela of an increased percentage of petroleum. Since the implementation of the new Venezuelan policy, the growth of the refining capacity has in the Antilles been slow and scarcely sufficient to employ the growing labor force. The diversification program includes courting foreign capital through tax exemptions and promotion of the tourist trade. A ten-year tax holiday has been given new industries, and the tax rate on the profits of investment trusts and security holding companies has been lowered to 2.4 per cent. Free-trade zones have been established on both Curaçao and Aruba,[31] in accordance with the Free Zones Ordinance of 1956. Both islands have several private storage warehouses and several government bonded warehouses. In 1954 the new storage warehouses were finished at the new government harbor at Curaçao.

In a bid for a share of the increasing Caribbean tourist trade, island authorities are welcoming foreign capital for the construction of hotels. A $2,750,000 luxury hotel, built with United States and Antillean capital, was opened recently in Curaçao and another, partly government financed, is being constructed at a cost of $3,000,000 in Aruba.[32]

In the case of Surinam, the South American mainland political partner of the Netherlands Antilles, future trade possibilities appear more promising than in the Antilles in view of the vast territorial extent and the variety of resources. Surinam is the largest exporter of bauxite, production and shipments in 1956 totaling 3,483,528 metric tons valued at Sf (Surinam florin) 45,536,000, although production has not been expanding so fast in recent years as in Jamaica and in French West Africa. Bauxite has for years been the major export item, constituting 75 per cent of the value of all exports and going chiefly to the United States. The United States also usually furnishes the largest share of Surinam imports—35 per cent in 1956, followed by the Netherlands, 28.8 per cent. During 1956, however, although Surinam exports to the United States increased, the Netherlands' share of Surinam's exports increased slightly more.

Although Surinam continued to show a net deficit in foreign

31. First National City Bank, "Memo. on the Netherlands West Indies," October 26, 1956.
32. *The Netherlands Antilles,* p. 31.

trade at the close of 1956, the long-term picture appeared re-assuring to the Department of Economic Affairs. The Department pointed out that, using 1949 as base, imports over the last 8 years had risen 65 per cent, whereas exports had climbed 73 per cent. In 1949 imports amounted to Sf 37.8 million, and exports, Sf 34.1 million; but in 1956 imports totaled Sf 62.6 million (net Sf 61.4 million), and exports (including re-exports) totaled Sf 59.0 million.[33]

In addition to bauxite, leading exports from Surinam in 1956 were plywood, valued at Sf 3,628,800, and husked rice, Sf 3,-426,700. In that year Surinam's export pattern showed a trend change because of a significant increase in rice exports and the sale of forest products, attributable to higher prices. These gains appeared to indicate good results from the Ten-Year Plan instituted for development of resources in 1954. A new item, frozen shrimp, entered Surinam's exports in 1956; and citrus shipments, destined mostly for the Netherlands, showed increases over 1955. The local clothing industry kept its export position at about the same level as in 1955. The greater part of the Sf 1.2 million re-export business was with Brazil, comprising chiefly refrigerators, radios, motors, automobiles, and other luxury items.

Gains in agricultural exports during 1956 were attributed to an increase in the area under cultivation, to certain administrative changes in the government's agricultural service, and to an active program of agricultural education, and to good weather.

During 1956 Surinam enjoyed a favorable trade balance with the United States, Canada, and the Caribbean islands other than Trinidad. In value this amounted to Sf 17.2 million in the case of the United States, and Sf 4.0 million each for Canada (bauxite) and the Caribbean islands (prefabricated houses, forest, and agricultural products). The Netherlands, Trinidad, the United Kingdom, and West Germany were the four major areas which had advantageous trade balances in their Surinam

33. U. S. Department of Commerce, "Economic Developments in Surinam, 1956," World Trade Information Service, *Economic Reports,* Part I, No. 57–78 (Washington, September, 1957), pp. 3 f.

trade.[34] The Surinam guilder or florin value remained constant in 1956 at Sf 1 for U.S. $0.54.

Comparative agricultural export figures for 1955 and 1956 are given in Table 7.[35]

TABLE 7

SURINAM AGRICULTURAL EXPORTS, 1955–1956
(In 1,000 guilders; Surinam guilder or florin = U.S. $0.54)

COMMODITY	1955	1956
Rice	2,798	3,428
Cocoa	63	102
Sugar	—	182
Coconuts	53	76
Citrus	336	771
Coffee	802	596
Plantains	24	21
Other	78	51
	4,154	5,227

Fishery production has been increased with funds from the Ten-Year Plan, especially from the government's system of leased fish farms on reclaimed plantation areas, and sufficient fish meal produced to reduce considerably the importation of that commodity. Following the opening of a modern shrimp processing and freezing plant in 1956, one major shipment of about 35,000 pounds of frozen, cooked, and peeled shrimp were made to the United States. In order to facilitate expansion of the industry the government signed a contract for an offshore shrimp survey, using a modern trawler from the United States. Ten-Year Plan funds are being used for opening new fishing stations at various points. Forest exploitation is a growing industry which has become a major factor in the economy of the colony. Roads are being built in order to open up additional forest resources. The total production of plywood in 1956 was 12,565 cubic meters, valued at Sf 3,628,527, compared with 10,471 cubic meters, worth Sf 3,308,882 in 1955. An order for 3,000 prefabricated

34. *Ibid.*, p. 4.   35. *Ibid.*, p. 5.

houses found markets in the Caribbean, principally in Grenada, to replace houses destroyed by a hurricane.

A second experimental project, which may open a new market for Surinam timber products, was the shipment late in 1956 of a limited quantity of mirenhout wood for pit props for a West German coal mine. Another experimental export was utility poles for Trinidad. Hopes were also placed in a major American timber project at Albina on the Marowijne whose promoter expected to produce sawn lumber and eventually to ship plywood logs to Trinidad, where a plywood factory would be established.

In 1956 Surinam's Ten-Year Plan (TYP), started in 1954, had begun to show some tangible results, and as the government and the Aluminum Company of America neared agreement on the long-term Brokopondo hydro-electric project, the prospects for the country's economy appeared promising. Of a contemplated total expenditure of Sf 127 million, Sf 18.2 were programmed for the fiscal 1957 authorization. Chief TYP activities during 1956 were in the fields of agriculture, roads and transportation, and public health. Under a general agreement between the Netherlands and the United States Government, signed in January, 1954, assistance in the TYP is being given by the resident Operations Mission of the United States International Cooperation Administration, with major emphasis on training local persons for key economic and social tasks. For example, three United States technicians have been assigned to cooperate with the Surinam Department of Public Works in training mechanics and operators of heavy equipment for Brokopondo and TYP projects.[36]

III. The French Areas

The foreign trade of the French Antilles—Martinique and Guadeloupe—and French Guiana is chiefly with France and is traditionally in a state of imbalance. The economy and trade

36. Anon., "United States Coöperation in Caribbean Development," *The Caribbean,* XI (Trinidad, February, 1958), 146.

of Martinique and Guadeloupe have the same characteristics: more than 90 per cent of production is represented by sugar cane products (sugar, molasses, and rum) and bananas. The islands produce virtually nothing needed for the consumption of the population, consequently must import nearly all required merchandise and equipment.

The balance of trade of Martinique has always shown a deficit, but this deficit was smaller in 1956 than during the previous two years, as shown in Table 8.[37]

TABLE 8

Martinique—Trade Balance in Millions of Francs

Years	Imports	Exports	Balance
1949	8,637.2	5,184.6	– 3,452.6
1954	12,699	8,289	– 4,410
1955	13,422	8,972	– 4,450
1956	13,079	9,893	– 3,186

Table 9 shows France as the premier supplier of imports in both 1949 and 1956, and the United States as second in the former year, but fourth in the latter.

TABLE 9

Martinique—Imports in Millions of Francs

Country of Origin	1949	1956
France	6,036.8	10,040 (76%)
Trinidad	143.5	767
French Overseas Territories	937.6	474
United States	1,126.8	348
Belgium	53.5	275

37. Statistics concerning Martinique, Guadeloupe, and French Guiana, in the absence of other references, are derived from a "Memorandum" prepared by the Division of Overseas Territories of the French Embassy, dated New York, November 22, 1957, made available through the courtesy of M. Pierre L. Massin, Chief, Overseas Territories Division.

Food products are the most important imports, constituting 22.1 per cent in 1956, and 24.5 per cent in 1949. Construction material ranks next, and also important are automobiles, trucks, gasoline, and tires.

Exports include chiefly bananas, canned pineapples, sugar, fruit juices, and rum, going to the following countries in the order given: France (85.9 per cent), Algeria, Tunisia, and Morocco; French overseas territories; and the United States.

There has been an increase in the quantities and values of these exports since 1949 as indicated in Table 10.

TABLE 10

MARTINIQUE EXPORTS

MAIN PRODUCTS	1949	1956	1949	1956
	(Metric tons)		(Millions of francs)	
Bananas	38,551	70,835	991.7	3,153
Canned pineapples	192	3,072	51.5	672
Sugar	17,950	72,138	1,014.4	4,188
Fruit juices	8	355	1.	43
Rum			2,663.9	1,578
Total all exports	89,172	169,629	5,184.6	9,893

The foreign trade picture of Guadeloupe is similar to that of Martinique with an unfavorable balance of trade in French francs of 2,514 millions in 1956. In that year France received 65.9 per cent of the exports and was the chief supplier of imports. Shipments to the United States were negligible, as were imports from that country.

The economies of both islands are basically agricultural, with sugar the predominant industry. The situation of sugar growers has been a difficult one in recent years, because of low prices for sugar and a falling demand for rum. The French government endeavors to absorb the exports of sugar and subsidizes the industry heavily. In 1954 France was buying sugar from the Antilles for about 70,000 francs per metric ton, whereas the world market price was only about 25,000 francs per ton. The subsidization, accordingly, cost the French government approximately 7,350 million francs or $21 million. In addition the government paid a freight rebate of 4,500 francs per ton, or about 50 per cent of the freight charges on all sugar exported to France from the Antilles. The French government also endeavors to absorb the banana exports. Prospects for the rum industry in the French Antilles have been dimmed by the anti-alcoholism decrees of the French government.[38]

The French government, although encouraging expansion of both the sugar and banana cultivation, has since 1956 advocated diversification of agriculture and the establishment of manufacturing. Attempts have been made to introduce and develop new food products and textile-fibre plants, and to develop animal husbandry and forestry. One of the industries reported to be increasing output in 1954 was pineapple canning.

Tourism in Martinique and Guadeloupe have not been developed sufficiently to produce sizeable income. Although several thousand tourists visit Martinique and Guadeloupe during an average year, tourism is still retarded by lack of accommodations. The winter season, 1954–55, brought eleven cruise ships to Martinique which placed 5,937 passengers ashore. An additional 2,000 British tourists and about 1,000 Americans arrived by plane or yacht for visits to the island during the same period. In the winter of 1954–55 Guadeloupe was visited for the first time by four cruise ships, carrying about 2,000 passengers; and perhaps 2,500 additional tourists arrived by plane and yacht.[39]

Since World War II both French and American individuals or groups have attempted to build hotels or otherwise provide tourist facilities, but without success. In December, 1956, the French government formed a company which is known as "Société Immobilière et Touristique des Départements d'Outre-mer" (S.I.T.O.) with an office in Paris. The French govern-

38. U. S. Department of State, Despatch, American Consulate, Martinique, June 24, 1955, pp. 6 f.
39. *Ibid.*, p. 32.

ment has announced that foreign companies, especially American companies, which desire to go into the hotel business in Guadeloupe and Martinique should communicate with this office.

French Guiana's chief trade is with France, and customarily there is an adverse trade balance. Table 11 indicates that the deficit deepened between 1949 and 1956.

TABLE 11

FRENCH GUIANA TRADE BALANCE IN MILLIONS OF FRANCS

YEAR	IMPORTS	EXPORTS	BALANCE
1949	1,031.3	219.3	– 812
1954	3,550	175	– 3,375
1955	2,700	362	– 2,338
1956	2,815	293	– 2,522

The country is largely dependent upon imports—$9 million in 1955 and $10 million in 1954.

French Guiana's imports rose in value from 1,031.3 million francs in 1949 to 2,815 million francs in 1956. In the latter year principal imports with their respective percentage of total imports were as shown in Table 12.

TABLE 12

FRENCH GUIANA IMPORTS, 1956

PRODUCT	PER CENT OF TOTAL
Food products	20.2
Concrete	1.4
Textile manufactures	7.4
Petroleum and products	6.2
Electric machinery	3.3
Machinery	6.1
Vehicles	7.0

The main suppliers of these imports and the percentage of the total furnished by each were as follows: France, 69.9 per cent; British territories, 6.7 per cent; United States, 5 per cent; Brazil, 3.8 per cent; and French overseas territories, 3.3 per cent.

The chief export products of French Guiana are rum, rosewood oil, tropical woods, and gold. Total exports amounted to about $500,000 in 1954 and $1 million in 1955. Trade with the main importing countries is shown in Table 13.

TABLE 13

FRENCH GUIANA—MAIN COUNTRIES WHICH RECEIVE EXPORTS

(In millions of francs)

COUNTRY	1949	1956
France	176.2	127
French West Indies	24.1	53
United States	0.3	18
Brazil	0.3	33
Surinam	0.7	49

Trade with the United States is not large, as will be noted in Table 14.[40]

TABLE 14

UNITED STATES TRADE WITH FRENCH GUIANA

(Thousands of dollars)

U. S. EXPORTS	1953	1954	1955
Tobacco and mfrs.	5	36	24
Petroleum & prds.	5	15	57
Metal mfrs.	6	17	61
Constr. and mining mach.	58	152	92
Other machinery	54	66	67
Tractors	62	69	32
Vehicles	54	121	25
All others	17	26	24
Total	261	502	382

40. First National City Bank, "Memo. on French Guiana," August 22, 1956.

TABLE 14 *(Continued)*

U. S. IMPORTS	1953	1954	1955
Wood	23	1	3
Veg. oils	9	3	3
Tantalite	30	68	63
Non-metallic minerals	2	—	—
Machinery, returned	—	—	47
Total	64	72	116

Possibilities of production and trade in French Guiana do not have the limitations which geography imposes upon the French West Indies. Although agricultural production is small-scale, the arable land which lies along the coast (about 75,000 acres) produces coconuts, castor-oil plant, cotton, ramie, coffee, cocoa, pineapples, fruits, and sugar cane. Rice growing has been encouraged and recent production is in the neighborhood of 500 tons a year. A sugar cane industry is being developed.

The French government launched a ten-year plan for social and economic betterment in 1946. The main objectives are the increasing of agricultural production as far as possible in such terrain, construction of roads and port facilities, and the building of a hotel. The Mortabo, a modern hostelry, was opened in Cayenne in 1954.

The Ten-Year Plan has already achieved results in agriculture and forestry, but the best promise of future economic development and consequent trade expansion is in mining. French Guiana is already the world's second largest producer of tantalite —10,000 tons in 1955—and recently discovered bauxite deposits have been estimated at 65 million metric tons, or 4.1 per cent of the world's reserves.[41]

A state controlled company, the Bureau Minier Guyanais, which recently completed surveys of bauxite deposits, has studied the problem of mining, processing the ore, and manufacturing

41. H. F. Kurtz and D. D. Blue, "Aluminum and Bauxite," undated reprint from *Mineral Facts and Problems, Bulletin 556,* U. S. Bureau of Mines.

and shipping the alumina, possibly with the utilization of American private capital. If these deposits were exploited, they would at present prices bring an additional $8 million in foreign exchange each year and would provide a strong impetus to economic development.

Rich forest lands are one of the principal resources of French Guiana. Four-fifths of the entire surface of Inini are covered with virgin forest containing 500 or more varieties of valuable woods: acapu, teak, various cabinet woods, gum, and other trees. Rosewood oil and balata gum (which resembles gutta-percha) are produced for export, and there are many varieties of medicinal plants.

The French government is encouraging the inhabitants to raise livestock as part of a long-range program to increase production and make the country less reliant upon imported food stuffs. The present herd numbers 3,500 head of cattle.

IV. Puerto Rico

The radical economic change which has come to Puerto Rico since the inauguration of "Operation Bootstrap" in 1946 has evoked the admiration of leaders in other Caribbean colonial areas. As a British observer has pointed out, ". . . British West Indians look with envious and admiring eyes at the achievements of Puerto Rico which, by the expenditure of large development funds and by the grant of lengthy income tax holidays, has made the past decade the most fruitful and inspiring of its whole history. As poor at the end of the war as Jamaica, and harder pressed for land for its expanding population, it has attracted an astonishing number and variety of establishments from the American mainland, and has lifted itself well above the living standards of most of the British colonies. The example of Puerto Rico is of the first importance because the British Colonies always have their eyes upon it, though they recognize that they cannot hope for Puerto Rico's advantages in the availability of large development funds, and in its proximity to, and Customs union with, the metropolitan country."[42]

This writer sums up succinctly the salient features of the Puerto Rican achievement. The industrialization program, with its aim of freeing the Commonwealth from dependence upon sugar and rum as the chief source of income, has in scarcely longer than ten years brought many new manufacturing establishments to the island, raised the standard of living for many of the population, and produced an increased volume of trade.

Perhaps the biggest talking point in favor of the American manufacturer's going to Puerto Rico is exemption from federal income tax and a further exemption of most companies for ten years from Puerto Rican taxes. Exemption from federal income tax derives from Puerto Rico's status under the American Constitution. Since the Commonwealth has no vote in Congress, federal income taxes cannot be collected from individuals under the jurisdiction of the Commonwealth. Another persuasive argument is the lower industrial wage scale in Puerto Rico and the relatively high productivity of the workers. In the last fifteen years Puerto Rico has doubled its educational facilities and tripled its special technical and vocational training enrollment. An additional advantage afforded the manufacturer who establishes his business in Puerto Rico is the shipping costs to United States markets, which in certain cases are lower than those from many plant locations in the United States. Finally, the Commonwealth is in the United States tariff system.[43]

For the foregoing and other reasons several hundred new enterprises have been established in Puerto Rico. Some 450 were in operation in August, 1957, and industrialization is said to be responsible for a new annual net income of $223 million.[44]

42. A. A. Shenfield, *The Statist,* p. 26.

43. Commonwealth of Puerto Rico, Economic Development Administration, *Puerto Rico: 1956 Review of Manufacturing Growth in Puerto Rico* (San Juan, January, 1957), p. 1; also *Facts for the Manufacturer* (San Juan, 1956), pp. 5, 7, 11.

44. Puerto Rico, Economic Development Administration, Press Release, San Juan, August 20, 1957.

Among the larger and better known firms which have established plants and offices in Puerto Rico are three divisions of General Electric, W. R. Grace & Company, Phelps Dodge Corporation, Indian Head Mills, Lovable Brassière Company, and Union Carbide Corporation. Major industries now operating on the island include electronics, plastics, apparel, textiles, chemicals, and metal work.

The industrialization program has been supplemented by successful efforts to promote the rum trade. In fiscal 1957 for the first time since the Economic Development Administration began its efforts to stimulate this industry, rum shipments exceeded the 2 million wine gallon mark, a 6 per cent gain over fiscal 1956. It is estimated that 70 per cent of all rum consumed in the United States now is brought in from Puerto Rico.

Despite altered constitutional relationships, the United States continues to be the chief trade partner of Puerto Rico, receiving annually from 90 to 95 per cent of the products of the Commonwealth. The island in return depends upon the United States for some food products, some apparel, building materials, raw materials, semi-finished products for industry, machinery and equipment, petroleum products, and chemicals.

In recent years Puerto Rico has become more rather than less dependent upon the United States. The Commonwealth has not had a favorable merchandise balance of trade with the United States since 1937–39, when the former had a surplus of $5 million. In the period 1948–50 this had become a debit balance of $140 million,[45] and during each of the last three fiscal years, 1955–57, the gap in merchandise trade exceeded $200 million. A portion of the deficit can be ascribed to heavy importation of equipment for increasing productive capacity. Such an imbalance, however, reflects strength in the economy rather than weakness. As statistics show, there has also been a substantial deficit on current account because of payments made for freight charges and insurance premiums, as well as for the transfer of

45. Caribbean Commission, p. 11.

profits and dividends on the increasing volume of investments from the mainland. For example, during fiscal year 1957 these transfers totaled $50 million.

Nevertheless, at times Puerto Rico is able to do even better than offset the gap in trade and services because of expenditures in the island by the United States government and by reason of the inflow of capital. The transfer of earnings of seasonal labor employed in the United States, remittances of Puerto Ricans who have settled on the mainland, and the spending of visiting emigrants and tourists are important sources of income. Furthermore, just as the British West Indies receive financial help from the United Kingdom, so does this former American possession benefit from various payments of the United States government on the island: the return of customs duties, grants-in-aid for health, transportation, and other programs, spending by the military on maintenance and new defense projects, and outlay for maintenance of non-military federal agencies. Expenditures of the armed forces at the bases and veterans' benefits—the latter reaching $60 million in 1946—assist further in meeting the deficit. And to top these sources of credit items, during the last five years Puerto Rico has attracted an average of $70 million annually in investment capital. In consequence of this influx of funds to the island, from fiscal 1949 through fiscal 1955 the Commonwealth actually increased its assets held abroad. This was not repeated in fiscal 1946, however, when because of the need for temporary financing of numerous large projects Puerto Rican investors and institutions had to draw upon foreign held assets.[46]

The increase in the number of manufacturing industries is the principal factor responsible for the expansion of Puerto Rico's productive base. The growth of these activities in turn has served to stimulate construction, trade, and transportation. Income originating from manufacturing rose from $86 million in fiscal 1947 to $213 million in fiscal 1957, a figure almost 40

46. *Ibid.;* and Office of the Commonwealth of Puerto Rico, *The Commonwealth of Puerto Rico* (Washington, 1954), p. 41.

per cent above the income from agriculture during the same period.

Official Puerto Rican statistics published in 1956 indicate the contribution of the new industries to the expanding volume of exports. The exports of a selected list of commodities produced by the new industries in 1954–55 were valued at $113,327,000 compared with a valuation of $54,545,000 in 1950–51, and only $20,408,000 in 1947–48.[47] Export products from the new industries with highest valuation in 1954–55 were the following: wearing apparel (except handkerchiefs and gloves), $23,365,000; corsets, brassières, and girdles, $14,459,000; and electrical machinery and apparatus, $12,901,000.

Figures on trade with countries other than the United States seem small by comparison. Other leading customers of Puerto Rico include Cuba, which bought commodities to the value of $2,289,227 in 1954–55; the Dominican Republic, with purchases of $1,707,741 in the same period; and smaller purchasers like Haiti, Jamaica, the Leeward and Windward Islands, Belgium and Luxemburg, and Greece.

As a supplier of Puerto Rico in 1954–55, Canada ranked next to the United States with sales of goods valued at $9,662,738. The Netherlands Antilles ranked third, with sales of $4,289,133; and Belgium and Luxemburg fourth, with exports to Puerto Rico of $3,582,908.[48]

Puerto Rico's planners have not overlooked the income possibilities of the tourist trade. Climate, scenery, proximity to the United States, and a combination of Old World and American atmosphere attract thousands of tourists to Puerto Rico every year. Between 1946–47 and 1954–55 the number of visitors increased from 40,380 to 134,625. These guests in 1954–55 spent in the neighborhood of $20,413,000. This figure does not include expenditures of servicemen on leave after maneuvers estimated at $1.5 million for 1952, and at $2.5 million for 1953,

47. Puerto Rico Planning Board, Office of the Governor, Bureau of Economics and Statistics, *Statistical Year Book—Puerto Rico, 1956* (San Juan), p. 342.
48. *Statistical Year Book, 1956,* pp. 300 f.

1954, and 1955, respectively.[49] During fiscal 1957 approximately 186,000 visitors to the island spent $20 million.[50]

In strong contrast to the situation in Puerto Rico at the end of World War II, when only a few hundred visitors could have been furnished with modern tourist facilities, today first-class hotel accommodations are available for 2,500 or more. The 300-room Caribe-Hilton Hotel, for example, now seems as much a part of San Juan as El Morro fortress. The opening of this luxuriously appointed hostelry in the winter season of 1949–50, and the subsequent response of vacationers, encouraged other new ventures. The visitor now has a wide choice of new hotels or renovated old ones, and of apartments, restaurants, and night clubs. The Caribe-Hilton was built with funds of the Puerto Rico Industrial Development Company (PRIDCO), with the Hilton Hotel Corporation as lessee and manager. PRIDCO is a 50-million-dollar corporate agency of the Economic Development Administration, set up chiefly to carry out the factory construction program.[51]

Despite the phenomenal manufacturing activity in Puerto Rico, agriculture is still the primary source of wealth. Sugar cane is the chief agricultural crop and recent production runs from 1,166,000 to 1,182,000 tons a year.[52] The United States is the island's best customer for agricultural products. In the 12-month period ending June 30, 1953, products of agriculture made up $167,000,000 of total exports to the United States valued at $310,000,000. Ever since Puerto Rico became a part of the economic system of the United States, local growers have benefited from American tariff legislation. Under the Sugar Act passed by Congress in 1934, the United States guaranteed purchases of stipulated quantities of sugar at prices higher than those in world markets. This measure, however, although

49. *Ibid.*, p. 265.
50. First National City Bank, *Puerto Rico*, p. 17.
51. Office of the Commonwealth of Puerto Rico, "Tourist Trade," *The Commonwealth of Puerto Rico* (Washington, October 31, 1954), p. 43.
52. U. S. Department of Agriculture, Foreign Agricultural Service, *Foreign Agricultural Trade-Statistical Handbook* (Washington, August, 1956) p. 272.

realizing its objective, namely the reduction of unemployment in the sugar industry, tends to discourage future expansion of output, because since 1953 productive capacity has been geared to annual quotas. For example, the allowable yearly shipment to the Mainland set for the 1957 season was 1,158,000 short tons, plus whatever was needed to satisfy local requirements— usually about 110,000 tons. Chiefly on account of damage caused by Hurricane Betsy during the 1956–57 crop year, which ended in July, 1957, Puerto Rico failed to meet its annual quota by approximately 250,000 tons.[53]

A problem which has faced Puerto Rican sugar growers and Commonwealth planning authorities is whether the sugar cane industry can prevail against foreign competition without mechanization and modernization. One of the deterrents to mechanization in sugar cane and in other agricultural industries is the fear of increasing unemployment.

Tobacco ranks second as an agricultural export, and like sugar gained tariff protection when Puerto Rico became part of the United States. Compared with large producers of tobacco Puerto Rico's industry is minor. In Puerto Rico about 40,000 acres produce 30 to 34 million pounds per harvest as compared with Cuba's some 154,000 acres and 109,900,000 pounds. Traditionally, Puerto Rico's tobacco has been a cigar-filler type, but other types of tobacco are being introduced. Cigar manufacturing on a large scale has been resumed, partly as a result of the government's program to attract new industry. Since 1944–45 the quantity of cigars consumed locally has exceeded in great degree the quantity exported. The United States takes most of the export, in 1954–55 valued at $4,591,884.

Coffee is Puerto Rico's third largest agricultural crop, but coffee growing has struggled against adverse conditions since 1900. Puerto Rican coffee is known for excellent flavor but low yields. In Spanish days coffee was a leading export, and was booming in 1895–97 when sugar production was low. After American occupation the industry lost its tariff-protected Euro-

53. First National City Bank, *Puerto Rico*, p. 5.

pean market, and was also set back by a hurricane. The industry had recovered sufficiently to enjoy relative prosperity during 1910–15, when World War I dealt it another blow. Recovery was again halted by a hurricane in 1928, followed by low prices in a competitive market. In recent years the industry has been aided by the Unified Coffee Program, supported by both the Commonwealth and the United States governments. Exports of coffee are customarily taken mostly by the United States. In 1954–55 the United States imported 2,189,211 pounds, valued at $1,542,273.[54]

Other agricultural exports include fresh and canned pineapples, and coconuts, sent mostly to the United States. Small quantities of vegetable crops have been exported to the United States. Sweet potatoes, cucumbers, tomatoes, and peppers are believed to have export possibilities.

54. *Statistical Year Book, 1956,* pp. 340 f.

15

Cornelius J. Griffin: ENERGY IN
CARIBBEAN PROGRESS

THE THEME OF THE CONFERENCE suggests that it
would be in order to discuss "Energy in Caribbean Progress"
with the term "Caribbean" being confined for the purposes of
this paper to the British, Dutch, French, and United States areas.
This is an important matter to Esso Standard, S.A., which I
represent. Therefore, first a word about who we are and what
we do. Standard Oil Company (New Jersey) has been selling
petroleum products in the areas under discussion for many
decades. At the beginning of 1952 we merged our operations in
most of the Caribbean area into the company I represent. For our
purposes we in effect merged 32 different political jurisdictions,
including the Bermudas and the Bahamas. This action obviously
has no political implications, but with the Federation of the
West Indies and the Organization of the Central American
States subsequently coming into being, we seem to have acted
in the spirit of the times.

Our area of operations includes British Honduras, Central
America, Panama, British Guiana, French Guiana, Surinam,
all of the Lesser and Greater Antilles, the Bahamas, and the
Bermudas. Note that Venezuela, Colombia, Curaçao, and
Aruba are not included; we have other affiliates who operate
in these areas.

We are a marketing, refining, transportation, and exploration

225

company. Marketing is our most important and extensive activity. We have a refinery in Cuba and presently have exploration parties at work in Cuba and Guatemala. We think of ourselves as suppliers of energy, and in our own minds we assume a responsibility for making this vital element of economic progress available in the quantity and quality needed at prices which will enable people to put machines to work for them at a maximum feasible level of utilization.

I. Significance of Energy Consumption

Returning to energy in Caribbean progress, I may appear to be uttering a truism when I say that energy is essential to progress. Strangely enough, however, it has only been in recent years that the relationship of energy consumption to progress has been recognized and clearly defined. In this context, progress actually means productivity to improve standards of living and to supply the increasing needs and wants of growing populations. All around us we see the effect of expanding use of energy in transportation, industry, farm mechanization, and the home.

When we look at the per capita energy consumption figures for most of the countries of the world, we invariably find that where per capita consumption of energy is relatively low, economic and social development are retarded—that is to say, that the standard of living is not high enough to satisfy a majority of the people.

When we convert the consumption of coal, petroleum fuels, and hydroelectric power into barrels of oil, we find that United States energy consumption is 43 barrels of oil per capita per year. Canada is second in the world with 40 barrels of oil per capita per year. The United Kingdom consumes the equivalent of 26 barrels per capita, France consumes 13 barrels, and The Netherlands 12 barrels per capita per year. In the areas under consideration, excluding Curaçao and Aruba, we find that energy consumption averages a little less than 3 barrels of oil per capita per year, exclusive of wood for which we do not have any reliable consumption data.

Before taking up the specific areas, I offer for better understanding some general considerations of their energy sources. First, there is no coal being mined in the British, Dutch, French, and United States areas. Oil is produced in only one place—Trinidad, which has a growing oil producing and refining industry.

Forests are a poor or improvident source of energy fuel in all but British Guiana, French Guiana, British Honduras, and Surinam. Wood and charcoal, however, are still burned for energy; but where necessary there are rigid controls to prevent further deforestation and subsequent soil erosion which destroys the productivity of the land.

Hydroelectric power has been developed in only two places—Jamaica and Puerto Rico. Solar and atomic energy are still in the future. This leaves the area dependent on petroleum for its most suitable energy fuel. With the exception of Trinidad, petroleum must be imported.

I mentioned earlier that my company thinks of itself as being a supplier of energy, and one can easily see now why this is so. One can see, too, why we think of this as a responsibility of considerable magnitude.

The people of the area are full of hope and ambition. By virtue of a number of stimuli, they have in recent years been stirred into determination to make a better life for themselves. How this is to be achieved—much has been achieved—depends greatly on the individual resources of each country and colony. These resources vary. In many places more intensive and diversified cultivation of the fruits of the soil appears to be the only way to progress. In other places development of mineral resources is producing substantial rewards with promise of more. Some are finding that industrial development can supplement traditional agricultural economies. By some, tourism is being intensively cultivated as a "money crop."

All this being true, then, the way to appraise the future of these areas is in terms of the progress they are making. In the oil business we derive our impressions of progress from the number of barrels of oil consumed this year as compared with last year and other years ago, because as already pointed out, oil is the chief source of energy, and energy consumption is a measure of progress. One will understand, then, why I talk of energy in terms of barrels of oil, not ignoring, of course, that wood, other vegetable fuels, and farm wastes are still a real, though diminishing, source of energy in all the Caribbean areas.

Oil consumption in most of the entities embraced in these areas is increasing at a rate faster than in the United States. This was not true immediately after World War II but it is true today—a fact which gives us an impression of accelerating progress.

In the ten years since 1947 consumption of petroleum in the four areas has increased at the average rate of 6.8 per cent per year. But in 1956 it increased 13.8 per cent over 1955, and we estimate an increase of 11.4 per cent this year over 1956. The 1957 increase over 1956 in the United States is estimated at 2.5 per cent and in Europe at 3.7 per cent.

II. British Areas

Now, let us consider the specific areas. There are great differences in the potentials of the colonies of this area, especially when we look at natural resources. Per capita consumption of energy is increasing substantially in Jamaica, British Guiana, and Trinidad, and our figures show very little increase in Barbados and the Windward and Leeward Islands colonies. In the past ten years oil consumption in Trinidad has increased 106 per cent, in Jamaica 400 per cent, and in British Guiana 168 per cent.

Stimulating factors in these countries are intensified agricultural production, encouraged by the British market, and natural resources development—bauxite in Jamaica and British Guiana

and petroleum in Trinidad. In Jamaica tourist trade is also
a stimulus.

The Windward and Leeward colonies have the lowest energy
consumption in the British area and, with Barbados, are advancing very modestly.

III. Dutch Areas

The Dutch area embraces Surinam and the Netherlands
Antilles, the chief islands of which are Curaçao and Aruba.
We are intentionally omitting comment on Curaçao and Aruba
as their economies and progress are so intimately associated
with large refining installations. Surinam is basically agricultural
in its economy, though there is a large bauxite mining operation.

Consumption of energy is constantly growing in Surinam
as reflected in a 179 per cent increase in oil consumption in
1957 over consumption in 1947 and an increase of 15 per cent
in 1957 compared with 1956.

Like British Guiana, Surinam has a substantial hydroelectric
power potential, and will shortly begin to develop it with construction of a dam and plant at Brokopondo to cost 57 million
dollars and produce a billion kilowatt-hours per year. Its chief
customer will be a new aluminum smelter with a capacity of
40,000 tons a year.

IV. French Areas

The French area embraces the Department of French Guiana
and the Departments of Guadeloupe and Martinique. Energy
consumption in these departments of metropolitan France is
not rising very fast, relatively speaking. In respect to Martinique
and Guadeloupe it would be a mistake, however, to say that
their agricultural potential, which is their mainstay by way of
sugar and bananas, has been completely developed.

French Guiana has undeveloped mineral and forest resources
of substantial measure, possibly equal to British Guiana or

Surinam. Bauxite reserves of adequate quantity and marketable quality have been proved up by the government geologists. The vast forest reserve has only been modestly exploited.

V. United States Areas

The United States area of the Caribbean includes Puerto Rico, a free associated state, and the Virgin Isles of the United States which were bought from Denmark in 1917. I will confine my comments to Puerto Rico which has developed, in its relations with the United States, a special personality as the only free associated state in the world.

In terms of oil consumption Puerto Rico is 104 per cent ahead of 1947, and according to our estimates will in 1957 use 9 per cent more oil than in 1956. When we compare this with a per capita increase in the national income from 271 United States dollars in 1946 to 421 dollars in 1956, we can see the relationship of energy consumption to standard of living.

VI. Appraisal of Energy Demand

Looking to the future of the areas under discussion, it is apparent that we have reason to be optimistic. Energy consumption is going to continue to increase in these areas just as long as the people persist in their all-out effort to improve their standard of living, because employment of energy of whatever kind is essential to the realization of their ambitions.

A highly efficient common form of energy is yet to be developed for man's use in the presently known instruments of utilization. For instance, only one-quarter of the potential energy in gasoline is utilized when it is exploded in the combustion chamber of an automobile engine. Nuclear fuels, more popularly known as atomic energy, are not yet highly efficient. As recently as September of this year a leading British specialist in application of nuclear fuels to production of electric power said their reactors could burn only one-third of 1 per cent of the uranium fuel. He expected this to be raised to 1 per cent in newer reactors.

Technicians in our organization expect that nuclear power will be carrying some 3 per cent of the total free world energy demand two decades hence. We do not look for this to reduce the demand for oil. We feel, rather, that the use of atomic energy for power generation and heavy industry in the areas where it will come into important use is more likely to enhance than diminish the demand for other energy sources. It does not seem likely that relatively small consumers of energy, such as the basically agricultural areas we are discussing, will find nuclear power economically practical within the near future. Industrial development will have some bearing on its feasibility.

Another source of energy, of course, is water for hydroelectric power, but the circumstances which make it usable are rather special. In the areas we are discussing, Jamaica and Puerto Rico draw energy from hydroelectric power. The potential elsewhere does not appear substantial, except in British Guiana and Surinam.

So we come back to petroleum which is widely available in all forms through a number of companies which compete intensely for the consumer's favor. The areas mostly use Trinidad or Venezuela oil refined in Venezuela, Trinidad, Aruba, Curaçao, or Puerto Rico.

Intensive and, in some cases, costly effort has been made to find oil in these areas. Extensive drilling has been done in Jamaica and Barbados with no positive result to date. Puerto Rico has been combed over many times by oil geologists and will be again, I am sure. British Guiana and Surinam have been examined and, I understand, a well-known company is right now negotiating for exploration rights in British Guiana. Unfortunately none of the exploration effort has produced any result to date; and I emphasize "to date," because with new techniques and ideas we are constantly finding oil in areas where it was believed to be nonexistent.

VII. Conclusion

For the future we see a continued growth in energy requirements in the areas under consideration. On the average we
believe this growth will continue at a higher rate than the growth
in the United States. The growth will vary widely in the areas,
being much greater in colonies or countries where mining and
industry are being developed. To satisfy this growth, we believe
that petroleum will be the principal energy source.

In reviewing the overall development planning in the areas
we are discussing, our observations lead us to the conclusion
that a sound and constructive approach is being utilized. These
plans include mining, industry, transportation, housing, schools,
electric power, agriculture, highways, public health, experimental
planting, education, and a thousand and one more things—all
being pursued to improve the local economy and increase the
standard of living which is the end objective of all of the
programs.

Energy is the essential key to this better living, for after
the dreaming, planning, and financing, effective realization relies
on energy. The areas are manifesting their progress by their
increasing demand for energy fuel.

16

Peter M. Stern: POPULATION FACTORS

PEOPLE ARE our greatest resource" is a frequently heard slogan in overpopulated countries. But people are only a potential resource, just as unmined minerals are only potential, in their contribution to the economy. In order to realize that potentiality, a country's population must be healthy and long-lived, educated and skilled, and endowed with land and capital in productive quantities and combinations. In short, it must be developed.

One of the dangers facing areas like the Caribbean which embark on new programs of economic development is that although production may be gradually increased, the mounting needs of a rapidly growing population will swallow up these gains as fast as they are made—leading only to the sustenance of a larger population on the old, meager level of existence.

Since population growth under certain conditions tends to retard the betterment of man's material condition,[1] this paper addresses itself to the demographic dilemma that confronts all of the dependent Caribbean areas (British, French, Dutch, United States) with almost equal urgency. It discusses the three variables—fertility, mortality, and migration—that are responsible for population movements, and it examines critically various measures aimed at slowing down the rate of population growth.

1. "First, it increases the pressure of numbers upon a nation's land and resource equipment as of any given time. Second, it tends to accentuate

I. Present Demographic Position

The present population of the Caribbean territories stands at
7 million, or twice the population of Florida. Crude densities
are high in the islands (Table I),[2] with Barbados' 1,400 per
square mile a near world record. If the United States had the
density of Barbados, it would contain over twice the population
of the planet. The mainland territories, on the other hand, with
less than 6 persons per square mile would fall in the "underpopulated" category but for the fact that most of the people
in the Guianas are crowded into coastal clusters, while the vast
interior remains almost uninhabited. Further, when "cultivated
area" is substituted for "total area" to give a more significant
man-land ratio for countries that are primarily dependent on
agriculture, then many of the Caribbean units show densities
of the order usually associated with urban concentrations.

Crowded as they are today, the Caribbean territories have
suffered from a chronic scarcity of people—at least in the eyes
of the ruling class—for the better part of their history. Neither
the slave trade of the eighteenth century nor the immigration of
indentured East Indians in the nineteenth century could satisfy
the needs of plantation owners or provide for much more than
a replacement of the population.[3] Thus the uncoiling of the
population spiral which we are witnessing today is a phenomenon
of the twentieth century. To be exact, it dates from the decade

---

this pressure through time by accelerating the rate at which the store of
exhaustible and non-replaceable natural resources is used up and the costs
of their use are increased. Third, it diminishes the rate at which capital
can be accumulated, and this diminution is greatly accentuated when, as is
the case in most overpopulated countries, much potential capital is utilized
in maintaining for a few years children who eventually die before they
reach a productive age. Fourth, given the rate of capital formation, the
rate at which the equipment of the labor force can be increased is reduced."—Joseph J. Spengler, "The Population Obstacle to Economic Betterment," *American Economic Review,* XLI, 2 (May, 1951), 350–351.

2. Tables are on pp. 238–241.

3. For an excellent summary of the region's demographic history, see
G. W. Roberts, "Some Demographic Considerations of West Indian Federa-
tion," *Social and Economic Studies,* University College of the West Indies,
Jamaica, VI, 2 (June, 1957), 262–269.

immediately following World War I. Census data for the British territories, where the longest uninterrupted record is available, are used to tell the story. In the 30 years *preceding* 1921 the population increased by less than 25 per cent; in the 33 years *following* 1921 it grew by 70 per cent, with a marked acceleration after 1946. In terms of annual increments the 1921–46 rate of growth was 1.4 per cent, while after 1946 it was much greater, 2.4 per cent.

Two factors are clearly responsible for this acceleration in the rate of population growth. The first is the control over an ever widening range of diseases, expressed in steep declines in mortality. The second is a continuation of high fertility. The way in which these factors complement each other to produce rising rates of natural increase in all of the Caribbean territories is illustrated in Table I.

This progressive swelling of annual population increments is often described as the acute phase of a region's demographic transition from a wasteful equilibrium of high fertility and high mortality towards a more efficient and lifesaving balance of low fertility and low mortality. If, then, we could be assured of steady progress towards the new, low-level equilibrium, we would look with confidence for an end of the population explosion.

In the Caribbean, however, there is as yet no appreciable evidence of declining birth rates,[4] while thanks to the spectacular successes of public health programs and the extension of medical services throughout the territories, death rates are now nearly equal to those of the metropolitan countries. Moreover, conspicuous reductions in infant mortality rates (Table I) are reflected in the ever widening base of the area's population pyramid. In Jamaica, for example, infant deaths declined from 127 per 1,000 live births in the late 1930's to 60 in 1955, a reduction of over 50 per cent.

The grafting of a Western mortality on populations with "young" age distributions and high fertility rates can only lead

4. The only evidence so far comes from Puerto Rico, where crude birth rates have fallen from about 42.2 in 1947 to about 34 in 1956.

to still higher growth rates in the future. With the probability that a death rate of 9 per 1,000 will be general within the next few years and with the prevailing fertility, the Caribbean is moving toward an annual rate of natural increase of the order of 3 per cent. Unless large-scale emigration intervenes, the region may thus look forward to a doubling of its population in less than the span of a generation.

II. Population Projections

A number of population projections prepared for the Conference on the Demographic Problems of the Area Served by the Caribbean Commission, held in July-August 1957, bear out this conclusion. The estimates up to 1970 and the assumptions on which they are based are presented in Table II. Three different projections have been prepared for the British territories; they foresee increases of 41 to 50 per cent for the period 1955–70. Even assuming emigration from the more crowded islands on a scale comparable to Jamaica's recent emigration experience to the United Kingdom (Table II), the British territories may have a 1970 population of 5 million, as compared with 3.5 million in 1955.

Puerto Rico alone among the dependent Caribbean territories is shown as reaching a stationary population level. It should not be concluded, however, that Puerto Rico is on the verge of balancing its fertility and mortality; rather, the projection assumes a movement to the mainland of 50,000 Puerto Ricans per annum through the 15-year period under scrutiny.[5]

The French and Dutch territories, whose projections are not as refined, and therefore not as useful as those of the British areas, also face the prospect of sizeable accretions to their populations with no downturn in the rate of natural increase in sight.

A population increase of 40 or 50 per cent within the next fifteen years means that there will be ever larger numbers of

5. This assumption, in turn, is predicted on a continuation of full employment in the United States.

potential workers for whom jobs will have to be created at considerable capital cost.[6] It also points to a growing strain on educational and welfare facilities as the number of school-age children increases.

III. Some Approaches to Population Control

With a record of high fertility and steeply falling mortality, with limited acreage of cultivable land and a shortage of capital to provide employment for a rapidly expanding labor force, the territories of the Caribbean can no longer postpone the search for new ways to alleviate the rising population pressure. Although there has been no conscious effort so far to formulate an integrated population policy within the Caribbean area, several approaches have been advanced from time to time for public discussion.[7] Three of these prospects—migration, industrialization, and fertility control—will now be examined for their potential effectiveness.

At different times during the recent history of the Caribbean, migration has played an important role in slowing down population growth in several of the densely settled islands. Between 1911 and 1921, for example, the outward movement of people to the United States and Latin America successfully retarded growth rates throughout the region. Again in 1955 the departure of thousands of Jamaicans for the United Kingdom took away

6. The vicious circle of poverty and overpopulation is such that the burden of dependent children precludes a larger rate of individual saving and thus of investment, which in turn is needed to provide equipment for new jobs and higher productivity per worker.

7. For example, Roberts, "Some Demographic Considerations. . . ," pp. 275–85; G. W. Roberts, *The Population of Jamaica* (Cambridge: The University Press, 1957), Chap. 9; Clarence Senior and Douglas Manley, *Jamaican Migration to Britain* (Kingston: Government Printer, 1955); H. D. Huggins, M. G. Smith, L. Braithwaite, G. E. Cumper, J. M. Stycos, and Arthur Brown, "Possible Solutions of Problems of Over-Population," Paper 3(d) prepared for the Technical Conference on the Demographic Problems of the Area Served by the Caribbean Commission, Port of Spain, Trinidad, July, 1957; J. M. Stycos, Kurt Back, and D. O. Mills, *Prospects for Fertility Reduction: the Jamaica Family Life Project, a Preliminary Report* (New York: The Conservation Foundation, October, 1957), mimeo.

TABLE I

POPULATION AND VITAL STATISTICS FOR THE DEPENDENT CARIBBEAN TERRITORIES

TERRITORY	(1) 1955 POPULATION ESTIMATE	(2) 1955 DENSITY (Number of inhabitants per square mile)	(3) CRUDE BIRTH RATE (Number of live births per 1,000 pop.) 1935-39 av.	(4) 1955	(5) CRUDE DEATH RATE (Number of deaths per 1,000 pop.) 1935-39 av.	(6) 1955	(7) RATE OF NATURAL INCREASE (Col. 3 less col. 5) 1935-39 av.	(8) (Col. 4 less col. 6) 1955	(9) INFANT MORTALITY RATE (Deaths of infants under 1 year of age per 1,000 live births) 1935-39 av.	(10) 1955
Federation of the West Indies										
Barbados	229,000	1,380	32.2	33.2	20.6	12.6	11.6	20.6	209.9	134.6
Jamaica	1,543,000	350	32.8	36.3	16.6	9.9	16.2	26.4	127.3	60.3
Trinidad	720,000	364	32.4	41.9	16.6	10.4	15.8	31.5	103.7	67.9
Antigua	52,000	306	34.6	33.1(a)	19.4	10.6(a)	15.2	22.5	....	63.3
Montserrat	14,000	424	31.7	30.0	14.4	12.1	17.3	17.9	116.8	116.8
St. Kitts-Nevis	54,000	355	32.8	46.2	21.3	12.3	11.5	33.9	....	67.4
Dominica	62,000	203	33.2	41.0	15.4	14.0	17.8	27.0	99.0	120.3
Grenada	88,000	662	36.0	44.4	17.2	13.7	18.8	30.7	104.7	76.0
St. Lucia	87,000	373	35.1	40.7	17.6	11.9	17.5	28.8	106.4	98.1
St. Vincent	76,000	507	39.9	47.5	16.2	14.5	23.7	33.0	116.3	118.1
British Territories outside of Federation										
British Guiana	485,000	6	32.5(b)	43.2(b)	21.9(b)	11.9(b)	10.6	31.3	129.7	70.3
British Honduras	79,000	9	35.3	43.6	21.1	10.9	14.2	32.7	139.9	99.3
Virgin Islands (Br.)	8,000	119	33.0(c)	40.5(a)	16.2(c)	10.0(a)	16.8	30.5	....	....

TABLE I *(Continued)*

POPULATION AND VITAL STATISTICS FOR THE DEPENDENT CARIBBEAN TERRITORIES

TERRITORY	(1) 1955 POPULATION ESTIMATE	(2) 1955 DENSITY (Number of inhabitants per square mile)	(3) CRUDE BIRTH RATE (Number of live births per 1,000 pop.) 1935–39 av.	(4) 1955	(5) CRUDE DEATH RATE (Number of deaths per 1,000 pop.) 1935–39 av.	(6) 1955	(7) RATE OF NATURAL INCREASE (Col. 3 less col. 5) 1935–39 av.	(8) (Col. 4 less col. 6) 1955	(9) INFANT MORTALITY RATE (Deaths of infants under 1 year of age per 1,000 live births) 1935–39 av.	(10) 1955
French Overseas Departments										
French Guiana	29,000	1	...	...	...	...	...	...	....	....
Guadeloupe	236,000	353	35.3(d)	40.2(e)	16.9(d)	12.4(e)	18.4	27.8	79.0	60.0
Martinique	244,000	634	36.9(d)	39.5(e)	21.7(d)	10.8(e)	15.2	28.7	....	53.0
Dutch Territories										
Netherlands Antilles	182,000	497(f)	33.7(e)	33.1(e)	10.9	5.1	22.8	28.0	83.8	20.3
Surinam (Du.Guiana)	254,000	5	30.9(e)	41.5(e)	12.4(e)	8.6	18.5	32.9	60.5(b)	36.0(b)
U.S. Territories										
Puerto Rico	2,264,000	659	39.1	35.0	19.1	7.2	20.0	27.8	122.9	55.0
Virgin Islands (U.S.)	30,000	227	29.3	30.8	20.0	10.7	9.3	20.1	127.0	48.2

Source: *Statistical Abstract to the Conference on the Demographic Problems of the Area Served by the Caribbean Commission.* Port of Spain, Trinidad: Caribbean Commission, July 1957.

(a) 1954 data
(b) excludes aborigines
(c) 1941 data

(d) 1946 data
(e) excludes live-born infants dying before registration

(f) the crude density of Curaçao is 676; that of Aruba, 812 per square mile

239

TABLE II

POPULATION PROJECTIONS FOR DEPENDENT CARIBBEAN TERRITORIES,* 1955–1970

(In thousands)

	BRITISH TERRITORIES Projections			PUERTO RICO	FRENCH ISLANDS Martinique & Guadeloupe	DUTCH TERRITORIES Neth. Antilles	Surinam
	I	II	III				
1955	3,513	3,513	3,513	2,264	480	182	254
1960	4,023	3,943	4,013	2,293	539	198	300
1965	4,594	4,409	4,541	2,290	611	217	366
1970	5,269	4,960	5,134	2,254	694	238	447
Projected population increase or decrease, 1955–1970	1,756	1,447	1,621	−10	214	56	193
Per cent increase, 1955–1970	50.0	41.2	46.1	negligible	44.6	30.8	76.0
Projected average annual rate of increase	3.3	2.7	3.1	negligible	3.0	2.1	5.1

Source: *Technical Conference on the Demographic Problems of the Area Served by the Caribbean Commission, Second Subject: Projections.* Port of Spain, Trinidad: Caribbean Commission, July 1957.

* Projections are not available for the Virgin Islands (U.S.) and French Guiana, but their combined 1955 population is less than 1 per cent of the region's total.

PROJECTION ASSUMPTIONS

British Territories: *Projection I* (high)—Assumes continued uniform decline in mortality, fertility constant at 1955 level, and no migration.

Projection II (low)—Assumes some mortality and fertility movements, supplemented by a steady emigration from the more densely settled islands to countries outside of the Caribbean on a scale derived from the Jamaican emigration experience of 1954.

Projection III (medium)—Assumes a transfer of population from the crowded islands to the settled mainland territories of the British Caribbean instead of abroad, as well as a smaller movement from Barbados to Trinidad; also assumes a modest decline in fertility (by 5 per cent within each quinquennium) predicted on the gradual spread of fertility control among the population.

Puerto Rico: *Mortality*—Puerto Rican age-specific mortality in 1975 approximately same as United States in 1953

Fertility—Puerto Rican age-specific fertility in 1975 approximately same as United States in 1953

Migration—50,000 annual migration to mainland distributed by age and sex according to total migration in 1953–55. The projection assumes that U. S. will continue to maintain a condition of near full employment under which Puerto Rican "marginal" labor will remain in demand.

French Islands: Mortality and fertility constant at 1952–53 level; no migration.

Dutch Territories: *Netherlands Antilles*—Mortality and fertility constant at "present level" (1956?); emigration of retired non-native oil industry workers at an accelerating rate. The projection assumes that the oil refineries will continue to be supplied with sufficient raw material to maintain current level of output until 1970.

Surinam—Continued decline in mortality at a rate of about 1 per cent per annum for ages 5 to 59, and a higher rate for ages below 5; continued rise in fertility at a decreasing rate; no migration.

43 per cent of the island's natural increase. And Puerto Rico's postwar experience with migration on a massive scale has given the island a "breathing spell" from population pressure that has been fully utilized to promote education and economic development. Puerto Rico's population would be larger by 25 per cent than it is today had not out-migration accounted for almost 500,000 persons or two-thirds of the total natural increase during the years 1946–56.[8]

But the negative aspects of migration must also be considered. In the Caribbean large-scale emigration has tended to deplete the most valuable segment of the sending territory's labor force at a time when skill and enterprise are crucial to local development. In Jamaica, for instance, the number of skilled workers lost through emigration in 1955 was more than twice the number of accessions to the ranks of these workers.[9] The accumulation of workers abroad with the danger of a return flow in the event of a recession in the receiving country is often cited as another negative function of migration.

In addition to external migration it has been frequently suggested that populations might be transferred from the crowded islands to the sparsely settled mainland territories of the Guianas. Estimates of the capital investment required to establish one new worker in an undeveloped area vary considerably, but all such estimates are many times the cost of emigrating to the United Kingdom in search of employment. Serious students of the British territories have therefore concluded that:

The strong abstract argument for transfer of population from the islands to British Guiana is in practice contradicted by the difficulty of opening up the hinterland . . . , by the lack among potential emigrants of the qualities needed for such a pioneer life and by the rapid current increase of the Guianese population.[10]

8. Clarence Senior, "Demography and Economic Development," paper delivered at the Economic Development Conference, University College of the West Indies, Mona, Jamaica, August, 1957, p. 26.
9. G. W. Roberts and D. O. Mills, "Study of External Migration Affecting Jamaica, 1953–55," unpublished manuscript.
10. Huggins *et al.,* "Possible Solutions . . . ," p. 9.

The same writers are equally realistic about prospects for new large-scale migrations to areas outside of the Caribbean *other* than the metropolitan countries: "The West Indian is objectionable on racial grounds to many of the countries which stand in theoretical need of settlers, while various practical and political difficulties cut him off from others."[11]

Industrialization *per se* is not a cause of population change. But over the past two centuries in the Western countries industrial development has induced not only a rise in production, but also the kind of social and economic changes that pave the way for voluntary limitation of fertility. The question before us, then, is whether the Caribbean territories can rely on industrialization and concomitant urbanization to provide a solution to their population problem.

In our search for an answer we are fortunate to be able to turn to a living case study within the region itself. Puerto Rico's mid-twentieth-century industrial revolution is known to many as "Operation Bootstrap." It should be noted, however, that Puerto Rico's unique advantages with regard to the availability of capital and the accessibility of the United States consumer market may limit the applicability of the island's recent experience to other territories. It is common knowledge that Operation Bootstrap has already resulted in a substantial increase in the island's output and living standards. The effects of industrialization on fertility levels, however, are not as clear-cut. Ten years is too short a time for slight changes in attitude to be *clearly* reflected in the statistical record.[12] Emigration, for instance, has certainly contributed to the modest decline that has been observed in both the crude birth rate and the age specific fertility of the female population in Puerto Rico; its effect has simply been to reduce the chances for mating of the female population staying on the island.

11. *Ibid.*

12. Fertility is a function of so many variables that it often becomes very difficult to determine the quantitative contribution of any specific factor affecting it, because it is impossible to hold all the others under adequate control.

Two other factors that bear on Caribbean fertility prospects must also be considered, for they may be instrumental in bringing about results different from those achieved in the West in the course of industrialization. First, we have some indication that the massive attack on certain diseases (with DDT on malaria and with penicillin on venereal disease), apart from its immense effect on the health and well-being of the population, is also the cause of a recent rise in fertility in many Caribbean territories. The possibility of a relationship between improvements in health and the levels of fertility remains an extremely important subject for study.[13]

The second factor that may have an effect on fertility contrary to that expected from a development program has to do with patterns of fertility that are peculiar to the Caribbean. On the basis of recent censuses, three types of family unions can be distinguished: the formally married, the common-law union, and the keeper relationship. All available studies seem to confirm that fertility is highest in the married and lowest in the least stable keeper relationship.[14] This pattern tends to make current overall fertility rates somewhat lower than they might otherwise be. Hence, any economic or social development that would pave the way for more stable unions would have a tendency to promote a rise in the level of the population's fertility. As Roberts put it:

For possibly with the rising standard of living, greater urbanization and improvement in social conditions that may follow industrialization, the idea of marriage as a binding element of family life may spread, and the general stability of the family unions increase.[15]

Thus it seems clear that in the Caribbean area any assumptions of imminent and inevitable declines in fertility as a result

13. Roberts, "Some Demographic Considerations . . . ," p. 282.
14. Roberts, *The Population of Jamaica*, Chaps. 8–9; Judith Blake, J. M. Stycos, and Kingsley Davis, *Family Structure in Jamaica: the Social Context of Reproduction*, to be published in 1958.
15. Roberts, "Some Demographic Considerations . . . ," p. 284.

of economic development must remain open to question, and that therefore the avenues for accelerating widespread acceptance of voluntary family limitation should be seriously investigated.

In assessing the chances for the adoption of family planning in the Caribbean we must consider, first, the attitudes of the population towards smaller families and their motivation to reach that goal, and second, the degree to which the means for family limitation are available in the area.[16]

It had been generally assumed in the past that Caribbean women desire as many children as possible, that they feel they must fulfill an ordained reproductive quota, or that they have no opinion as to desirable family size. A numer of recent studies of this question disclose how wrong were these assumptions.

In Puerto Rico[17] the average lower-income mother maintains that two or three children are the ideal number; in Jamaica,[18] three or four. Moreover, few women who have had at least this number desire more children, and virtually none want an unlimited number. While we must not overestimate the intensity of such desire for the smaller family, it is clear that the large family ideal is not a value which would seriously hamper the introduction of family planning.

With respect to the *economic* availability of the means for fertility control, only Puerto Rico fulfills the criteria of adequate supply, distribution, and price of birth control techniques.[19] Barbados and Jamaica have a few private clinics dispensing information and materials, but only a network of *public* facilities providing materials free of charge could effectively service the entire population.

16. This section is based on Huggins et al., "Possible Solutions. . . ." There is no information on the outlook for family limitation in the Dutch and French territories of the Caribbean because of their governments' official objection to birth control on moral and ethical grounds.

17. J. M. Stycos, *Family and Fertility in Puerto Rico* (New York: Columbia University Press, 1955), p. 243.

18. Stycos et al., *Prospects for Fertility Reduction* . . . , p. 49.

19. Free supplies of the more commonly used contraceptives are made available in 160 health units scattered over the island.

Effectiveness, furthermore, depends on the spreading of information. In order to use the facilities, the public must have at least a rudimentary knowledge of birth control techniques and their availability at the clinic. In Jamaica, for example, most women are not even aware that methods of contraception exist; and they tend to associate "birth control" with abortion, a practice that meets with almost universal condemnation. This shows that a sustained educational effort is a prerequisite to an effective program of family planning in the Caribbean.[20]

Inevitably such a program will be expensive. It needs to be "tailor-made" for each territory, even for each segment of the population. This requires research, training of case workers and nurses, and an investment of capital funds. But compared to the cost of providing for the yearly arrival of 250,000 new Caribbean citizens, to the cost of mass population transfers to the empty lands of the Guianas, or even to the construction of new medical, welfare, and educational facilities, a fertility control program would seem a bargain indeed.

20. An experimental educational program was carried out in Jamaica in 1957 under the auspices of The Conservation Foundation. Pamphlets, discussion meetings accompanied by an educational film, and case work methods were tried out. Two major conclusions stand out: (1) an educational program in the area of fertility control meets with little community resistance; and (2) a sustained educational program can be assured of considerable success in promoting family planning.

Roland Dennis Hussey: HISTORICAL FACTORS

ANY VERY BRIEF EXAMINATION of three centuries of the history of the present Caribbean dependencies must necessarily generalize so sweepingly as to cast doubt upon the validity of any conclusions. Some two dozen islands and the mainland Guianas differ greatly in size, in geological and geographical character, and in the systems under which they have been governed. (British Honduras would introduce another type of colony but has been little considered in this conference. Its basic geographic and population problems are different from, though not smaller than, the others.) Loosely they fall into two groups, the old "sugar islands" and Trinidad, Puerto Rico, and the Guianas. Those in the second group are much the larger, and they have always had important bases for life other than sugar. Jamaica is a "group" all by itself, a cross between the other two types. Nevertheless, the dependencies as a whole have a broadly similar pattern of life, and it is not more inaccurate to ascribe that pattern to all the area than to talk about an "American" pattern of life for the United States. The difference between Massachusetts and the Ozarks, or Florida and Idaho, is much too striking to be used as a comparison; the Caribbean dependencies probably differ no more than do, say, Florida and California. And a historical approach is always valuable, however summary. It can give a better basis for evaluation

247

of either good or bad than is afforded by several surveys of
current conditions, and it can bring out more clearly than has
been easily possible for those surveys that there is much more
than an economic or a recent problem involved. The dependencies are not mere laboratory specimens today for the rational
experimentation of social scientists and devoted civil servants.
They are boiling cauldrons of human miseries and resentments
likely to blow their lids off at any careless stoking of the heat.
An examination of resources, population, and pattern of life
for the period from the seventeenth to the early twentieth
century shows why. It adds up to a pretty discouraging background.

I

The resources of the dependencies were and are limited. Nearly all the islands are small in area and very rugged of relief, with
even less agricultural land than appears to exist if one checks
merely square miles. Much of what remains under forest, even
in the three large islands, would not easily be reclaimed for
farming; and the great expanses in the Guianas are poor soil
for almost any purpose, being apparently mostly laterites. Iron,
coal, and copper are unknown, and such mineral resources as
bauxite, oil, asphalt, sulphur, or lime phosphate were largely
unknown, or if known unvalued, until recently. The water
supply varies sharply, but contrary to what is often supposed
merely because the areas are in the tropics, rainfall is often
deficient, and a few of the smaller units lack ground water.
Students have "proved" in recent years, no doubt correctly,
that a tropical climate need not lead to physical or moral deteri-
oration, but no one who has ever lived in the southern Caribbean
is likely to question that it is at least enervating.

The population of the present dependencies also got off to a
bad start. The planters were a pretty materialistic lot in themselves. So far as they lived upon sugar, they lived also by
slave labor until the mid-nineteenth century, and the Negro

population vastly outnumbered the whites. Only Puerto Rico was, as it still is, a big exception as to Negro dominance. (Bermuda and the Bahamas were about half and half at the end of the eighteenth century, but they are hardly relevant here.) It seems likely that even in the early nineteenth century a great proportion of the field Negroes had either been born in Africa or were only a generation or two removed from it. About 1777 the Frenchman Romanẹt (*Voyage à la Martinique* [Paris, 1804]) noted that "Of all the generating beings either savage or civilized—except the elephant, which does not mate in the state of slavery—the negro slaves are the only ones that do not reproduce themselves." His comment was more picturesque than most, but many other witnesses testify that slaves had steadily to be reinforced from Africa under the conditions of work on the island plantations. And however close or far their African ancestry, in America they necessarily learned to live on very little and to have very little ambition. The potential of this Negro population was low when it had to adapt to nineteenth-century freedom. No competent anthropologist, ethnologist, sociologist, or psychologist today questions the Negro's ability to live in the same manner, and with the same aims and capacities, as the white man. The degree of advancement made long before general emancipation by freed persons of color in many of the islands shows the possibilities. But neither would those scholars nor any historian question that it takes a long time to change the whole ethos of a "people" even under the best of conditions. Such conditions would include being a minority dispersed among people of a superior culture and being offered full opportunity, education, and encouragement. It scarcely needs saying that conditions were in fact almost the exact reverse.

The pattern of life developed during the first two centuries was also "bad" from the viewpoint of the present. Safety and security were not good domestically, and they were worse as to foreign dangers. Only Barbados can claim never to have been under more than one nation's control. Wars and privateers, buccaneers and pirates (not the same thing, but equally uncomfortable neighbors), and contraband traders were a constant source of peril and disturbance, with five major claimants to overlapping territories. (There were eight claimants from 1698-1700, and from 1784 to 1878 Sweden made it six, not to mention the disturbing interpositions of the United States.)

Domestic life was economically highly developed on the sugar islands, but also highly specialized, narrow, or "distorted" from what would later be a norm. Basically the plantations produced sugar which was sold abroad for everything else needed, doing so often for absentee landlords. Any of the islands might produce cacao, or spices, or tobacco, or indigo, or cotton, or subsistence foodstuffs; and Jamaica, Puerto Rico, and Trinidad were notable for cattle and hides. Any other economic activity was very limited. Low priced, low quality food processing, including brewing and crude sugar refining, and some leather and wood work or blacksmithing might go on, but only on a small scale and for local use. Professional men were few, and even merchants were likely to be agents of houses in Europe or England or New England or the Middle Colonies. Productiveness was high for the sugar islands, though low elsewhere. But everywhere the proceeds were badly distributed from the modern viewpoint, and production was wastefully achieved. The soil was exhausted by poor techniques; the planters were wildly extravagant, careless about their accounts with their agents overseas, and increasingly in debt.

Other aspects of life were poorly developed. Everywhere there was a small upper class, a large lower class, and practically no middle class, with the legal stratification very sharply held to because of the tendency of class lines to coincide with color lines and because of well-grounded fear of revolt by the Negro and mulatto group. There was no real self-government except in the English colonies, and there it was representative only of the planter class. Intellectual and esthetic activities were on a low level or nonexistent. There was no higher education anywhere on an organized basis until Codrington College opened in 1745 in Barbados, and no printing until Robert Baldwin came to Jamaica, probably from England, in 1718. As for religion, it is worth noting that there was no bishop anywhere in the present dependencies except in Puerto Rico, although the bishop was the main source of inspiration and discipline for both clergy and parishioners. The clergy everywhere tended to be poorly trained, worldly, or lax, if not European misfits or outright immoral. Their flocks were scarcely good even in outward observances, and certainly not in doctrinal training or personal morals. The Negroes of course were even worse from the Christian viewpoint. Many of them were supposedly Christian, but even they had adopted their new religion largely as a veneer upon their native obeah, ophiolatry, and fetichism.

The whole picture of West Indian life in the first two centuries sums up to one of a disorderly, violent, materialistic, crude, and sometimes cruel type of life. Planters might enjoy a good deal of rude luxury, and there were many exceptions as to the character of individual people. But on the whole and to say the best, one finds in it little training in self-discipline and little reaching for the stars. It is summed up, even if somewhat maliciously, by Leslie in his *History of Jamaica* (London, 1740), in words that apply as well, except for detail, to areas other than Jamaica. They have plenty of support in Father Labat's picture of the French West Indies about 1700, or in that of Abad y Lasierra on Puerto Rico at the end of the century. To abbreviate Leslie and change a word or two for the reader's ease:

In the towns there are several houses which are of two stories, but that way of building is disapproved of, because they are seldom known to stand the shock of an earthquake, or the fury of a storm. The negroes have nothing but a parcel of poor miserable huts built of reeds, any of which can scarce contain upwards of two or three.

The common dress here is none of the most becoming. The heat makes many clothes intolerable, and therefore the men generally wear only thread stockings, linen shorts and vest, a handkerchief tied round their head, and a hat above. . . . The negroes go mostly naked, except those that attend gentlemen, who take care to have them dressed in their own livery. . . .

The morning habit [of the ladies] is a loose negligee, carelessly
wrapped about them; before [afternoon] dinner they get out of
their dishabille, and show themselves in all the advantage of a
becoming, rich neat dress. . . .

Learning is here at the lowest ebb. There is no public school
in the whole island. . . . The office of a teacher is look'd upon
as contemptible, and no gentleman keeps company with one of
that character. To read, write, and cast up accounts is all the
education they desire, and even these are but scurvily taught.
. . . There are indeed several gentlemen here that are well
acquainted with learning . . . but these are few. . . . To talk
of a Homer, or of a Virgil, . . . is quite impolite. And it cannot be otherwise, for a boy till the age of 7 or 8 diverts himself
with the negroes, acquires their broken ways of talking, their
manner of behaviour, and all the vices these unthinking creatures
can teach. Then perhaps he goes to school. But young master
must not be whipped; if he learns 'tis well; if not, it can't be
helped. . . .

The ladies read some, dance a great deal, coquet much, dress
for admirers, and at last, for the most part, run away with the
most insignificant of their humble servants. *Their* education
consists entirely in acquiring these little arts. . . .

The farther one goes into detail about the period before 1815,
the clearer it becomes that it furnished a poor background for
living by the ideas of the more peaceful, orderly nineteenth
century, devoted to individual freedom and to something other
than material ends. It failed especially to develop the social
unity or certain abilities—those of an educated electorate and
tested leadership—needed if the islands were to run their own
affairs or even to meet their own economic and technical needs.
Another problem existed which has not been prepared for in
earlier parts of this discussion, and has never been much studied.
But it is implicit in all the records of the period that the dependencies lacked capital of their own, which they would need
if they wanted to, or had to, develop an independent basis for
their economic life. Slaves obviously would have no habit of
thrift. Neither had the planters. Yet an expert rule of thumb

today would require savings of *at least* 10 per cent for normal development in a rising population, and more surely would have been required in that earlier period when business risks and normal interest rates were higher.

II

The nineteenth and early twentieth centuries may have improved the above rather gloomy picture for the future. To contemporaries conditions seemed to be, and probably were in many ways, worse.

New forces and factors had entered the picture from the later eighteenth century, and they created a new political and economic situation for the Caribbean. New nations in America (the United States, Haiti, Latin America aside from Cuba and Puerto Rico) offered examples of freedom and of at least proclaimed democracy. The United States, long before it was a world power, was an important political and trading entity in the Caribbean. Into the bargain, European trade with Spanish America, which had passed through the West Indies while legally barred from the Spanish colonies, now went direct to the new States, to the loss of the West Indies. Ideologically the appearance of the new nations was accompanied by a wave of exciting new doctrines: liberalism, egalitarianism, humanitarianism.

Aside from the above, both the economic situation of the West Indies and the status of slavery in general were changing. There was still a little virgin land, especially in Jamaica, Trinidad, Puerto Rico, and the Guianas; but in general land fertility was far declined throughout the dependencies. At the same time competition became serious for the old island monopolies. Partly that came from the development of the sugar beet—a less efficient but temperate-zone source of sugar—and from the free trade doctrines of the nineteenth century. (British sugar could not compete with French sugar even in the eighteenth century, except for the protection of the Empire laws.) In addition,

areas which failed to shut off the importation of slaves as
early as did some of the others, benefited greatly. Louisiana and
Cuba took over important segments of the sugar market; and
first Brazil, then the United States with plentiful slave labor
plus the cotton gin, took over the brief tenure of the West Indies
as the chief supplier of the British textile mills. As for slavery
itself, opposition grew steadily from the later eighteenth century.
The slave trade was legally ended by Denmark in 1792, by
Britain and the United States in 1808, by Sweden in 1813, by
the Netherlands in 1814, by France in 1818, by Spain in 1820,
and by Portugal in 1824. (There was, as is well known, much
evasion of the laws, as in Brazil, the United States, Cuba, and
Puerto Rico.) The resulting attrition in numbers and a general
trend in favor of voluntary manumission were producing an
effect upon the number of slaves long before slavery was legally
abolished. (Curiously enough, Dutch law tried, though without
much success, to discourage manumission.)

Since the background factors were similar for all the dependencies, it is not strange that their history during the nineteenth century shows common trends. One of these was the
decline and final end of slavery. As has just been said, the
decline began with favor for manumission, including gradually
effective laws providing for free births. Abolition so evidently
would create serious problems in so many fields that even sincere
advocates might hesitate, and emancipation laws usually tried
to set up a gradual process with provision for a period of "apprenticeship" for the freed slave and some sort of indemnification
for the former owner. Slaves often had cause to be suspicious
of the good faith of the *baas* class, and often became so without
cause, from misunderstanding or mere impatience. Violence, or
the threat of it, therefore marred the period. It often speeded
up the final measure, but it left behind, or at least revealed,
class and race tensions of an ugly sort. The finally effective
laws for the English colonies were dated 1833–38, for the
French, 1845–48, for the Danish West Indies, 1848, and for
the Dutch, 1863. Spain promised the end of slavery for her

Antilles in 1869, but did not make this effective in Puerto Rico until 1873, and later in Cuba.

Another common trend was the decline of the West Indian plantation system. Emancipation undoubtedly was one cause, but one among many. At least as important must have been the soil exhaustion, the changed markets, the growth of free trade, and the lack of capital noted earlier; and it is easy to believe that an inflexibility of the planters' minds was as important as anything else.

Nevertheless, some efforts were made to overcome a major problem: the shortage of labor. It must be remembered that the newly freed men had become used to living on very little and to producing with considerable skill most of that little on small patches of land in their "spare time." In the larger islands they could get land for themselves after emancipation, simply by squatting, and were not necessarily deprived elsewhere of the plots of their slave days merely because they became free. They saw little purpose in long days of steady sweating toil in the fields simply for what would now be called a slightly higher standard of living. The use of apprenticeship laws in connection with emancipation was part of the effort to find an answer to this, but necessarily was only a temporary expedient. A French decree of February 13, 1852, required work of all who lacked a proper *livret*. But this sort of thing fostered social unrest and was offensive to "liberal" sentiment in the mother countries, however reasonable it seemed to the planters in the colonies. An effort to attract white labor, which began even before emancipation, failed to solve the problem, and probably it would have done so even had there been no Canada, United States, Australia, Argentina, or Brazil in competition for land-seeking immigrants. Britain, France, and the Netherlands therefore turned to Asia. A cargo of Hindus from Calcutta reached British Guiana even in 1838. Such migration was soon banned, but was legalized again in 1845. The enormous Indian migration into both British Guiana and Trinidad that has so changed the demographic makeup of those areas followed. Some Chinese appeared about the same time. Jamaica also tried Asiatic labor, but to a less degree. The French tried Asiatics also from 1853. There were 16,000 Indians in Martinique alone in 1870, and large groups arrived there or elsewhere, along with some Chinese, in the 1880's. The Dutch brought to Surinam many Chinese from 1853 to about 1870, and many Asiatic Indians from 1873 to 1916 (when India forbade the trade) and some Indonesians in the later period. These Asiatics proved a good solution for the labor shortage, but they created or reinforced many other problems.

Nothing really could save the old plantation system. More and more land went untilled. More and more owners sold for what they could get and retired to the mother country. The Great Houses decayed, empty, in sun and rain; wind and water mills creaked to a stop; irrigation ditches broke down; and a distinctive pattern of human life slowly disappeared. Lands were taken over for subsistence, and the names of new men rose to prominence of such sort as was possible under the new conditions. The process of course was gradual and varied with the island and nationality. French Guiana was still, apparently, a prosperous plantation society when its gold rush of 1853 stripped its plantations of labor. As late as the agricultural report of the West Indian Royal Commission of 1938 land in most of the British West Indies was classified as being still two-thirds in "estates" and one third in "peasant holdings." (Size was only one basis for classification, although important.) In St. Kitts, Montserrat, and Barbados practically all land was in "estates." Only the British Virgin Islands had no "estates," but these were also less numerous in British Guiana than in the old sugar islands. It is known from other sources that at least in Jamaica, being unable to sell their lands for enough to clear their debts and go home to England, the less successful planters stayed on perforce, tended to intermarry with the leading families of the small but often very able bourgeois, or middle, class that had arisen even in the later decades of the slavery era, and settled down to a patriarchal existence usually as cattlemen. Their descendants might have some distant color stain, but they still were living in the Big House. When good studies are someday made for all the islands of all the nations, we may well find that more of the land remained under the old holders, and more of the old families retained a semblance of their old social status, than has been supposed. Certainly sugar is still widely the major crop.

Another common trend centered in the mother countries' changing relations to their colonies. That the latter lost their high status in the minds of statesmen is obvious. (Admittedly other than domestic West Indian factors were involved, including the unremitting insistence of the United States upon hegemony in the Caribbean and the greater opportunities seen by the European powers in Africa and Asia.) Great Britain finally backed down before the United States even in Central America, by a series of treaties with the Central American nations, 1858–60, although she adroitly safeguarded British Honduras in her dealings with Guatemala. About the same time she revised downward her defenses of the West Indies, and James Froude records that about 1870 at least some statesmen had become so disgusted with the whole problem of the islands that they were considering setting them adrift. In 1867 Denmark failed to sell her Virgin Islands to the United States only because the United States Senate refused to ratify the treaty. Denmark made several more offers before success in 1917. In 1878 Sweden did get out from under by selling St. Barts to France.

Meantime the home governments had been struggling with adjustments of the old colonial system. Part of the adjustments were toward better administration as such by the introduction of a colonial civil service and other devices. Part concerned taxes or trade. Much was as to form of government itself. Previous papers have mentioned enough details on that. Perhaps it will suffice here to point out that changes in the system or its administration were aimed primarily at keeping control from the hands of the newly emancipated class. For most of the mother countries this is not too easily to be proved since control had always rested in the mother country. But for Great Britain it meant even the sacrifice of the old and prized autonomous government of Jamaica (1866) and of all the other islands, except Barbados, in the next generation. A concomitant attempt at federation for the Windward Islands (1879–1885) broke down, partly because of lower class suspicion of both government's and planters' motives.

One final common trend must be observed, from the later nineteenth century and increasingly in the twentieth: an honest, if too small, effort to improve the living conditions and personal lives of the lower (mostly colored) classes. In part this came from sincere idealists in the mother countries, in part from the force of world events, in part from outright fear of the consequences if improvements were not made. Land distribution either by tolerating squatters or by positive policy of the government, better educational opportunities, programs of social welfare and health, and admission to the civil services were all part of the story, everywhere. They achieved useful results, but it must unfortunately be added that they were "given" to the people, not "earned" by them, so that a connection between merits and benefits was not made clear. Worse than that, the health program led to the explosion of population that is perhaps the most critical of present day problems, and the educational opportunities promoted or speeded the appearance of a few great leaders and of very many who were not great. Some for good motives, and some for other, have led a demand for genuine self-government, for control of their own lives, long before the people could possibly be ready to stand alone.

III

All of the above adds up to the statement that by around the 1920's the conditions had all come into being—at least, all the Caribbean ones—that are the basis of the problems and the reforms of the present day. And one is inclined to say that there are far more problems than solutions, though we have been hearing about attempted solutions at this conference for three days. The human problems include the laziness and lack of thrift and ambition that may, as some people have thought, be a "Negro" problem, but can as well be explained as a carry-over from slave and sugar days and from centuries of malnutrition. Resources that were always scanty have become worse than ever, so far as the islands still depend upon the soil. (And despite such things as oil or bauxite in some areas, they mostly do so depend.) The soil is exhausted, and yet it must support more people. The total acreage—not total arable acreage, which may be only half or a quarter as much—even at its best as in Guadeloupe or Jamaica is today only two acres per person; Martinique, Puerto Rico, and others have about one acre to one person; Barbados has two persons to each acre! Even were the soil the black land of the central Mississippi Valley, what sort of life could be supported on that basis?

So one will introduce industry? If so, he must also import raw materials and the sources of energy, and he must have a supply of highly skilled and hardworking labor and of capital. New England, which never had much natural resources, lived for a long while because its great thriftiness and its amazingly adaptable and skilled labor enabled it to pay the price needed for raw materials and energy, but New England has been in trouble for two generations as skills and capital became common elsewhere. Britain, which for a long time had raw materials as well as capital and skills, has been trying to get along chiefly on the last two for the last generation and has been increasingly in trouble all that while. And finally, the capital needed in the West Indies can come only from outsiders, whether or not the outsiders belong to the same national family. The desire of investors to have profits and therefore some control over their investment has aroused enmity even among people who are not strongly divided into creditor and debtor classes which coincide with color classes. In the West Indies it would rouse, even without demagogic incitement, violent emotions over "colonialism" and over "racism." The latter has been too little mentioned in this conference; it is one of the most powerful moving forces in the world today.

One must be pessimistic, but one does not want to be hopeless. The presently forming British West Indian federation can help by pooling resources. (For that reason, relatively well-off areas like Jamaica, which fear that it may mean for them pooling poverty, are being stand-offish.) But there is no great precedent in confederation for the other national areas, for there have been greater barriers to French or Dutch colonial migration to their respective Guianas than have been suspected. Continued subsidies from the mother countries, even if in the form of preferential taxes or import quotas, might be a less emotional form of "loan" than one involving bonds and contracts. But the mother countries need subsidies themselves! Emphatically there are no utopias or paradises just around the corner.

One simply must not overlook the fact that the two shining examples of improvement in the last generation, Puerto Rico and the Dutch West Indies, are not standing on their own two feet. Admirable as is the plan and well performed as is the work that has been done under the remarkable leader Luis Muñoz Marín in Puerto Rico, the plan is based upon an enormous hidden subsidy: capital and managerial know-how from the United States can there dodge the savage taxation of the United States and sell their products in the United States market as domestically produced goods. As for the Dutch West Indies, though one does not doubt that their thrifty merchants make the most of Curaçao's fine harbor, the prosperity comes from Venezuelan oil exploited by American capital. Venezuela has already "persuaded" the oil companies involved to agree not to *expand* the islands' share of the business, and one would be unwise to assume that those islands' prosperity can continue indefinitely even on the present basis.

Emphatically such hopeful prospects as there are will require a long, hard, patience-taxing pull for achievement. And that raises the biggest question of all: will or can the "people" (the "under-privileged" or the "masses") wait to learn all the things that

they have to learn before they can run their own affairs satis-
factorily, or will they ruin the hope that they have by impatience for their pie-in-the-sky, or by a natural but too great
suspicion of their present off-island controllers and guardians?
Anyone worried about the answer to this question is not necessarily suggesting that they will be less rational than the rest of
mankind, but only the fear that they may not be more rational.

Rexford G. Tugwell: THE CARIBBEAN COMMISSION: NOTES ON ITS BEGINNINGS

SINCE THIS IS AN OCCASION for surveying the situation in the whole of the Caribbean, it has seemed to me appropriate to look back at the beginnings of the institutions we now have and the conditions out of which they arose. In the last two decades the relationships between the former colonies and their metropolitan governments have been drastically altered; and the relationships between the peoples themselves have been appreciably changed.

Two events of world-wide importance shook the Caribbean in recent times—the Great Depression and the Second World War. The first of these brought disaster and misery at first, but its results were so inhuman that steps for relief were finally taken. The second had the effect, curiously enough, of drawing the island peoples closer together and even of setting up a certain institutional cooperation. There is a long history of linkings between the islands and mainland cultural and market areas. This has often served to keep even the closest neighbors separated. Peoples only a few miles apart often have fewer contacts with each other than they do with European or North American ports and capitals. There has been a certain change in this respect. I think it might be interesting to recall for this generation some of the adventures of those who dreamed of change and helped to bring it about.

262

I

There are two characters, now both of them dead, whose work ought not to be forgotten. Many others helped them, as I did, but the rest of us were always secondary. I refer to Charles W. Taussig and Sir Frank Stockdale. Let me tell you a little about them and about what they did. They would, I suppose, be called minor statesmen and rate no more than a short footnote in the histories of their respective nations. Yet such integrity and determination used in the interest of those who were themselves helpless offers an example of noblesse raised to a very high degree. Neither was very adventurous, although each had a lively intelligence; but each arrived at a firm conclusion concerning his country's duty and did what he could to see that it was fulfilled. Neither had any political ambitions. One was a fine example of the technical civil servant; the other was a businessman using his knowledge and talents to further a wholly selfless ideal.

I knew Charles Taussig much better than Sir Frank Stockdale. In government and business I was associated with Taussig for many years; Sir Frank came to the Caribbean late in life and had his headquarters in Barbados. I met him rather often and we had many interests in common—notably agriculture—and these led us from acquaintance into friendship. Taussig, he, and I made three in the early days of the Caribbean Commission. There were other members who came to be friends too. But none made the lasting impression that Charles and Sir Frank have left with me.

We came together in most unhappy circumstances; we worked together at problems we never succeeded in solving; and we were separated from the work we cared so much about in quite different ways. But I find in my recollections of our service together a genuine satisfaction. We did what we could, each in his own way, to make life better for the people of the Caribbean.

You will perhaps recall what the circumstances were. There

had been unrest throughout the islands in the thirties. The Great Depression had borne very hard on that part of the world. Sugar and the other products of the region had become, quite literally, about as cheap as dirt. And since the outside world was depended on for much of the food supply, not much food could be bought. In fact the economies of all the islands were at an incredibly low level. This finally revealed itself, as was inevitable, in desperate protests. In 1935–37 there were riots of almost insurrectionary violence in the British islands, and in the others the protests were almost as serious. In Puerto Rico, in spite of New Deal relief efforts, there were similar incidents aimed at authority.

But it was not only the Depression which was at work. People were demanding much more than bread and clothing. They wanted political and economic rights which had too long been withheld. They were exasperated with a closely guarded governing class which refused to open the way to advance. They associated their ills with the support of their oppressors in Washington, in London, and in the other capitals. Even the liberals there seemed not to sympathize with their demand for the kind of liberties and privileges Americans and Europeans had long ago won for themselves.

Within the next decade or two this would all be changed. Now there is not a single government that has not been more or less democratized; there is not a single home government that does not grant Caribbean peoples the same status as their fellow nationals. And there is full or substantial self-government everywhere. Very seldom in the world's history has there been a peaceable transformation of comparable rapidity and depth. When I speak of Taussig and Stockdale, I speak of individuals who contributed measurably to this transformation by a constant constructive partisanship. But they were also responsible for setting in motion, or helping to set in motion, other devices, agencies, and plans which had the effect of transforming economic life. If there has been a political renaissance since the late thirties, the economic changes have been equally striking.

Nothing that has happened during these striking years was outside the lines laid down in the earliest anticipations of Taussig and Stockdale; and there is yet more to come that I recall them to have appraised and judged necessary. When the riots of the thirties were only recently past and no real changes had yet taken place, the war disrupted all the planning and created new emergencies. There had to be plans not only for the far future but also for meeting the exigencies of present commercial chaos and blockade. It may be that the Caribbean Commission might not have been authorized if it had not been for the war. I have heard that said by those who wanted it to disappear when the war was over. But I do not believe this to be so. Taussig intended to create it; his campaign in that interest was determined and intensive; and he soon enlisted Stockdale. Its first deliberations and duties were determined by the needs of war; but the long-run problems were never forgotten. While the war was still going on, meetings and investigations of wholly peacetime problems were being undertaken. The agenda of our meetings showed remarkably little connection with the war, as we survived the first months; the war, after that, might almost as well not have been going on. For Taussig knew, as Stockdale did, that the deeper problems of the Caribbean had nothing to do with the battles then in progress. They required to be solved in any case. The Commission was invented to solve them.

II

What Taussig had to go on was observation and experience. He was a sugar merchant, and his business had taken him to Barbados, St. Vincent, St. Kitts, Nevis, and the other islands very often since his early youth. He had seen the West Indies put at a disadvantage by the subsidizing of sugar cultivation in Europe; he had seen the area fall behind both politically and economically. The planter and merchant classes were conservative and slow to change; the workers were not advancing with others elsewhere in the world.

Sir Frank Stockdale was an agricultural expert. Long before
I knew him I had kept a textbook for which he had been largely responsible on my desk for reference. His experience had been
in the East; but if you will look at a globe you will see that
Ceylon, where he worked so long, is almost directly opposite
the West Indies. It has much the same climate, much the same
vegetation, and therefore many of the same problems. There
could hardly have been a better choice for the Comptrollership
of the Development and Welfare Funds.

That fund, established in 1940, was the result of recommendations made by a Royal Commission—the so-called Moyne
Commission—set up to investigate the causes of the prevailing
unrest in the British islands. It will be noted that the commission did not report and the fund did not become operative until
after the beginning of the war. Because of this its findings were
not published. The enemy would have found in them rich
material for propaganda. But the contents were well enough
known. And the recommendations reversed the traditional
colonial policy in several respects. The most important of these
was that the island treasuries should no longer be required to
produce surpluses, but might depend on outside help, especially
for welfare services. And a special fund for this purpose and for
development was voted by the Parliament.

In that same year, the West Indies began to have a new
meaning for the United States. President F. D. Roosevelt had
more geographical sense than many of his political contemporaries. And when he approached the British with the suggestion
that bases on the various islands were essential to continental
defense and the destroyer-bases deal was concluded in September
of 1940, he was acting on lessons learned long ago from Mahan
and other geopoliticians. But it had not occurred to him to look
into the condition of the people in whose midst the bases would
be placed. It was Charles Taussig who asked him whether it
was not important to see that the installations were accepted as
a friendly rather than a hostile move by the United States.

As a result of this question and the obvious answer to it,

Taussig was asked to visit the various islands and report. This he did in the fall of 1940. His terms of reference are reminiscent of emergencies now happily past. That, if you will recall, was a season when there was real question whether Britain would survive. And one of the possibilities was that a new disposition might have to be made of the Caribbean islands belonging to Britain, as well, of course, as those of the French and the Dutch which were already in a kind of twilight state since their home territories were already occupied. He was asked to inquire into the attitude prevailing toward the United States. It was not said that this had reference to a possible change of sovereignty. It was, however, understood that it did. But, besides this, his terms were very wide. He was to find out why there was so much unrest, what was being done about it, and what further ought to be done.

The President made Taussig the chairman of a group—this too was called a Commission—the other members being junior officers of the armed services. This gave him status. And the Navy furnished a destroyer. From November until January this ship poked her nose into harbors all up and down the islands. Taussig talked with governors and their subordinates, with experts of various kinds, and with political and labor leaders. I am inclined to think that he found what he expected. There was, however, before he finished, a considerable documentation for his conclusions; and his report was a model of restraint. I was inclined to argue that it was too restrained. Yet, in spite of his respect for authority and tradition, and his disinclination to suggest more than reform of existing institutions, he saw that those reforms would need to be drastic. I should like to quote a paragraph from a communication he sent to Sumner Welles, Undersecretary of State, from Antigua on December fourth when he was no more than well begun on his investigative journey:

The widespread disturbances throughout the West Indies from 1935 to 1937 [convinced the government] that a complete change in attitude was necessary. Much of the [resulting] legislation is modeled consciously or unconsciously on that of the United States during the last eight years. If the President should decide to assume active leadership in world social and economic reconstruction the British islands of the Caribbean would undoubtedly fall in line. . . .

There was more of this. He was rather surprised to discover that the acquisition of the bases was rather popular than otherwise. It made West Indians feel more secure. And more than once he was told that if circumstances should bring it about, a transfer of nationality would not be objected to. This was naturally a very touchy subject; and he realized that it had implications he could hardly appraise in a brief visit. There had been a very good start made on social legislation; and the work of Stockdale and the Fund were just then beginning. But things at that moment did look bad for Britain, even if the resources had been found to set up many welfare projects; and everything was in flux.

In that same dispatch to Welles this line of speculation was abandoned for another—the one that resulted in the setting up of the Caribbean Commission. I quote a passage which shows quite clearly where the initiative came from:

We put out feelers to ascertain whether the various British Colonies here would look with favor to the setting up of a joint permanent Caribbean social and economic fact-finding and research government organization that would explore our mutual problems. The response to this was always in the affirmative.

The governors to whom he spoke were less enthusiastic than Stockdale. They were inclined to suggest that this was a matter for the Colonial Office. Stockdale may have been just a little exasperated with that Office and its stiffness, although he was a correct civil servant himself. At any rate he turned out to be, not only a supporter, but the one chosen to be the first British Co-chairman.

The dispatch to Welles reflected some thoughts Taussig did

not put into his recommendations to the President. But those had their own interest. He said it ought to be more clearly recognized that only if they acted as a regional unit could the Caribbean countries have any considerable influence in any world economic deliberations. Those deliberations he felt sure would become more frequent. This led to the passage in which he said that the time was then propitious for establishing closer relations between the United States and the British West Indies "with a view of finding common ground for a cooperative approach to world economic problems."

Perhaps I should re-emphasize that at that time it was hard to believe on this side of the Atlantic that, brave and stubborn as the British were, they would come out of the war victorious. It looked more as though a German invasion would be successful. This was disturbing the President's nights as he considered what might happen to the British navy. And thinking about it led on to the possibility that not only bases on the islands would have to be acquired, but perhaps the islands themselves.

III

It was not long before I was introduced to Caribbean affairs. Secretary Ickes, of the Department of the Interior which was the headquarters of the Division of Territories and Island Possessions, found himself involved in Puerto Rican matters in ways he seemed powerless to extricate himself from; and he asked me to investigate. While Taussig was taking a hard look at the British islands, I was trying to untangle the intricacies of Puerto Rican politics and economics. Incidentally I developed some ideas about the whole Caribbean. The affairs of the West were in pretty serious case; and I felt that no sufficient understanding had developed of the potential importance of the islands—Puerto Rico being only one.

A little later I discussed the matter with the President. He was ahead of me, as I might have known he would be since the idea of the bases had developed in his own head and nowhere else. But he had a good many other matters on his mind; and when I suggested that bases might not be enough and that perhaps the strategic situation called for complete occupation, he said to me just what he had said to others—that he saw no reason why, if it was not absolutely necessary, we should relieve Britain of some of her worst headaches. We might have to, but he hoped not.

He told me that he had had some suggestion from Churchill, while the bases were being discussed, that the United States was a more logical attachment for the islands than Britain. Churchill must have been in one of his union-now moods if he ever really said anything of the sort. It is certainly not reflected in his memoirs.

Closest to such a suggestion is a passage which recognizes the relationship of the islands to American security; and he was also thinking of the dire British need for the old destroyers which Britain was to get in return for the bases.[1]

Profound and anxious consultation had taken place at Washington, and in the first week of August [1940] the suggestion was made to us through Lord Lothian that the fifty old but reconditioned American destroyers which lay in the east coast navy yards might be traded off to us in exchange for a series of bases in the West Indies islands, and also Bermuda. There was, of course, no comparison between the intrinsic value of the antiquated and inefficient craft and the immense strategic security afforded to the United States by the enjoyment of the island bases. But the threatened invasion, the importance of numbers in the Narrow Seas, made our needs clamant. Moreover, the strategic value of these islands counted only against the United States. They were, in the old days, stepping-stones by which America could be attacked from Europe or from England. Now, with air power, it was all the more important for Ameri-

1. Although Churchill choked a little over the President's suggestion of a "deal." He wanted the destroyers as a gift; and he wanted to present the bases without bargaining. He was forced finally to recognize the President's need for political evasiveness, but he did not like it. There is something almost comic in the sparring that went on between the two over this matter. See *Their Finest Hour* (New York, 1949), Chap. 5.

can safety that they should be in friendly hands, or in their own. But the friendly hands might fail in the convulsive battle now beginning for the life of Britain. Believing, as I have always done, that the survival of Britain is bound up with the survival of the United States, it seemed to me and my colleagues that it was an actual advantage to have these bases in American hands. I therefore did not look upon the question from any narrow British point of view.

Churchill in London, however, and British officials in the Government Houses in the colonies had different views. Taussig, I felt myself, when he asked me to read his report, was inclined to defer far too much to the official and traditional point of view. The governors Taussig met had shown their stiffness by protesting in one instance at a published news report of the President's winter trip which spoke of him as visiting the "new American possessions," and in another instance by showing annoyance that flights had been made over his island without asking permission. As the bases began to be developed, too, there were irritations everywhere over the arrangements made by the contractors. Wages were too high and other employers protested; and there were other annoyances natural to such a peaceable invasion. The officials in the islands by no means reflected Churchill's gratification at the American initative.

It seemed to me that Taussig took these protests too seriously and was too sympathetic to the interests of disturbed colonials. It was, I felt, a time for drastic measures. I am afraid that I said plainly that the British were at the moment incapable of protecting—and had shown themselves incapable of developing —their West Indian possessions. Indeed, I wrote a memorandum to this effect, a kind of answer to Taussig's own. My thoughts certainly ran contrary to his soft suggestions for consultations. In fact I said our safety and the needs of the Caribbean peoples called for an action which the logic of history and geography also required. There are very few moments, I said, when exactly what everyone knows *ought* to be done *can* be done. This was one of them. The whole Caribbean ought to be brought into one federation under American auspices. At this moment this was a strategic necessity for the Allied world, now so woefully shrunk; if Britain should fall, as seemed likely, it would need to be done anyway; and in the future, when peace had returned, it would weld the Caribbean into that unity without which it could neither prosper nor find political satisfaction.

The conversations between Taussig and myself during the year 1941 tended to degenerate into a kind of friendly acrimony. I accused him of having been taken in by Colonial Office pretensions; he said that I had no respect for tradition. The differences between us were complicated by a devious maneuver he tried to carry out which would deprive Secretary Ickes of jurisdiction over insular possessions. This he thought necessary to insure the success of the intergovernmental agency he was conspiring to set up. He made me promise not to tell Ickes what was in his report to the President; but of course Ickes heard about it anyway and accused me of conspiring against him. I then showed Ickes my own memorandum and told him about the controversy. Some time in the course of the involved affair the President sent the Taussig memorandum to Ickes, and then Taussig accused me of having betrayed *his* confidence.

I did not succeed in pacifying either one, I am afraid, although I count it as one of my minor *tours de force* in government that I did once get them both into the same room for a talk. They came away just as hostile as ever to each other; but both, I think, had exonerated me. I never did quite convince Taussig that the Department of State, devoted to foreign affairs, was the wrong administrative residence for an agency with jurisdiction over insular possessions; and Ickes was not persuaded that Taussig had abandoned his subversion. In this he was quite correct.

Taussig's infatuation with the Department of State had its origin in his friendship with both Secretary of State Hull and Undersecretary Welles. They took his advice seriously and would, he knew, support his intention to establish the intergovernmental and intercolonial cooperation he was gradually elaborating. The scheme, as it unfolded, seemed to me impossibly complicated. It was proposed to induce not only the home governments and the colonial administrations, but the elected legislatures as well, to confer and to cooperate. I was aware of the suspicion between the appointed officials and the elected ones; I thought it unlikely that the Colonial Office would sponsor meetings in which the elected representatives could have contact with those from other islands and, worse even than that, with Puerto Ricans.

But it was accomplished. Within a year, when I had become Governor of Puerto Rico, when Britain had won the battle against invasion, and when the United States had entered the war, Taussig made a special trip to see me. My solution was now out of the question. The sense of uncertainty and emergency was not yet relieved; but the tension was less. And Taussig had persuaded everyone, including the Colonial Office, that an Anglo-American Caribbean Commission was desirable. It was, in fact, in process of being set up.

It seemed that I was to be a member. I was necessary to the scheme because I was Governor of Puerto Rico. With Stockdale in Barbados, having a kind of roving authority in the British islands, and me in San Juan, a start could be made. I was reluctant; and I found the Puerto Rican politicians even more reluctant than I was. There was nothing in it for them and nothing, so far as they could see, for Puerto Rico. But I finally consented, and we had our first meeting in Trinidad in the spring of 1942 under the joint chairmanship of Taussig and Stockdale.

IV

More time than I have at my disposal would be necessary to convey to you even the gist and spirit of the discussions during those first meetings. We were governed by a sense of urgency; we were then under blockade. But we also had a feeling that both the Colonial Office and the Department of State were looking over our shoulders. And just outside, looking in, were the representatives of the people who were a long way from trusting, or being trusted by, the appointed officials.

I am a little ashamed to admit now that from the first I sympathized rather freely with the representative of the outsiders who were looking in. This was because of the policy I was developing in Puerto Rico, I suppose, of pushing for more political liberty. It seemed to me even more applicable in the British islands. I realized well enough that it was actually none of my business; and I knew well enough too that the gradual, even if reluctant, movement toward a federated dominion was as far as the British could go toward a unilateral solution. But generally speaking, I was on one side of most questions and the British on the other. Stockdale, I felt certain, shared my prejudices; but he was fitted out with a staff whose opinions were as obvious as their Oxford accents. The sharp antagonism between them and the West Indians gave me many a moment of pleasure.

The British, I now feel, advanced into constitutional reform and federation somewhat faster because of their association with us. Our insular citizens were broadened by the discovery that there were Caribbean peoples with problems even worse than their own. And quite aside from any contributions we made to the easing of the war-emergency, the technical interchanges we arranged must have served to improve the economic and social conditions of all the islands.

Now that the matters to which we first addressed ourselves have advanced so far toward solution, it is sometimes suggested that the need for formal organization has disappeared. It seems to me that the contrary is true. As technology advances, the need for the interchange of information is greater rather than less. And, of course, the Dutch and the French became part of the Commission within a few years and have added their contribution. This accession rather delayed matters for a while. The British and ourselves had just reached a tolerable understanding when we both had to begin all over with the others. At that time I felt that we ought also to invite the membership of the independent nations; and I still wish that had been done. We might all have learned from each other; and we would have had a truly Caribbean body instead of a truncated one.

I still hear suggestions that the Commission now be abandoned. I have the temerity to suggest instead that its work be enlarged by bringing in the independent countries.

When I think of the time and effort spent so unselfishly by the pioneers of the Commission—especially Taussig and Stockdale—I find myself very reluctant to see the institution they created abandoned. I do really hope it may go on, as it is capable of doing, to a greater future usefulness.

Frances McReynolds Smith: THE CARIBBEAN COMMISSION: PROTOTYPE OF REGIONAL COOPERATION

THE YEAR WAS 1942—the season was spring. It was a dark spring for the Allied cause. In North Africa Rommel was on the loose; in Russia vast territories had come into German hands; in the East, Great Britain had lost Singapore and the United States had been hit by the attack on Pearl Harbor. On March 10 the retreat from Burma had begun.

At 12:00 noon Eastern War Time, March 9, 1942 a war-grey announcement was made simultaneously in London and Washington. The joint communiqué was brief. It read:

For the purpose of encouraging and strengthening social and economic cooperation between the United States of America and its possessions and bases in the area known geographically and politically as the Caribbean, and the United Kingdom and the British colonies in the same area, and to avoid unnecessary duplication of research in these fields, a commission, to be known as the Anglo-American Caribbean Commission, has been jointly created by the two Governments. The Commission will consist of six members; three from each country, to be appointed respectively by the President of the United States and His Majesty's Government in the United Kingdom—who will designate one member from each country as co-chairman.

Members of the Commission will concern themselves primarily with matters pertaining to labor, agriculture, housing, health,

276

education, social welfare, finance, economics, and related subjects in the territories under the British and United States flags within this territory, and on these matters will advise their respective Governments.

The Anglo-American Caribbean Commission in its studies and in the formulation of its recommendations will necessarily bear in mind the desirability of close cooperation in social and economic matters between all regions adjacent to the Caribbean.

The following appointments of co-chairmen have been made:

> For Great Britain:
> SIR FRANK STOCKDALE
> For The United States:
> CHARLES W. TAUSSIG

The remaining members of the Commission will be named later by the Governments concerned.

Thus the Anglo-American Caribbean Commission was officially established.

The joint communiqué made no reference to the war other than there was to be a strengthening of "social and economic cooperation between the United States of America and its possessions and bases in the area . . . and the United Kingdom and the British colonies in the same area." The Commission was to advise the governments on "labor, agriculture, housing, health, education, social welfare, finance, economics, and related subjects." Clearly these subjects indicated a permanent agency for these were not related to immediate war needs. Parenthetically, it is interesting to note, however, that when the Congress in 1947 was considering enabling legislation for United States participation in the four-power Caribbean Commission it described the old Anglo-American Caribbean Commission as a "temporary undertaking, based upon what the President regarded as his emergency powers flowing out of the war situation."

But whether the AACC (as it became known) was regarded as a temporary wartime agency or a permanent body, the Caribbean area needed attention both on an emergency and on a long-range basis. Both the United States and the United Kingdom governments realized that serious problems existed. The standard of living of the peoples in 1942 was low. Unemployment and underemployment existed in most areas. The Caribbean was (and is) not one of the fertile areas of the world. Its soil had been depleted by centuries of overcultivation; many areas were badly eroded, and the population in relation to usable land made some parts of the West Indies among the most densely populated in the world. There were few minerals and a scarcity of water for power. Agriculture was the mainstay of the economy.

Chronic sickness—tuberculosis, hookworm, yaws, venereal diseases, malaria—were an accepted part of life. Most of these diseases were closely associated with adverse social conditions— poor and overcrowded housing conditions, primitive sanitation, and lack of education. Because all of these diseases were serious and debilitating, they constituted an economic problem of magnitude.

In March, 1942, the economic woes of the Caribbean had become crises. The immediate problems were ship and food shortages. Even in normal times large reserves of food are not stored in the tropics. The maintenance of supplies became extremely difficult in war time.

I

At its first meeting held March 26–31, 1942, in Trinidad, the Commission took steps to establish an organization for the bulk purchasing of imported foodstuffs, to encourage the production of all kinds of food in substitution for imported supplies, and to arrange for a system of inter-island distribution of supplies.

The Commission early devised the technique of utilizing experts on an *ad hoc* basis to advise it on a particular subject. It convened a Conference of Supply Officers in Jamaica, May 15–18, 1942. The drastic curtailment of usual steamship services and the submarine infestation made it imperative to concentrate on the organization of emergency shipping, including the substitution of overland hauls for water transport wherever possible and the utilization of local schooners in the waters of the Caribbean Sea. The establishment of an Emergency Land-Water Highway was one of the prime results of the Supply Officers conference. The first section of the Highway was a shuttle service between Florida and Gulf ports and Havana, Cuba. The remaining links were a railroad from Havana to Santiago de Cuba; small boat service from Santiago de Cuba to Port-au-Prince, Haiti; a truck service from Port-au-Prince to San Pedro de Macorís, Dominican Republic; and a small boat service from San Pedro de Macorís to Mayagüez, Puerto Rico. This land-water highway eliminated an 800 mile exposure to submarines. Jamacia participated by operating a shuttle between Santiago de Cuba and Port Antonio—a distance of 120 miles. The highway operated for about a year when a letup in the submarine warfare made it possible to discontinue its operation.

Associated with this rerouting of shipping were two other operations: (1) a stockpile operation of emergency foods and medicines at strategic points, and (2) a West Indian Schooner Pool. The schooner pool was organized by the AACC to operate inter-Caribbean trade in the eastern group from the Leeward Islands in the north to British Guiana in the south. Its purposes were to centralize the movement of sailing vessels in order that the most urgent services received priority. The pool collected a fee for each ton of cargo carried, and from these funds it met the charges to keep schooners and sloops in operation, to indemnify owners for loss of vessels sunk by enemy action, and to pay gratuities to families of crew members who lost their lives in such sinkings. The schooner pool was a dramatic example of a successful cooperative effort between a wide range of interests—British colonial governments, shippers, warehousemen, shipping agents, schooner owners, masters, and crews. At the height of its operations some 85 per cent of the schooners of the Caribbean area were participating. The long-range advantages of the pool were recognized, and after the war it was reorganized as the Schooner Owners' Association and as such is operating today.

The Commission at its first meeting also began attacking one pressing aspect of the health problem with vigor. It recognized that the prevention and cure of venereal diseases was both a civilian problem of a long-term character and a problem of immediate urgency among the armed forces which were stationed in the Caribbean. In 1944 the Commission established in Trinidad a Venereal Disease Control Center which later became the Caribbean Medical Center. This joint Anglo-American center carried on mass blood tests, public education by means of films and lectures, and the training of local doctors, laboratory technicians, nurses, and midwives from neighboring islands. Representatives of medical departments in the area were called in for periodic conferences. Results of tests were counterchecked at laboratories in the United States, and the Caribbean area was able to utilize the most modern techniques of medical science. The Caribbean Medical Center after 1945 continued to operate in Trinidad, maintained entirely by Trinidadian and British funds. In 1956 a total of 69,688 blood tests were made by the Caribbean Medical Center Laboratory. These tests showed that the positive rate for syphilis and yaws was 4.9 per cent— while in 1945 when the Commission conducted its first blood tests the positive rate was 25.8 per cent. The Medical Center is an outstanding example of progress in the field of public health.

The psychological impact of Axis propaganda beamed to the Caribbean had already had an effect upon the morale of Caribbean peoples by the time the AACC was established. All of the social, economic, and political shortcomings of centuries were exploited in radio programs beamed especially to the Caribbean. The Nazis announced the gory details of every ship that was sunk and used the broadcast slogan "He who sails for North America sails certainly to death." On December 1, 1942, the AACC began transmitting its own program for the West Indies from the United States to supplement the BBC coverage. Known as the "West Indian Radio Newspaper," this daily program brought international news, American jazz, folksy bits of information about West Indians abroad and made them feel less isolated. This daily program was discontinued in 1946 largely because of the expense involved and the increase in national programs in the post-war period.

II

The emergency projects cited were dramatic illustrations of the cooperation on a regional basis to meet immediate situations. The war crises demonstrated to the Caribbean peoples the necessity and the procedures for meeting pressing problems of themselves and their neighbors. But basic problems remained in the area and remedies had to be found. This in turn called for long-term planning. The Commission even in the distress of war found time to set long-term objectives and to begin basic work. A series of high-level meetings in Washington, London, and the West Indies resulted in an exchange of notes in 1942 spelling out a ten-point long-range program:

(1) The economic problems of the Caribbean should be regarded as regional rather than local problems.

(2) Generally speaking, a single-crop economy in the West Indies is undesirable. Although the continuation of cash crops must be relied upon to a considerable extent, mixed farming and animal husbandry should be encouraged everywhere, both on a large scale (whether by private enterprise or on a cooperative basis) and by peasant holders.

(3) Inter-island trade throughout the entire Caribbean region should be encouraged.

(4) The possibilities of industrial development, although probably limited in the majority of territories, should not be overlooked.

(5) Advantage should be taken of fishing grounds in and adjacent to the Caribbean, and local fisheries with facilities for storage and distribution should be developed and organized.

(6) While an adequate literary and cultural standard must be maintained, a greater vocational bias should be introduced into the educational system.

(7) There is an urgent need for a wide improvement of housing and sanitary conditions and for an extensive school building program.

(8) Transportation to and within the Caribbean is inadequate and should be improved.

(9) Tourism intelligently developed can become a substantial source of income to the area. Its potentialities should be carefully studied with a view to action.

(10) An immediate and effective approach to the nutritional problem might be met by providing midday meals for children at school.

The rather dramatic examples just cited of meeting wartime emergencies and the more prosaic long-range planning required some kind of machinery. The concept that two nations, recognizing their common economic and social problems, should pool resources, imagination, experts, and finances to solve the problems of ten widely scattered territories on a regional basis was a new and bold political concept. The body was, moreover, only advisory and consultative. Its strength, in these early days, lay to a very large extent in the soundness of its advice and the wisdom of those who gave the advice.

The men who devoted their energies to this initial effort were men who combined technical knowledge with administrative experience, strong personal convictions with the ability to persuade and above all the capacity to devise new techniques. Mr. Charles W. Taussig, the first United States Co-chairman, was a highly successful businessman with a social conscience. An authority and writer on Caribbean matters, he had served as chairman of a special Presidential commission to survey the economic and social problems of areas where the United States had acquired naval and air bases in the Caribbean. Although Mr. Taussig was primarily to look into the attitude of the West Indian peoples toward the establishment of the bases in particular and toward the United States in general, the survey was to give consideration to the basic problems of the region as far as possible. The survey group visited the area between November

15, 1940, and January 5, 1941, and took testimony from 150 individuals. The group submitted a report to the President on January 7, 1941, pointing out among other things that the Caribbean territories could benefit from working as a unit in meeting both war emergency and long-range problems. Mr. Taussig suggested the type of organization required to do such a job. From his brain and pen came this first regional body.

The first British Co-chairman—Sir Frank Stockdale—was an eminent scientist who had had wide experience in the agricultural field in many parts of the British Empire. In addition to his new duties he continued to carry on his regular responsibilities as Comptroller of the British Colonial Development and Welfare Organization, whose headquarters were located in Barbados.

The Anglo-American Caribbean Commission, in accordance with the terms of the joint communiqué, consisted of two national sections, British and United States, of three members each. A small staff of American and British personnel and commissioners located in Washington and attached either to the United States Co-chairman or to the British Resident Commissioner in Washington, constituted in effect a small secretariat.

III

At its fourth meeting, held in August 1943, the Commission invited a number of technical experts from Britain, the United States, and the Caribbean to meet with it. At that session the Commission announced the establishment of a Caribbean Research Council to provide it with the technical advice it would need in furthering scientific, technological, and social advancement in the area. The objectives of the Research Council were "to survey needs, determine what research has been done, arrange for dissemination and exchange of the results of research, provide for conferences between research workers or extension workers and recommend what further research and cooperation should be undertaken." An agricultural sectional committee was created to begin work at once in the fields of agriculture, nutrition, fisheries, and forestry. This sectional committee was conceived as a first step any place in the world in implementing the findings of the Hot Springs Conference on Food and Agriculture on a regional basis. In 1945 the Commission established four additional committees in specific fields and named them Research Committees. They covered (1) public health and medicine, (2) industrial technology, (3) building and engineering technology, and (4) social sciences.

With the appointment in 1945 of a full-time and able British West Indian as Deputy Chairman of the Research Council, the nucleus of the research organization of the AACC was established. A series of technical booklets was approved, and the long-range work of the Commission was under way.

Thus far the machinery did not provide for participation of the local peoples, except a few technicians on the Research Council and its committees. The two governments recognized in 1942 that they needed "to broaden the base for approach to Caribbean problems to include consultations with local representatives—not necessarily officials—of the territories and colonies concerned." This democratic approach to solutions of the Caribbean problems found enthusiastic advocates, and on January 4, 1944, another communiqué was issued by the United States and the United Kingdom announcing a regular system of West Indian conferences to be inaugurated under the auspices of the AACC. Each territory or group of territories was entitled to send two delegates to the conference which would have "a definite continuity of existence" despite the fact that the delegates would probably change as the subject matter changed. The conference was to convene from time to time wherever subjects arose which would be "at once alive and capable of being profitably discussed at such a conference." The communiqué dealt with certain procedural and staffing questions. The most significant paragraph read: "The Conference shall be advisory but it would be hoped that it would attain a really influential position, and it would be open at any time to the interested

Governments to agree among themselves to delegate to it any specific powers which they might think desirable."

The first session of the West Indian Conference was held in Barbados in March, 1944. Twenty delegates and eighteen advisers from all of the areas covered by the AACC—the Bahamas, Barbados, British Guiana, British Honduras, Jamaica, the Leeward Islands, Trinidad, the Windward Islands, Puerto Rico, and the Virgin Islands of the United States—attended. There were also respresentatives from the United Kingdom and the United States and observers from the Netherlands and Canada. The agenda covered a wide range of subjects including nutrition, re-absorption into civil life of persons engaged in war employment, health protection, industrial development, and the Research Council.

Although the Conference did not consider political questions, the very act of convening such a conference was of political significance. For the first time in the history of the world, a formal international conference had been convened whose delegates were representatives of dependent peoples. It provided a meeting place for Caribbean peoples to get acquainted with each other, their political institutions and philosophies. They also learned that their neighbors faced the same problems. They exchanged ideas on solutions to these problems. This first conference stimulated regional thinking. It would have been significant if all that the delegates had done was to sit down together and talk. They passed resolutions and sent the resolutions to the two member governments of the Commission and to all the local governments. Out of these recommendations came a joint statement of Britain and the United States of basic economic policy for the region.

The peoples of the area participated not only in the West Indian Conference but in the Commission itself after June 30, 1945. A modification of the original joint communiqué was issued on that date in another joint statement of the two governments. The membership of the Commission was increased from three to four members on each side. The expansion of membership was "for the purpose of associating the peoples of the Caribbean area more closely with the work of the Anglo-American Caribbean Commission and of including in its membership representatives of those peoples." A separate United States announcement said that the additional member of the United States section would be nominated from Puerto Rico and appointed by the President. The British Government declared that it had full sympathy with the demand which had existed for some time for the appointment of a British West Indian unofficial member and that the expansion would permit the appointment of two unofficial members. They further proposed that the British unofficial delegates to the second session of the West Indian Conference elect these two commissioners. Two commissioners from the British West Indies were chosen during the second session of the West Indian Conference and began serving in 1946. Thus, the Anglo-American Caribbean Commission early reflected the new political awakening in the West Indies.

IV

The Commission emerged as a truly regional body in 1946, for France and the Netherlands had accepted invitations in December, 1945, to join the organization. It was renamed the Caribbean Commission. The new areas brought within the scope of the Commission's activities were the old French colonies of French Guiana, Guadeloupe, and Martinique and the Netherlands islands of Aruba and Curaçao and the mainland territory of Surinam.

The first regional activity was participation in the second session of the West Indian Conference February 21-March 13, 1946, in St. Thomas. The agenda for this second Conference was drawn up by the Commission in consultation not only with the member governments, but with all of the territorial governments. It covered a wide range of technical subjects such as agricultural and industrial diversification, trade, tourism, and such organizational questions as how the Commission could best serve the area, the role of the Caribbean Research Council, and the procedures and agenda for future West Indian conferences.

Concurrently with the second session of the conference, the new Caribbean Commission held its first meeting. The recommendations of the Conference were given some preliminary consideration. But the first meeting devoted even more attention to the preparation of proposals for the formal establishment of the expanded Commission, the organization and financing of a Central Secretariat, and procedures for the conduct of business of the Commission and its two auxiliary bodies. These latter questions were referred to the member governments with the suggestion that a meeting with specially designated representatives should be convened.

A special meeting, convened in Washington in July 1946, drafted, negotiated, and initialled the text of the Agreement for the Establishment of the Caribbean Commission, selected Trinidad as the site for the Central Secretariat, appointed a Secretary General, and established a formula for the assessment of member government contributions to a joint fund for the operation of the Commission. The Agreement was formally signed in Washington on October 30, 1946, was ratified by the four governments, and entered into force August 6, 1948. (United States membership and participation was authorized by Public Law 431, Eightieth Congress.)

During the years 1942-46, it had become evident that the Commission required a central secretariat in the Caribbean area, and the delegates to the second session of the West Indian Conference made a strong recommendation along this line. The first secretary general, Mr. Lawrence W. Cramer, assumed his duties in September and immediately moved into the headquarters at Trinidad. His enthusiasm, energy, and administrative ability attracted an unusual staff which was representative of most of the races and nationalities of this diverse area. This multi-racial, multi-lingual group was welded into an efficient working secretariat within four months.

A group representative of each nationality had been assigned

the task during the St. Thomas Conference of undertaking the
detailed work involved in the planning and establishment of
a secretariat, the administration of a joint fund, the formulation
of rules of procedure, and the many other organizational tasks.
The first chairman was Dr. Ralph Bunche, who was then a
United States Commissioner. This working committee became
a formal part of the machinery of the Commission and met
as frequently as necessary in Washington during 1946. It proved
to be an effective means of planning, of devising techniques, and
of getting prompt decisions on a variety of urgent matters which
would have taken months to settle by correspondence between
the co-chairmen and the other commissioners.

The new Caribbean Commission got busy. It already had a
history and precedents. It now had a staff and funds. While
it remained an advisory and consultative body, its functions were
precisely defined:

[1] To concern itself with economic and social matters of
common interest to the Caribbean area, particularly agriculture,
communications, education, fisheries, health, housing, industry,
labor, social welfare and trade, [2] to study, formulate and recommend . . . measures, programs and policies with respect to
social and economic problems designed to contribute to the well-
being of the Caribbean area, [3] to assist in coordinating local
problems which have regional significance and to provide technical guidance from a wide field not otherwise available, [4] to
direct and review the activities of the Research Council, [and
5] to convene the sessions of the West Indian Conference.

The two auxiliary bodies, which had served the old AACC, are
specifically provided for in the Agreement—the Caribbean Research Council in the field of scientific, technological, social,
and economic research and the West Indian Conference as
"a regular means of consultation with and between the territories
on matters of common interest within the terms of reference of
the Commission."

The Research Council consists of not less than seven and not
more than fifteen members appointed by the Commission because

of their scientific competence. The principal functions of the Council as enumerated in the Agreement are "to ascertain what research has been done, to survey needs, to advise concerning desirable research projects, to arrange and facilitate cooperative research, to undertake research assignments of a special nature which no other agency is able and willing to carry out, and to collect and disseminate information concerning research." Among its other functions were to recommend the holding of meetings of the several research committees and "also of meetings of scientific, specialist and extension workers and to facilitate an interchange of experience among the research workers of the Caribbean."

The continuity of the West Indian Conference is ensured by means of regular sessions which are held biennially. The venue of each session is by a system of rotation selected according to English alphabetical order of the member governments. The chairman of each session is the chairman of the national section in whose territory the session is held. Each territorial government is entitled to send not more than two delegates and as many advisers as considered necessary. Delegates are appointed in accordance with the constitutional procedures of the appointing government.

V

At this stage some mention should be made of the nomenclature used in the Agreement and up to this time in this narrative. Article XX of the Agreement is labled "Definitions" and reads: "In this Agreement the expressions 'territories' or 'territorial government' shall be deemed to relate to the territories, possessions, colonies, or groups of colonies of the Member Governments in the Caribbean area or to the administrations or governments thereof." The terms "possessions," "colonies," "territories," have become since 1946 outmoded and inappropriate in the Caribbean area because of the development of new political relationships between these parts of the Caribbean and the member governments.

The Commission has adopted the phrase "countries served by the Commission." The areas covered by the expanded Caribbean Commission are: *British*—Barbados, British Honduras, British Guiana, Jamaica, the Leeward Islands, Trinidad, Tobago, and the Windward Islands (the Bahamas participated actively the first few years when the Commission was Anglo-American, but has not participated since 1946); *French*—the French departments of Guadeloupe, Martinique, and French Guiana; *The Netherlands*—the Netherlands Antilles and Surinam; *the United States*—the Commonwealth of Puerto Rico and the Virgin Islands of the United States.

While these areas vary in the rate and direction of their social, economic, and political development, the peoples and their leaders are keenly aware of the nature and complexity of their basic problems. All are determined to take every measure within their power to overcome them. The small governmental units and the almost universal lack of natural and physical resources continue to be handicaps in applying modern technology to overcome recurring, although fully recognized, problems. The area may be characterized as "underdeveloped" or "less well-developed," but it has reached a stage where even small amounts of technical and financial assistance yield large amounts of economic and social improvement. The problems are there, but so are dedicated leaders. The Commission is one instrument by which solutions can be found through a regional approach.

VI

The Commission has just passed its tenth year as an international body with dignity and standing among the international organizations of the world. It cannot lay claim to a specific percentage increase in standards of living; it cannot assert that per capita income has increased one cent because of its existence; it cannot justify its existence on the basis that underemployment has ceased or that life expectancy has been increased. Such claims would be foolish and unfounded.

The Caribbean Commission has been a moral force in the area; it has provided a forum for the discussion of age-old problems and modern solutions; it has developed a regional awareness of common problems and common solutions; it has evaluated needs and brought technical guidance. In the words of one leading West Indian:

The Caribbean Commission is the expression of a lofty concept and plan for regional cooperation between the four Metropolitan Governments directly interested in Caribbean territories and those territories. Limited in activity to advising in the social and economic field, it has made a handsome contribution to Caribbean progress by marshalling the needs of the area, formulating a massive collection of data on which plans for meeting those needs may be based, and arousing a greater consciousness in all governments concerned and in the United Nations and its specialized agencies as to their opportunities and duties in the area.

The international conferences which it has arranged on governmental, technical, and commercial levels have made very real contributions to progressive thought in the area and have influenced political action. The Commission may justly claim to have made some contribution to British Caribbean federation. It may justly claim to have enriched the life of the area by making it very much more knowledgeable about its several parts. It has not been without criticism; but however valid that criticism may be—and which human organization has done all that it might have done?—it has to its credit solid achievement which the Caribbean area would have been all the poorer without. (Garent Gordon, *The Caribbean*, November, 1956.)

The Caribbean Trade and Industry Annual of 1956 (published in British Guiana) states:

Prior to the coming of the Commission, the inhabitants of the Caribbean lived their lives as complete strangers. Each colony was almost ignorant of the other; life in the area was more on an insular basis with scattered ideals and bewildered objectives. But the Commission's arrival brought the people and their affairs together. The Commission was indeed the harbinger of the Caribbean Federation: it showed the inhabitants of the region an example of working together for the common good.

The concrete accomplishments of the Commission can best be shown by current projects which are illustrative, but not all-inclusive, of the present program.

1. *Agriculture.* The Executive Secretary for Agricultural Economics suggested to the Commission that it organize field demonstration tours in tropical products to gain on-the-spot knowledge. The program brings together technical workers, growers, and commercial representatives. The tours have been held in cocoa, bananas, and coffee, and others are planned in pineapples, cattle, and grasslands. They provide mutual exchange of data, visual demonstration of new or modified practices and specialized procedures as are governed by the special topography and environmental conditions prevailing in the Caribbean. The Commission organizes the tours, supplies technical documents and the necessary administrative services. The local host government underwrites many local costs, and the local governments or private industry pay the transportation and other costs of the delegates. This is technical cooperation rendered direct by the Commission.

2. *Aided Self-Help Housing.* The need for more, better, and cheaper housing is everywhere evident in the Caribbean. Housing technicians have been loaned by the United States International Cooperation Administration to the Commission since 1952. They have built hundreds of low-cost, hurricane-proof, and termite-proof houses with the aided self-help technique adapted from Puerto Rico. They have advised local governments upon problems of construction of several thousand houses, investigation of local building materials, upon the financing and management of low-cost housing projects, and have trained local men as supervisors and foremen. The technical guidance furnished in cooperation with ICA has been one of the most successful of Commission activities.

3. *Home Economics.* With the cooperation of the Food and

Agriculture Organization of the United Nations, which loaned a home economist to the Commission's staff, an intensive program for home and family improvement has been started in the Caribbean. As a result of this work over the last five years, home economics departments have been added to many local governments; short training courses in nutrition have been held throughout the Caribbean for teachers and family welfare workers, and two training courses of several months duration have been conducted, one in English and one in French. These were practical courses—designated to meet the special problems of the Caribbean peoples where illegitimacy, poverty, and a weak family unit present a serious social problem. A concrete result of this program was the designing and making of simple household furnishings, including a waist-high stove, from scrap and discarded material. A home economics textbook illustrating Caribbean foods and Caribbean conditions will shortly be published by the FAO and the Commission for use in the schools of the region.

4. *Education.* Since 1949 the Commission has assisted in the selection of students from British, French, and Netherlands areas for the ICA "Caribbean Training Program" scholarships in Puerto Rico. Scholarships are granted mainly in teacher-training in agriculture, vocational education, and home economics. Over 300 students have received this specialized training since the inauguration of the program.

An expert loaned by UNESCO to the Commission in 1956 has established an "Education Clearing House" within the Secretariat, primarily in the field of instructional material.

A technical library primarily devoted to the principal fields of the Commission and a documentary film library are maintained by the Commission in Trinidad. The Commission's library has been carefully developed into an important center of West Indian materials and is open not only to staff members but to students and the general public.

The government of the Commonwealth of Puerto Rico and the University of Puerto Rico have joined forces with the Commission and FAO in regional training courses in tropical forestry, cooperatives, home economics, and an Aided Self-Help Housing Seminar Workshop.

5. *Technical Conferences and Technical Services.* In 1946 the Commission inaugurated the system of convening technical conferences. Such conferences have been held in forestry, soil science, cooperatives, industrial development, fisheries, home economics, and education in nutrition, trade promotion, education, and small-scale farming, town and country development planning, meteorology, tourism, and demography.

The technical conference has proved to be a most useful technique for bringing together specialists from within and without the Caribbean. Technical reports coming from these conferences have often become guidebooks and manuals for specialists. The Caribbean Tourist Association, which promotes the Caribbean as a year-round regional resort area, grew out of one of these conferences. The establishment of a uniform hurricane warning system in the eastern Caribbean by the World Meteorological Organization resulted from another technical conference.

A technical Publications Exchange Service is maintained by the Commission as a service to planters, businessmen, and governments, and has grown out of the technical conferences. Publications by the Commission, governments, and scientists on bananas, cocoa, coffee, fisheries, small-scale farming, and nutrition are translated into French and English and supplied free to the area.

In addition the Commission maintains a Plant and Animal Diseases Reporting Service. A technician at Commission headquarters receives reports from all cooperating areas and sends out cabled warnings on disease outbreaks to all areas which might be endangered.

In many respects the Commission has become a large clearing house in the area, a body to which government, industry, and private individuals come for advice, information, or publications. Every year the Commission answers hundreds of requests for technical information, supplies seeds, cuttings, trees, and roots for experimental plantings, and furnishes publications and pamphlets.

Technicians on the staff of the Central Secretariat serve in advisory capacities on local boards, such as the coffee and cocoa industries, and undertake short-term assignments to local governments to aid in a market survey or advise on the establishment of a statistical unit.

Regular research activities of the Commission are carried out by the Secretariat in all of the major activities of the Commission. Several publications resulting from such research in the past few years have been used as manuals by governments, and some have been translated into many languages and distributed throughout the world. Examples are: "Guide to Commercial Shark Fishing in the Caribbean Area," "Handbook for Cooperative Personnel in the Caribbean" (jointly with FAO), "Aspects of Housing in the Caribbean," "Education in the Caribbean," "Caribbean Timbers, their Utilization and Trade Within the Area," "The Industrial Utilization of Sugar Cane By-Products," and "Industrial Development in the Caribbean." Parenthetically, I am happy to add at this point that the University of Florida Press is the sales agent in the United States for Commission publications.

VII

The Commission's work, as can be seen by the examples, has been steady, but not dramatic. As an international organization, bridging four languages and nineteen different country boundaries, it has come to enjoy the confidence of governments and individuals. It is in a unique position to obtain technical, economic, and social material. The enthusiasm, industry, and dedication of staff members to the work in no small measure accounts for its general acceptance in the area. Its staff includes a very high proportion of West Indians: about 50 per cent of the administrative staff, 62 per cent of the professional staff, and 96 per cent of the general service staff. As the West Indian Conference over the years has grown in importance, the stature of the Secretariat has increased in a kind of direct ratio. From the minds and hearts of the West Indian delegates to the West Indian Conference, and from the minds and hearts of the Secretariat staff, have come fresh ideas, new concepts of the role of the Commission in the life of the area.

The Commission's shortcomings proceed not only from an unrealistic financial ceiling, which was imposed in its first year, but from certain weaknesses inherent in its very structure. It is merely an advisory and consultative body. It has no executive authority. Three co-chairmen constitute a quorum, only the votes of co-chairmen count, and all substantive matters must be agreed to unanimously. The creation of national sections increases the tendency to think as four national groups rather than as a regional technical body. The appointment of commissioners who have other full-time positions (and sometimes in fields not related to Commission activities) has created less of a technical and more of a political body. While the Commission has recently concentrated its energies in the fields of agricultural and industrial development, housing and basic education, it has on its books a varied assortment of projects which were hastily conceived and hastily approved. Its two meetings a year, of about five or five and one-half working days each, usually permit only a superficial analysis of the problems involved. Its staff and funds could more effectively be employed if there were a greater concentration on fewer subjects, and if these were pursued until some practical achievement resulted. At present the Commission attempts to deal with almost all of the subjects handled by the United Nations and all of its specialized agencies. The Research Council has not fulfilled its expectations of being a counselor to the Commission on technical and scientific matters. Its members all have full-time jobs elsewhere; they are scattered throughout the Caribbean and the metropolitan countries and meet at the headquarters of the Commission once every two or three years. The need for the existence of such a body is dubious, especially since the Commission has adopted the system of convening small *ad hoc* groups of specialists to serve as preparatory groups for technical meetings. In addition, the development in the Secretariat of a staff of experts, serviced by a strong statistical unit and a library, has for all practical purposes supplanted the Research Council.

The West Indian Conference has developed into a regional forum where the hopes and aspirations of the delegates can be aired; where local technicians and politicans can sit down together to discuss their problems; where big and little areas meet as equals; and where the experience and knowledge of each country is available to the other. Its recommendations have become the work program of the Commission and have been translated into concrete projects.

It should have come as no surprise to the Commission in 1952 when delegates to the fifth session of the West Indian Conference meeting in Jamaica unanimously called upon the member governments to revise the Agreement Establishing the Caribbean Commission "in the light of the new constitutional relationships with the Caribbean area, and in the light of the demonstrated desire and ability of the peoples of the area to accept increased responsibility in solving the problems of the region." Even in 1952 new constitutions in several parts of the Caribbean had given to the local people autonomy in their own economic, financial, social, and educational affairs. Since 1952 other constitutional changes have gone into effect, and others will take place in 1958. The form and procedure of the Commission was considered by most delegates to the fifth session of the Conference as undemocratic and inconsistent with the aims of the Commission.

The four member governments have been studying this question since 1952. In December, 1956, in conjunction with the celebration of the tenth anniversary of the Commission, the four governments issued a joint statement. It read in part:

The four Governments consider that the purposes and objectives as set out in the present Agreement should continue to be the basis of any new organisation resulting from such revision; that is to say, it would be an advisory and consultative body set up for the purposes of studying specific economic and social problems common to the Caribbean area and making proposals thereon to the various Governments concerned for consideration in accordance with their respective constitutional powers and processes. It should however reflect appropriately the new responsibilities which the Governments of the area have undertaken since 1946 as well as those which some of them are about to assume.

In order to ensure the greatest possible expression of opinion by the Caribbean peoples, the four Governments invite the Governments of the area now served by the Caribbean Commission, to meet at the earliest practicable date and to discuss the formulation of a new Agreement. The draft of such an Agreement would be submitted to the Governments signatory to the 1946 Agreement as well as to the Governments participating in the special conference for consideration and approval in accordance with their respective constitutional processes and responsibilities.

In the meantime the Caribbean Commission, as presently constituted, will continue to serve the area in the best tradition of the Commission.

In February of 1956 the United States government had made a proposal to the British, French, and the Netherlands governments that the Commission be reorganized under a new name, such as "Caribbean Conference." All of the local governments now served by the Commission would become participating governments of the new organization. The present member governments would be entitled to send two observers with the right to participate in discussion but not to vote. The United States government suggested that the existing machinery of the West Indian Conference be utilized to serve as a revision conference. The United States further spelled out the procedure of adopting the new charter thus:

Upon adoption of a Draft Charter by two-thirds of the Members present and voting, each of the participating governments would decide, in accordance with its constitutional processes, whether to become a member of the proposed organization and would send to the headquarters of the present Commission an appropriate notification.

The United States proposal suggested that the draft charter would come into effect as follows:

When notifications had been received from two-thirds of the governments entitled to participate, the Draft Charter would be submitted to the four metropolitan powers now party to the Caribbean Commission Agreement for approval. (In the case of the United States, approval by the United States Congress will be required.) When the four metropolitan powers have taken the requisite constitutional action to approve the Draft Charter, the four powers will issue a joint declaration announcing the termination of the present Caribbean Commission Agreement and approving the new Charter. Upon the issuance of such declaration, the Caribbean Conference would acquire legal existence and the Caribbean Commission would thereupon be dissolved.

The procedures to be used in getting a new charter drafted, the agreement upon the wording of a new charter, and the acceptance of such a charter under the various constitutional processes present a problem of magnitude. Undoubtedly, the Caribbean peoples have advanced to a maturity—both political and economic—which makes the present Commission outmoded. It appears, therefore, that the Commission as presently constituted cannot continue to have the support of the people.

The United States proposal is a challenging and novel one. It has been put forward in the belief that some international organization, dedicated exclusively to this part of the Caribbean area, is desirable. It earnestly hopes that any new organization will reflect the aspirations and the needs of the Caribbean peoples and will be such as to command their respect.

20

W. Adolphe Roberts: THE CARIBBEAN IN THE PAN AMERICAN MOVEMENT

PAN-AMERICANISM IS the most far-reaching and effective political doctrine ever formulated for the guidance of the New World. A natural balance of power obtains between the United States of America to the north and the Latin countries to the south. The axis upon which this revolves is the Caribbean region, not merely because the inner sea lies with admirable exactitude at the geographical center, but because great interests are concentrated there. The Caribbean is the lobby between the Atlantic and Pacific Oceans. Trade routes converge from all points of the compass and are served by the vitally important Panama Canal.

The mutual benefits at stake have long been clear to statesmen. But the strategic value of the region and its commercial products, from the old sugar bonanza to petroleum and bauxite today, have caused it to be fragmented among European powers. Relics of the colonial system prevailed longer than in any other part of the hemisphere. This hampered the development of Pan-Americanism at the heart, but only hampered, for the march of so inevitable a destiny could not be stopped.

There is now being formed a federation of the British West Indian islands proper, excluding the Bahamas, British Honduras, and British Guiana. Elections are to be held in March, 1958, and a structure of semiresponsible government established im-

300

mediately thereafter, with dominion status promised in a few years. Autonomy, in one shape or another, must follow for the remaining colonies. The new nations can scarcely fail to come within the orbit of Pan-Americanism. Why do I say this? I answer by appealing to the records of history, for by inclination and training I am accustomed to seeking in that court the judgments that forecast the solutions of contemporary issues.

I

All the European colonizers of the Americas practised a statecraft which was bound, in greater or lesser degree, to create nations instead of satisfied colonies. The basic conception was of virgin estates, to be developed for the enrichment of the mother country with the interests of the settlers subordinated. The chief weapon of enforcement was the system known in history as mercantilism. This provided that a colony must trade only with its overlord, and in ships flying the latter's flag. It must not manufacture competing goods. Products urgently needed from foreign sources could be had solely by permit and through the commission agencies of the central power.

Details varied here and there. Spain went so far as to forbid her colonies to trade directly with one another. If Venezuela, for instance, wanted to buy from Cuba, the wares had to be sent to Spain and transshipped. The method was held to be common sense, since it served to keep Spanish vessels and sailors busy. But then Spain placed similar restrictions upon travel among her territories, and in many other ways reduced the colonial to the status of a second-class citizen.

England, France, and Holland had more liberal regulations, but there is no getting away from the fact that the three of them went in for mercantilism to an extent that their subjects overseas found intolerable. It will be well to establish what moved men of the different nationalities to become colonists in the first place.

Though Spain took the initiative as the pioneer conqueror in fixing an ironclad economic policy, she was not a commercial country in the sense that England, France, and Holland were. After the original mania for gold bullion had yielded to the realities, Spain wanted American products for consumption by herself and her subject states in Europe. She paid for them with her manufactures at artificial prices in her favor. But the business of buying and selling on an international scale was alien to her.

Nor had the Spanish emigrants to the New World gone there to be merchants. They desired to set themselves up as land-owners, served by Indian peons bound to the soil. The little hidalgo sought to become a great hidalgo. The man who could never have aspired to owning more than ten acres at home now dreamed in the terms of thousands of acres. To a considerable extent such ambitions were fulfilled, with professionals, artisans, and shopkeepers rounding out the picture.

Practically no Spanish settler wished to be an absentee pro-prietor. He had adopted his "New Spain," whether this was Mexico, which officially bore that name, or any other part of the vast dominion. If "Old Spain" had known how to treat his descendants, who felt precisely as he did for several genera-tions, all might have been well. But he plundered and isolated them.

The English colonist embarked on his adventure with much less of a feeling for permanence, at least in the tropical parts of the region. England was a maritime power and intensely com-mercial. Very early the department which grew into the modern Colonial Office was called the Lords of Trade and Plantations, the last word meaning not an individual plantation but a whole colony. Sugar in the West Indies proved to be for Englishmen the equivalent of the Spanish lust for treasure, and with a sounder basis of fact. The idea was to exploit a sugar island to the limit, pouring in African slaves regardless of the demo-graphic problem that would follow. Planters who did well ordinarily returned to England to live in luxury. The compara-tive failures remained perforce on their holdings.

Restricted shipping, taxation without representation, and other hindrances clogged the progress of the robust North American colonies, as well as that of the Caribbean outposts. Throughout the eighteenth century, the age of enlightenment, the conviction grew that freer institutions were essential.

The Dutch would have liked to imitate closely the policies of the English. But Holland fell behind in the race for colonial territory. She succeeded in maintaining only a narrow strip on the Guiana coast and a few footholds among the smaller Antilles. A type of middleman's commerce, partly founded on smuggling, was her long suit. She pioneered with local free ports, and she squeezed such profits as she could from the agriculture of her colonies.

The French position was midway between those of the Spanish and the English. France applied mercantilism sometimes avidly and at other periods with a certain carelessness. Her settlers were more inclined than the English to make lasting homes in the tropics. They were brutalized in the Caribbean, however, like other Europeans, by the methods of sugar planting that called for hordes of slaves outnumbering the masters by ever more fantastic figures from decade to decade. The French showed to better advantage in Louisiana and Quebec.

II

Allowing for political variations, a main condition prevailed throughout the Americas. Here were two continents divided into roughly forty captaincies general, provinces, island colonies, hinterland domains, or call them what you will, ruled by five peoples from the Old World, including the Portuguese in Brazil. The structure, as the last quarter of the eighteenth century started, had been built in a little over two hundred fifty years. There was no historical parallel, certainly not with Rome who had conquered the Mediterranean world slowly by making vassals of rival states. When Rome disintegrated, it was into component parts with ancient traditions of their own.

The Aztec and Inca civilizations never rallied from their over-throw, and the other Indian peoples were of minor importance in the government of the Western Hemisphere.

So the new countries were in a very real sense the children of Europe, made rebellious by tyranny. It would have been ideal if they could have organized as a closely knit league and then all have struck together for freedom. Facilities for doing this were lacking. Except in the thirteen North American colonies, the inclination to form even a localized union did not exist.

The first revolution was against England, and the United States of America was established. Advanced institutions, politi-cal and educational, had made this possible. But the foreign policy of the Union continued to be isolationist for many years. Entanglement in the affairs of Europe was avoided, the taboo extending to the remaining European possessions on this side of the Atlantic. Thomas Jefferson's astute statesmanship, how-ever, did not miss the opportunity of the Louisiana Purchase, when the difficulties facing Napoleon persuaded the Emperor to sell. Those difficulties had included the loss of Haiti (formerly Saint Domingue) in the second great regional upheaval to happen in America.

Haiti's struggle interrupted the pattern of the wars of in-dependence. It was the only successful slave revolution, and it destroyed that land-owning colonial caste upon which nations elsewhere were founded. Nevertheless, the Haitians developed a most fervid patriotism, and their leaders have generally been friends of the Pan-American doctrine.

III

We reach the overture of the central drama when insurrections began breaking out in 1810, from end to end of the Spanish-American domain. The immediate stimulus was the abdication of the King, under pressure from Napoleon, who placed his brother Joseph Bonaparte upon the throne in Madrid. Rebel committees declared against the French regime, and in favor of the legitimate heir Ferdinand VII. But this was merely a subterfuge. All the colonies had grievances, and before long they cast down the symbols of Ferdinand's rule and proclaimed free governments. They knew so little about one another that they did not see that the simultaneous revolts implied a common cause. Each went its own way. The tendency was toward crumbling into still smaller units.

The genius of Simón Bolívar, the Liberator, who had swiftly risen to leadership in Venezuela, found this illogical and intolerable. He tirelessly urged his own country and adjoining Nueva Granada to link their fortunes. That he did combine them, along with Ecuador, in a short-lived nation called Gran Colombia proved to be the most that could be accomplished at the time. But the victory of his ideas has been progressive in the century and a quarter since his death.

Bolívar's vision took in the whole of the Spanish-speaking territories. There is much evidence that he believed from the start that the rest of the hemisphere must eventually cooperate. In reading and quoting his words, it should be borne in mind that when he says America he usually means Spain's former colonies. He often speaks of his theories, however, as applying to the New World, and his meaning must then be taken as all inclusive.

While a political refugee in Jamaica in 1815, the year of Waterloo, Bolívar wrote one of the three key documents of his career, the so-called "Jamaica Letter." It is also described by historians as the "Prophetic Letter," so accurately does it forecast the results of the revolutionary movement. In it the Liberator pronounces: "I desire to see America fashioned into the greatest nation of the world." And a little further on we find the phrase: "Unity is what we need to complete our work of regeneration."

These things were said at an early date, when the wars of independence had almost ten years to run. Bolívar did not discover the perfect words for his conception until January 8, 1822, when he wrote, inspired, to Bernardo O'Higgins, the

Supreme Director of Chile: "This world of the Americas should be formed into a nation of republics."

The expression was new, subtle, and precise. Note that he says "a nation of republics," not a union or a federation. Actually, he did not endorse for Latin America the federal structure that had been established by the United States. He declared in the "Jamaica Letter" that it was "over-perfect" and that it demanded political virtues and talents to which his countrymen had not attained. What he preferred was a looser alliance, a confederacy, the members of which would be republics not provinces, yet be held together by a bond of obvious destiny. It was absolutely original with Bolívar to call such a league "a nation," though an outstanding example was to be furnished before long by the Confederate States of America.

That same year of 1822, just after he had become president of his Gran Colombia, but with the Battle of Ayacucho, the final victory over Spain, still two years distant, Bolívar took certain positive steps toward the realization of his ideal. He exchanged diplomatic envoys with Mexico, Peru, Chile, and Buenos Aires. A series of treaties followed, which pledged the signers to help one another in defending their independence. Bolívar regarded these treaties as preparatory stages of an All-American congress which he proposed to hold at Panama.

For the first time, also in 1822, he weighed the possibilities of driving Spain from Cuba and Puerto Rico, her two insular possessions in the Caribbean. Both had become restive and eager to strike for freedom, but were too heavily garrisoned to do anything about it. Bolívar planned a joint action with Mexico when transports were available. Because they were islands, he did not think that Cuba and Puerto Rico could be set up as independent countries. There would always be danger of strong Spanish naval expeditions to recapture them and use them as bases for new assaults on the continent.

As Bolívar saw it at the time, Cuba must be attached to Mexico and Puerto Rico to Gran Colombia. The two republics would then be obligated to defend the islands. He began negotiations, but they dragged interminably. The trouble was that Spain had warships afloat, and neither Gran Colombia nor Mexico could find even a squadron of armed merchantmen in which to send troops. The revolution in South America itself was far from being won.

Nevertheless, the Liberator also pushed ahead with the largest of his ideas, the Panama Congress that failed of its immediate end, but turned out to be the very source of modern Pan-Americanism. "Nothing interests the Government of Colombia so much," he said in 1822, "as the forming of a truly American league."

Late the next year the Monroe Doctrine was proclaimed from Washington. It pleased Bolívar, since it placed the United States in blunt opposition to the seizing of new American colonies by European powers. However, it was unilateral, and he seems to have regarded the motives behind it as selfish. He was irritated just then because diplomats of both United States and England declared that their governments preferred Spanish sovereignty to continue in Cuba and Puerto Rico.

Of the two he regarded England as a more valuable potential ally than the United States. This was natural enough. After the close of the Napoleonic Wars, England loomed overwhelmingly. She had important American holdings, and her attitude toward her former possession, the United States, was unfriendly on the whole. It rings curiously today that Bolívar should have told his associates that he wanted England to be represented at the Congress of Panama as "an American power," and that he hoped for a formal alliance with her. On the other hand, he said that the United States should not be asked to become a member of the projected league, because this "might offend England."

The calling of the congress was delayed by many difficulties. What it meant to Bolívar may be judged by the fact that he gave the final touches to a circular and signed it in Lima only two days before the Battle of Ayacucho, at which the last Spanish army on the continent was routed. The circular, or in some cases special invitations, went to all the new republics, and to Great Britain, the United States, the Netherlands, Brazil, and France. It read in part: "The day when our plenipotentiaries exchange their credentials will mark an immortal epoch in the diplomatic history of the world. A hundred centuries hence, posterity, searching for the origin of our public law and recalling the compacts that solidified its destiny, will finger with respect the protocols of the Isthmus."

Without waiting for answers, which could take months to reach him, Bolívar reopened with Mexico the plan for a double invasion to free Cuba and Puerto Rico. As he wrote to Francisco de Paula Santander, the Vice-President of Colombia, it was essential that this issue should come up before the congress. It would be well to have the military end of it under way. The result was a treaty signed in March, 1826, by Gran Colombia and Mexico to proceed in the Caribbean. But this was a bare three months before the congress actually convened. Arguments which maddened Bolívar were found by Mexico for delay.

The official delegates who met in Panama represented only Gran Colombia, Peru, Central America (then functioning as a single country), and Mexico. Great Britain and the Netherlands sent unofficial observers. One delegate from the United States died en route; the other was so dilatory that, as he prepared to start, he learned that the congress had closed.

It is not generally recognized how large an attempt was made at Panama, although there emerged from the debates a treaty of alliance nobly conceived. It would have established a workable confederacy, open to all American states. But by the time that the different legislatures got around to considering it, the prevailing atmosphere was more hostile to cooperation than it had ever been. Only Gran Colombia ratified the Panama pact, and that reluctantly. Every provincial leader wanted to break away and found a government. The union of Gran Colombia itself was close to dissolution.

Bolívar clung to the aim that the Antilles must, in any event, be brought into the American family. When he went to Venezuela to heal dissension in 1827, he got the word of General José Antonio Páez that the latter would lead his idle army of more than 10,000 men to Cuba and Puerto Rico, whether or not Mexico gave support. Again the plan came to nothing, because it was thwarted by selfish elements. Bolívar died, profoundly disillusioned, in 1830. He used the bitter phrase that he had "ploughed the sea," which history has contradicted. Despite his tremendous ego and belief in his glory, the Liberator fell short of realizing the potency of the Pan-American ideal he had left behind him.

I have dwelt upon points familiar to persons who have done general reading on the subject. It is not so well known that abortive conferences were held at intervals throughout the nineteenth century. There was one at Lima in 1847–48, another at Santiago de Chile in 1856, a third in Washington that same year of 1856, and a fourth at Lima in 1864–65. Problems of defence and the independence of New World countries were discussed at all of them. None attracted a sufficiently broad attendance of delegates from the republics, and the treaties proposed were not ratified. They served merely to keep the Bolivarian principles alive.

IV

A congress of jurists at Lima, supported by nine American countries, took the remarkable step late in 1877 of inviting the provisional government of Cuba, then engaged in a war to the death with Spain, to send delegates on a basis of equality with those of the independent states. It was but a gesture, for this first great Cuban revolution, called the Ten Years' War, was close to collapse and ended with the Pact of Zanjón in 1878, while the Lima Congress was still in progress.

Truly beguiling was a statement made by General Calixto García early in the Ten Years' War to James J. O'Kelly, a *New York Herald* correspondent, who interviewed him in a bush encampment. At the beginning of the revolution, English authorities in the region and in London had sympathized with the Cubans, García said. "They suggested the formation of a confederation of the Antilles. . . . Hopes were held out that England would abandon Jamaica, in order to facilitate the confederation."

O'Kelly included this statement, without further details, in his book *The Mambí Land,* published in 1874. It has been of great interest to me as a Jamaican and a writer of history. I have never found original documentary proof, but in James Anthony Froude's *The English in the West Indies* there are assertions about British Foreign Office and Colonial Office policies at the time which make General García's contention plausible. According to Froude, Whitehall was disgusted with the failure of the archaic pattern of government in the Caribbean colonies and was eager to be rid of them.

England's attitude quickly hardened, but the notion that all the Antilles might possibly work together as a single American unit took deep root in the 1870's. Actually it had been dreamed before, with emphasis on the Greater Antilles. The Puerto Rican, Eugenio María de Hostos, had cried in 1868: "Because I am an American, because I am a Puerto Rican, I therefore am a federalist. From my island I see Santo Domingo, I see Cuba, I see Jamaica, and I think of a confederation. I prophesy a providential confederation."

Other Puerto Ricans, notably Dr. Ramón Emeterio Betances and the poet Juan de Diego, as well as General Gregorio Luperón in the Dominican Republic and Anténor Firmín in Haiti, were strong advocates, during the Ten Years' War and after its close. The Cuban, Francisco Aguilera, supported cooperation. The great José Martí, father of the uprising (1895-98) that was to win independence for Cuba and at the start of which he gave his life, had declared generously in 1889: "Cuba and our America are one in my vision of the future and in my affection."

Democratic thinkers in the British, French, and Dutch territories remained silent. The regimes under which they lived were for the most part rigid. Jamaica, for instance, had surrendered its ancient constitution and become a crown colony after the Morant Bay Rebellion of 1865, which culminated in drumhead courts-martial and the hanging of the colored intellectual, George William Gordon, and the mob leader, Paul Bogle. As reprisals for the killing of 18 whites, 439 peasants had been summarily executed; 600, including women, had been flogged severely and others informally beaten; while over 1,000 dwellings had been burned.

V

On the initiative of Secretary of State James G. Blaine, the United States sent invitations in 1889 to all the sister republics of the New World to attend a conference in Washington. The result was the founding of the Pan American Union on April 14, 1890. I can refer now to this development only in the broadest terms. It requires separate treatment, and on a grand scale. The Pan American Union gave reality to the dream of Simón Bolívar. Starting as a loose entente, it crystallized steadily, holding conferences in various capitals at fairly regular intervals, and creating a body of inter-regional agreements that had the force of law. The Union maintained a secretariat in Washington, where it erected a beautiful building as headquarters, library, and museum.

Wars between member states could not at first be eliminated. There was fought, for example, the Chaco War between Bolivia and Paraguay in the early 1930's. But strife was held to a minimum, and it became understood that aggression from outside the hemisphere would be resisted by all American nations. Economic problems were worked out by means of pacts.

VI

The special importance of Pan-Americanism to the Caribbean countries was obvious. As soon as she had gained her independence, Cuba ardently supported the Union. Panama's very existence as a republic, and her subsequent prosperity, were due to the digging of the Canal, the safety of which is a supreme concern of the entire region.

Early in World War II before the United States had been attacked by Japan, conferences of the foreign ministers of American countries were held—and significantly in Caribbean capitals. These were not meetings of the Pan American Union, but would have been much less effective if the machinery of the Union— or the Organization of American States—had not existed. The first conference, at Panama, dealt with measures for mutual defense in case the conflict spread westward from Europe. The second, at Havana, posed an innovation of the greatest importance in New World diplomacy. What, it was asked, would the American republics do about the Caribbean colonies of European powers if Germany crushed England, as she had already crushed France and the Netherlands?

There emerged the statesmanlike Act of Havana, which provided that each colonial unit regarded as being in danger would be occupied separately by one or more American countries, whose representatives must adopt an organic law after consultation with the people in whatever manner possible. The resulting administration would in the first instance be limited to three years, and if it became necessary to extend it, a renewal for ten years would be the maximum. Only the unlikely circumstance of the war being still in progress could then postpone a decision—by the colonists themselves—between restoration to their former sovereignty and independence.

We know that this course did not have to be followed. But the Act of Havana stands on record as a precedent at a high level of political thinking, an indication of how, on the plane of action, liberty in the Americas may still have to be protected.

Fortunately a large part of the British bloc is on the verge of autonomy and will be able to negotiate for itself in any crisis. It happens that I do not like the structure adopted for the federated West Indies, as they have decided to be named. This statement is just by the way. My concern is that the new nation should clearly perceive its destiny, which is to be a western nation, an actual, if not an official, member of the Pan-American family. Such has long been the position of Canada. Membership was formally offered to her. She has allowed it to stay in suspense, doubtless so as not to ruffle the sentiments of the British Commonwealth. But Canada's political and trade policies are markedly Pan-American. Those of the federated West Indies should be no less so.

The French and the Dutch have introduced measures since the war to bind their holdings permanently to Europe. Martinique, Guadeloupe, and Cayenne have been created full departments of metropolitan France. The Netherlands Antilles and Surinam, have become constituent realms, partners of Holland, under the Throne. The units enjoy the right of individual membership in international organizations. These French and Dutch devices will probably not last long in history. Held together by language, the two groups I have named may become independent, or they may merge with other combinations. There is some talk of the three Guianas joining to form a South American state, but it is more likely that British Guiana will be drawn into the federation of the British West Indies.

VII

It may be asked what extraordinary merit I find in confederacies, or leagues. By this is meant the broad international unions, like the Pan American, and not the simple mergers for the purpose of establishing self-governing units.

The answer is that political relationships have expanded until they have taken in the whole world. Confusion can best be avoided and peace preserved if basic ideals are expressed by a few authoritative voices. Society always has been, and still is, founded upon the family. It used to be that a grouping of families formed the tribe, and a grouping of tribes the nation. Today the tribe has practically been eliminated, and a grouping of nations forms the ideological alliance. (We will not go into the unfulfilled aspiration for a universal regime of law through a perfect functioning of the body called the United Nations.)

The British Commonwealth is one of the outstanding examples that I have in mind. For us of the Western Hemisphere the most important is the league represented by Pan-Americanism, in which the United States admittedly is predominant.

Fraternity and power are implicit in the Act of Chapultepec, which was adopted on March 8, 1945, at a conference of the twenty-one American republics held at Mexico City. It broadened the Monroe Doctrine to include all the signatories in an agreement that every attack of a state against the integrity or the inviolability of the territory, or against the sovereignty or political independence of an American state, would thenceforth be considered an act of aggression against the other states.

Part VI

BIBLIOGRAPHICAL SOURCES

Lowell J. Ragatz: THE STUDY OF RECENT AND CONTEMPORARY CARIBBEAN DEPENDENCIES HISTORY

THE CARIBBEAN AREA has long enjoyed great popularity among research students in European expansion. The reason is readily apparent—the several groups of dependent territories found there were among the very earliest overseas possessions of the European countries venturing to tread the path of empire, and they speedily became the jewels of the old colonial empires. Innumerable knotty economic, social, and political problems attending overseas settlement were first encountered and resolved there. Indeed, colonial know-how was largely developed in the American tropics and experience gained in peopling, developing, and administering the New World sugar bowls was later successfully applied in even more remote lands in Africa, Asia, and Oceanica.

It is likewise in the long isolated Caribbean holdings, with their boundaries rigidly delimited by an encircling sea or jungle, that subtle changes in speech, laws, institutions, and ways of life attending emigration and its accompanying transit of civilization from European homelands can best be studied. It is, therefore, in no way surprising that a notable series of scholarly monographs bearing upon the Caribbean dependencies, especially in the period 1550–1850, should have appeared from such well-known research centers as Oxford, the University of London,

317

the Institute of Jamaica, the University of Paris, Yale, Columbia, and Wisconsin. Beginning early in the present century, the bulk of writings in the field was highly impressive by the late twenties, and a recent survey of Caribbean historiography during the past three decades demonstrates that interest has in no way abated. Indeed, occupation with the past of the West Indian dependencies has never been more active than today.

I

Professor Clarence Gould of Youngstown University in Ohio has ready for publication a masterly study of the fiscal system attending French enterprise in the sugar islands under the Old Regime which will revolutionize traditional concepts on the subject. G. Debien, currently a refugee in France from Nasser's terrorism, is making excellent use of enforced absence from academic life to further our knowledge of Santo Domingo in the seventeenth and eighteenth centuries. He has likewise begun work on an exhaustive guide to materials bearing on the colony, and a detailed general history is projected. Professor Ronald Sires of Whitman College is writing a constitutional history of Jamaica, and Dr. Clause Levy of Central Washington College is completing a monograph dealing with the growth of Britain's Caribbean policy in the half-century following Emancipation as shaped by contemporary events in Barbados.

Overshadowing all other current projects is a three-volume history of the West Indian Islands irrespective of sovereignty from Columbus' discovery to the present day being written by members of the History staff of the University College of the West Indies under grant from the Carnegie Corporation. The work has been conceived on a generous scale, with due attention to economic, social, political, and cultural developments. Noteworthy is the concept of the Caribbean area as a geographic unit with its distinctive environment, and the treatment of European penetration as a common process irrespective of the national state involved. This affords an unprecedented opportunity for a comparative study of problems attending immigration, administrative regimes, plantation economy, commercial policies, insular society, negro codes, emancipation techniques, and the growth of Caribbean mindedness, the objective being an interpretive synthesis of knowledge on the area. Several lesser projects, all pre-1900, are likewise in hand at American, British, and French universities.

Indicative of this persistent interest in the Caribbean past is the fact that more than 40,000 items in the Royal Dutch Archives in Amsterdam bearing upon Jewish life in Surinam and Curaçao have just been microfilmed for the American Jewish Archives. Further evidence will be found in the recent appearance of no less than three serious journals bearing upon the non-sovereign Caribbean lands, which are giving substantial space to the West Indian past—*The Caribbean,* published monthly by the Caribbean Commission (1947); *The Caribbean Historical Review,* organ of the new Historical Society of Trinidad and Tobago (1950); and *The Caribbean Quarterly,* sponsored by the University College of the West Indies (1957).

II

There is, thus, no lack of interest and research in tropical American dependency affairs up to two generations ago. The weak spot in West Indian area historiography today is the recent and contemporary period, roughly the twentieth century. "The story of our own times," to use a familiar phrase, has traditionally suffered neglect in the study of both national history and international relations, though far less so today than in earlier days. Some have argued that a narration of yesterday's and today's events is not true history, while others have held that the paucity of available source materials combined with lack of perspective renders impossible any such undertaking on a scholarly basis. In my reasoned opinion neither view is valid in its Caribbean application, and I wish, at this time, to suggest certain subjects of a recent and contemporary nature centering about the non-sovereign lands of today which are well worth historical appraisal, and for which adequate open materials and facilities exist to make such undertakings feasible.

The emergence of the United States as a Caribbean power, the opening of the Panama Canal, and the more recent establishment of leased bases in the tropical American area, have been three of the most momentous events in West Indian history; yet their implications and epoch-making consequences have yet to receive adequate attention from the historian. The investment of United States capital throughout the region, resultant changes in time-honored commercial relations, and the growth of northern neighbor influence through the development of new transportation facilities, as well as through the impact of tourist traffic, the motion picture, and radio and TV entertainment, merit close study. An able account of the conflict of cultures and its ultimate resolution in Puerto Rico and the American Virgins since their relatively recent acquisition by the United States would constitute a fascinating chapter in expansion history.

The emergence of two new Caribbean republics, Cuba and Panama, had profound influence in shaping political thought in the West Indian dependencies, yet this has never been appraised. The conflict between small planter and estate-owning corporations is clearly discernible, but has yet to be seriously reviewed. The turn from monoculture and the spread of diversification in agricultural enterprises have revolutionized rural economy in the non-sovereign lands and patently merit scholarly attention. Closely allied to this development are the introduction of new economic plants, of new strains among the old ones, and the unceasing struggle against insect pests and parasites, which, too, have received but scant attention from the historian. A comprehensive account of the founding of the Imperial College of Tropical Agriculture in 1921 and its multifarious activities is likewise badly needed.

The stimulus accorded handicraft industries in the Caribbean possessions as a whole and the successful campaign to encourage the migration of established industrial concerns from the continental United States to Puerto Rico make a fascinating tale. The dramatic story of "Operation Bootstrap"—Puerto Rico pulling itself out of the slough of stagnation and decay and achieving thorough economic regeneration—offers a challenge to the economic historian. The expansion of steamship service, the appearance of aerial navigation, and the revolution of internal transportation attending road construction, together with the rapid growth of motor-coach and freight facilities in the various dependent lands, have yet to be taken in hand.

Given the current vogue for business history, a study of the Panama Canal as a financial venture, a survey of the management and operation of representative properties, the ramifications of the fruit industry, banking structures, the phenomenal development of the bauxite and petroleum industries in the Netherlands Antilles, and the enterprise of giant corporations in the several dependencies, are naturals.

Spectacular population growth attending the introduction of sanitation and preventive medicine has precipitated grave social crises in all the non-sovereign lands, yet this basic factor in Caribbean social development has never been minutely scrutinized. Studies of comparative living standards at intervals during the past half-century are conspicuously lacking, as are surveys of shifting population make-ups and changes in predominant age groups and life spans. Altered educational facilities and job opportunities, the mounting drift from rural districts to urban areas, accompanying disruptions in family life, the growth of port slums, and the churches' shifting role in this welter of social transformations, invite attention by the social historian.

The nature of the several social communities in the dependencies—white European, white American, Red Man, Negro, Chinese, Indian, Jewish, and mixed blood of many degrees—their mores, their interrelationships, and their tensions, must be carefully studied if there is to be any real comprehension of social problems. Case histories of actual families in each group would admirably pinpoint the situation today. A dispassionate, factual presentation of the penal regime in French Guiana, too, is conspicuously lacking. Studies of health problems, of the emergence of social welfare organizations, of the vogue for sports, of the upsurge of strikes and riots in the mid-thirties, and of the resultant emergence of Trade Unionism, would all prove exceedingly rewarding and would contribute appreciably to our understanding of the Caribbean dependencies today.

Active political life in such non-sovereign political entities is a twentieth-century phenomenon and today plays a vital role in the life of each. Nonetheless, this notable development in tropical American affairs has gone all but unnoticed by the historian. What were the forces rousing the Caribbean peoples from their lethargy, forces which, in dependency after dependency, turned them to political action as a means of redressing their grievances and ushered in a new era of reform and reconstruction? Who were the molders of public thought; who were the party organizers; what situations shaped their platforms; what appeals were made for racial and religious support; what were the reactions of the several colonial administrations; what have been the actual gains; what changes in relationship with the parent states have followed? Surely these matters are of sufficient concern to warrant diligent investigation.

Problems arising from our administration of the Canal Zone and the United States' relationships with Panama over clashing jurisdictions and attendant petty annoyances have been hinted at by various writers, but have never been carefully explored. In little more than a decade we have witnessed four of the boldest experiments in the history of modern imperialism. These are the conversion of Guadeloupe, Martinique, and French Guiana into overseas departments of the French Republic in 1946, the elevation in 1952 of Puerto Rico to the status of a self-governing commonwealth freely and voluntarily associated with the United States, the admission in 1954 of Surinam and the Netherlands Antilles to the Dutch family circle, and the creation of the British Caribbean Federation as of 1958. All cry loudly for conscientious investigation and impersonal appraisal.

Exactly what lies behind Caribbean consciousness, and how

strong has this feeling become? No one has ventured to say. Frank realization that the tropical American dependencies faced common problems, and that concerted effort was needed intelligently to meet these, led to the creation, first, of the Anglo-American Caribbean Commission in 1942, and, with French and Dutch adherence, to the development of a four-power one in 1946. Yet this cardinal event in West Indian history and the critical evaluation of the body's undertakings have attracted but one scholar, and his admirable monograph, unhappily enough, is now badly out of date.

Lastly the cultural field. *Is* a distinctive Caribbean civilization emerging? A little has been written on the subject, but it merits far more attention. *Is* there a school of Caribbean writers, as some have suggested? If so, who are its leaders, what is the nature of their work, what is their philosophy, what are their unique contributions to world literature? The same is true in the fields of painting, music, and architecture. Any serious treatment of these subjects would almost certainly yield surprising results.

These are all basic subjects in the recent and contemporary development of the Caribbean dependencies deserving serious study with a view to gaining a more intelligent understanding of life and events in an area closely bound up with United States welfare. There are, of course, many others, and a highly inviting field lies all but wide open to tempt the discerning scholar eager to undertake pioneering research of the most rewarding kind.

III

The question of course arises: what materials are available for the purpose? The answer is: far more than for any other period of West Indian history. The general rule in historical investigation is that the nearer to our own time the problem under study, the greater the amount of evidence awaiting patient spadework by the researcher. The past half-century, the recent and contemporary age in Caribbean affairs, offers no exception.

While governors' dispatches are generally difficult of access
because of their recent date, more liberal archival policies in the
homeland are making them increasingly available. Annual executive reports for the several dependencies have commonly been
published by their respective home governments in our period
since the turn of the century. While varying in nature from
metropole to metropole, they invariably include an immense
amount of diverse information on the territory concerned and
are invaluable for our purpose. British Colonial Blue Books
which, in the cases of Barbados, British Guiana, and Jamaica,
go back more than a century and a quarter, were published for
the several British West Indian possessions in the recent period
up to the close of the Second World War, when they were
finally discontinued. Such official catch-alls, with an amazing
array of facts and figures, are also of basic importance. Occasional parallel publications will be found for the other groups
of possessions. The reports of numerous commissions of inquiry
sent to the Caribbean colonies have normally been made public
by all the motherlands involved and are of the utmost significance.

The journals of the several sets of dependencies having legislative bodies have appeared with regularity during the past half-
century, and current law codes have been published fairly
frequently. An immense amount of concise information on agriculture, industry, trade, administration, and social structures will
be found in the numerous general and single colony yearbooks
and reference works based upon official sources which have
appeared in large number during the past two generations.

Happily enough, the non-sovereign lands of tropical America
have supported a surprising number of vigorous newspapers in
the twentieth century. Between them, they admirably mirror
liberal, conservative, planter, commercial, labor, and racial
points of view. Their characteristic provincialism which might
well dismay the casual outsider chancing upon them is precisely
the feature giving them greatest value to the research student.
Column after column is filled with priceless data, and trenchant

editorials present decisive points of view on local matters innumerable. In marked contrast with older news organs of these territories, rather complete files of many of them have escaped the ravages of time, fire, and insect pests; and they can be freely consulted not only on the spot, but in such widely scattered centers as Washington, London, Paris, and the Netherlands.[1]

There are, likewise, considerable numbers of commercial bodies with Caribbean dependency interests whose records may be used with none too onerous restrictions by the serious student. In the British area may be mentioned the Incorporated Chambers of Commerce of the British Caribbean in Port of Spain, the British West Indies Sugar Association of Kingston, the West India Committee of London, and the West India Associations

1. Of particular value are the following, published daily unless otherwise noted; the dates are beginning dates. In the British West Indies. Antigua: *The Antigua Star* (Conservative, 1936); *The Worker's Voice* (Labor, 1944). Barbados: *The Barbados Advocate* (Conservative, 1895); *The Barbados Observer* (Labor, 1934). British Guiana: *The Daily Argosy* (Conservative, 1880); *The Daily Chronicle* (Liberal, 1881); *The Guiana Graphic* (Conservative, 1925). British Honduras: *The Daily Clarion* (Conservative, 1897); *The Belize Billboard* (Socialist, 1946). Dominica: *The Dominica Chronicle* (bi-weekly, Conservative-Catholic, 1909). Grenada: *The West Indian* (Liberal, 1915). Jamaica: *The Daily Gleaner* (Conservative-Liberal, 1834); *Catholic Opinion* (weekly, 1896); *Public Opinion* (weekly, Socialist, 1937). Montserrat: *The Observer* (weekly, Liberal, 1937). St. Kitts-Nevis: *The St. Kitts-Nevis Daily Bulletin* (Liberal, 1914). St. Lucia: *The Voice of St. Lucia* (Conservative, 1885). St. Vincent: *The Vincentian* (Conservative, 1919). Trinidad: *The Trinidad Chronicle and Port of Spain Gazette* (Conservative, 1825); *The Catholic News* (weekly, 1891); *The Trinidad Guardian* (Conservative, 1917); *The Evening News* (Conservative, 1936); *The People's Weekly* (Labor-Nationalist, 1939).

In the French West Indies. French Guiana: *Radio Presse*. Guadeloupe: *Le Miroir de la Guadeloupe; Le Nouvelliste de la Guadeloupe* (Middle-of-the-road weekly, 1945); *La Voix du Peuple de la Guadeloupe* (weekly, 1935). Martinique: *Le Courrier des Antilles* (thrice weekly); *L'Information* (1935).

In the Netherlands West Indies. The Netherlands Antilles: *Amigoe di Curaçao; Arubaansche Courant; Beurs & Nieuwsberichten* (Curaçao); *Boletín Commercial* (Curaçao); *De Morgenster* (Curaçao); *La Prensa* (Curaçao). Surinam (Netherlands Guiana): *De Nieuwe Tyd; Het Nieuws*.

In the United States West Indies. The American Virgins: *The Daily News* (St. Thomas, Independent, 1930); *St. Croix Avis* (Independent, 1844). Puerto Rico: *La Correspondencia* (Independent, 1890, defunct); *La Democracia* (Liberal, 1890, defunct); *El Día* (Independent, 1909); *El Mundo* (Independent, 1919); *El Imparcial* (Independent, 1933).

of Glasgow and Liverpool. Similar organizations exist in the United States, Dutch, and French spheres. Their minute books, in particular, deserve special mention.

In the official category are such bodies as the Regional Economic Committee of the British West Indies, British Guiana, and British Honduras (Barbados); the Colonial Development Corporation (London); the Caribbean Commission (Port of Spain); the Imperial Institute (South Kensington); and the Royal Tropical Institute (Amsterdam). Nor should the quasi-official Royal Empire Society (founded in 1868 as the Royal Colonial Institute) be overlooked. There are others, United States, British, French, and Dutch. Access may be gained to a surprising number of their papers. Indeed, the student of twentieth-century developments in the tropical American dependencies is confronted by an embarrassing wealth both of source and secondary materials.

IV

Speaking generally, it may be said that detailed specific studies, unit by unit, are the first need, and that each group of studies should then be integrated for the non-sovereign territories as a whole, to trace general trends, to work out common patterns, and to interpret and appraise them. The Pan American Union's recently concluded San Juan Seminar on New World plantation systems, while drawn on a somewhat wider scale, affords a brilliant example of integration in studying man in the tropics, and it might well serve as a model for all summarizations bearing upon the dependencies as a group. Dealing as they will with matters of living concern and often of vital significance, such studies will be found to have a practical application lacking in investigations of the remote past, however interesting.

There are four natural centers for the study of recent and contemporary developments in the tropical American dependencies—the University of Florida at the gateway to the Caribbean, and the University of Puerto Rico, the University College of the West Indies, and the research section of the Caribbean Commission in the area itself. Their geographic positions, affording basic understanding of the problems under review and easy access to primary materials, offer them leadership in the field. The eight Caribbean Conferences held in Gainesville have already brought under scrutiny a considerable number of matters affecting the West Indian non-sovereign lands today. Studies recently made and in hand in the two insular institutions effectively demonstrate their potentiality. Lastly, a notable series of research projects is sponsored by the Caribbean Commission, and these projects reveal a mounting awareness of the practical importance of surveys of "our own time" developments in the West Indian dependencies and argue that this long neglected aspect of Caribbean history is at long last coming into its own.

Index

[Prepared by Basil C. Hedrick]

AGRICULTURAL production, Caribbean, 79, 82, 111–116
Aluminum Company of America, 83
Anglo-American Caribbean Commission (AACC). *See* Caribbean Commission
Aruba, 66, 71–77 *passim*, 86, 88, 229

BARBADOS: trade, 196–197; energy consumption, 229
Bataafsche Petroleum Maatschappij (Royal Dutch Shell), 76
Bibliographical sources for Caribbean: Clarence Gould, 318; G. Debien, 318; Ronald Sires, 318; Clause Levy, 318; University College of the West Indies, 318–319; governors' dispatches, 324; commercial bodies, 325–326; governmental agencies, 326
British Guiana: industry, 19; forestry, 23–24; society, 27, 28, 32–33; trade, 195–196; energy consumption, 228, 229; oil exploration, 231
British West Indies: constitutional developments in, 3–10; federation of, 4; constitutional changes, 5–6; Crown Colony system, 6–8. *See also* Federation of the West Indies

CARIBBEAN Commission: background, 262–275; attitude of Washington, 269–273, 276–278; and health problem, 278, 280; propaganda program, 280–281; ten-point program, 281–286; as regional body, 286–289; nomenclature, 289–290; accomplishments, 290–297; as moral force, 291; reorganization, 298–299; as bibliographical source, 327

Caribbean Medical Center, 280
Colonial Development and Welfare Act (1940), 14; (1945), 16
Colonial Development Corporation, 16
Crown Colony System, 6–8
Curaçao: discovery, 54; Dutch in, 54; world trade, 57; West India Company, 60; oil industry, 60; Parliament, 65; political structure, 65–66; political parties, 71–72; geography, 73, 74; society, 75, 87; industry, 75, 76, 77; trade, 77–78; tourism, 78; products, 79; political life, 91; urbanization, 93–94; energy consumption, 229
Curaçao Independent Party, 91
Curaçaose Petroleum Industrie Maatschappij (C.P.I.M.), 76, 77, 203

DEMOCRATIC Party (Dutch Antilles), 91
Demography, Caribbean: present position, 234–240; population projections, 236–246
Dutch Guiana. *See* Surinam

EISENHOWER, Dwight David, 166
Electricity in Caribbean. *See* Energy consumption
Energy consumption, Caribbean, 226–228; in British areas, 228–229; in Dutch areas, 229; in French areas, 229–230; in United States areas, 230; future demands, 230–231

FEDERATION of the West Indies: formation of, 3; pattern of government, 4; Crown Colony system, 6–8; future of, 9–10; economic trends, 11–26; society, 32–33
French Antilles. *See* Martinique; Guadeloupe

329